D0195142

Touching
✳ *Spirit*

A Journey of Healing
and Personal Resurrection

Elizabeth K. Stratton, M.S.

Simon & Schuster

SIMON & SCHUSTER
Rockefeller Center
1230 Avenue of the Americas
New York, NY 10020

Copyright © 1996 by Elizabeth Stratton
All rights reserved,
including the right of reproduction
in whole or in part in any form.

SIMON & SCHUSTER and colophon are registered trademarks of
Simon & Schuster Inc.

Designed by Diane E. Dougal

Manufactured in the United States of America

10   9   8   7   6   5   4   3   2   1

Library of Congress Cataloging-in-Publication Data
Stratton, Elizabeth K.
     Touching spirit: a journey of healing and personal
resurrection / Elizabeth K. Stratton.
        p.   cm.
     1. Stratton, Elizabeth K.   2. Women Healers—United
States—Biography.   I. Title.
RZ403.P75S77   1996
615.8'52—dc20
[B]   96-26337
                                                     CIP

ISBN 0-684-83093-0

For My Mother
Karin Elizabeth Wallen Stratton

Contents

Introduction

The Meaning of Resurrection

Resurrection means "to rise again." It is something we would all like to do. We would like to rise from pain, illness, fear, and death to be born into a new life. Most of us believe we have to wait until the end of time for resurrection, as the Book of Revelation portrays in the New Testament, or as the Book of Daniel describes in the Old Testament.

I want to offer you a new vision of what it means to be resurrected, and one that you can apply to your life immediately, today, as you are living it. The reality of rising again is happening in your body, heart, mind, and soul right now as you're reading this page. Millions of cells are dying and new ones are being born. The body is constantly re-creating and healing itself. Each year 98 percent of the body's atoms are replaced with new ones. Every seven weeks we have a new liver. Our bodies are constantly resurrecting themselves.

The same is true for emotions and thoughts. From moment to moment throughout the day, we experience new and old emotions in different configurations. Our thoughts constantly shift and new ideas are introduced. Every night we have unique and original dreams, usually unlike those of the night before. Not only our bodies, but also our souls are healing and resurrecting themselves.

I want to take you on a journey of healing and resurrection from my own perspective as a spiritual healer over the past twenty years. I want to tell you about my life and the lives of the people I have helped during these two decades. Then, when you realize that resurrection and healing are tangible realities, you may believe that they are possible for you, your life, your body, and your soul—and that you can actively participate in this miraculous process.

The possibility of a true resurrection of body and soul has been envisioned in all mythologies and religions since the beginning of written history. The Egyptians created the myth of Isis and Osiris to portray the power of love and the energy of the feminine to bring back life from death. The Book of Genesis tells of the Tree of Life that will bring immortality to anyone who eats from it. The Hebrews foretold of a messiah who would bring healing and freedom from death to the Jews. The Greeks wrote of Persephone's descent into the underworld and subsequent return, bringing new life to the earth. The New Testament describes the life of Jesus and his death, burial, and resurrection, as well as the resurrection of the dead at the end of time in the Book of Revelation.

The desire to participate in Creation in a way that will lead to a resurrection of body and soul, a true eternal life, is innate in human nature. We seem to have an inborn creativity, from the natural generation of a new child in the womb, to the expression of a painting on canvas. Artists, healers, musicians, and sometimes even scientists remind us that the creative life force within us is a divine gift and its expression a natural consequence of our spiritual nature.

Even our dreams remind us that we are creating while we sleep. Every night we descend into their mysterious world to listen to the messages of our soul, even to listen to the voice of God. Many years ago, the Episcopal priest and Jungian analyst John Sanford wrote a book entitled *Dreams: God's Forgotten Language*. The Bible describes many instances of God's speaking through dreams, including Joseph's dream in which an angel tells him that Mary is carrying a child and that he is to name him Jesus. Dreams can allow us access to the messages that God gives us through the creative voice of our soul. They remind us that we have an inner connection through what Christians call the Holy Spirit and other religions call inner Divinity. This source is ever present within our physical body.

It is this inner Divinity that is continuously manifesting toward greater and greater expression. It is up to each of us to follow our inner guidance and find ways that we can cooperate with God in creating a new life and bringing the resurrection energy into manifestation here on earth. If we think of God as the Creator of all Life, then we are cooperating with the Designer of Creation to bring Life into greater and greater wholeness and harmony. Every spiritual path and religion grew from this Divine guidance wanting to find expression in physical form. When we attune ourselves to this inner Divine voice, we are surrendering to the will of God as it is expressed in our individual soul. We are each acknowledging our individual relationship with God, the true meaning of mysticism. Our choice can be to participate in Creation by operating with, cooperating with, God. We can choose to wait patiently, listen, see, feel, and follow the directions for healing and true life as God awakens the healer within us. Jesus, Buddha, Mother Theresa, Moses, the saints, Kuan Yin in China, and Tara in Tibet and India cooperated with God. At some point in their lives they each said: "Take my life, God, and do with it what you will. I will not resist. I will cooperate with you. My life is yours."

One of the most essential ways that we can cooperate with God is through the healing of our soul. Our soul is composed of all that we are, both in this life and, if you believe in them, in previous lives. Our soul is what lives on when our body dies. It is that configuration of energy that is constantly evolving toward wholeness. It contains all the unhealed emotions and thoughts that we carry with us from lifetime to lifetime; all the actions and mistakes we have not yet forgiven. It also contains all the lessons that we have learned, the wisdom we have accumulated. The soul is the creative matrix out of which our actions spring and our emotions and thoughts evolve. The creative life force within expresses itself as it rises again moment by moment, manifesting how we are evolving toward healing, toward wholeness in our connection with God.

As we all know, there are days when we feel that everything we do and everything that takes place seems to flow smoothly, as though this evolution is progressing as it should. And then there are other days when all the events and all our actions seem out of sync, as though we are caught in a bad dream. The evolution and healing of our soul is made up of peaks and valleys, clear paths, and rugged mountain climbs. Because we do not always understand the greater picture of our soul's progress, we should not judge the difficult times as bad. They are part of the process of awakening the healer within us. Illnesses, accidents, and losses are all wake-up calls to the soul to pay attention to its inner connection with God. It is this attention and this connection that allow us to wake up to the greater possibilities of healing available to us.

Healing comes from the Old English "haelen," meaning "to make whole." As we evolve through many different lifetimes, we learn the lessons that our soul chooses to learn. People who have near death experiences tell of "a being" of white light who helps them view their life. This being asks them: What did you learn? and Whom did you love? It seems that as our soul evolves through lifetimes, we are learning how to love, how to become whole, how to rise again and experience resurrection. Each new lifetime is its own resurrection. Our families, friends, career, illnesses, and crises are all challenges that confront us with opportunities to learn and love, and, thereby, heal the soul and the body as an expression of the soul.

This book will provide you with a vision of how you can awaken the healer within you and cooperate with God in the healing of your body and soul. It will encourage you to see your own healing process as a spiritual practice that you can make a part of your daily life. In participating in the creation of a new life, new body, and healed soul, you will be experiencing a true resurrection, a rising again that is available to us all when we focus on cooperating with God. Resurrection is taking place here and now, as well as being embodied in eternity. We are all evolving toward a true healing and resurrection of the body and soul of all humanity, the *anima mundi* or world soul that we all share, and the sacred ground on which we stand.

1
Awakening

I lay on the floor trembling, not quite sure what was happening
to me. I made a decision to surrender. The first in a long series of
surrenders that have composed my life. I let go completely into
the trembling. I let it happen to me, whatever it was. As I look
back on it now, I suppose I decided to cooperate with God. I lost
track of time and space, as I would find out later. And I had a vision. A lucid image of my mother's face directly in front of me,
and my right hand reaching out to touch her third eye, the energy
center between the eyebrows where clear vision, intuition, is
stored. I did not know what this meant.

One moment I was sitting in an audience of about two hundred
people, listening to several speakers on stage talking about their
views of healing, and the next I felt a sharp pain in my right rib
cage. I noticed the pain, but ignored it. The stabbing came again
and continued until I had trouble concentrating on the presentation. I shifted in my seat and decided to see my chiropractor on
Monday. The pain continued until I had to get up from my seat and
leave the room. On the way out the door an usher asked me
whether I was all right, apparently seeing the pain on my face. I

told him I didn't know, and he showed me to a room where I could lie down if only on the floor.

From that point on I remember going into some kind of altered state, my body trembling, my breath quickening, and my mind remaining completely clear. I was surprised by this turn of events and tried to control my breathing and calm myself. It didn't work. I tried to sit up. I couldn't. Nothing I did could control what was happening to me. As I lay there trembling from head to toe, I remember thinking how ridiculously strange this was. Something was happening to me that was beyond my control, yet I did not feel afraid.

Soon after I had the vision, a woman came into the room. The usher had left me alone to retrieve someone to help. I don't remember who she was or what she looked like, but I was to discover that she was extremely empathic, an intuitive, meaning that she could sense and explain what was happening to other people. She knelt next to me and stated "This isn't yours. Let it go." I was still lying on my back, and she helped me to sit up. "This isn't yours. Let it go." With that, the energy causing the trembling in my body started to rise up and out of my body, beginning with the soles of my feet. It was a strange feeling, as though a waterfall were flowing backward. I could feel this energy rise up and out of my feet, through my legs, torso, spine, neck and out the top of my head. For the first time in what I was later to discover was an hour and a half, my jaw stopped chattering and I was left completely still.

The woman kneeling to my right asked me how the condition started. I told her of sitting in the audience listening to the speakers, but she wanted to know who was speaking when I first felt the pain. I told her of the dark-haired man sitting all the way on the end to my left. She insisted I go speak to him and tell him what had happened to me. I balked. How could I? This was all so strange, so embarrassing. What *had* happened to me? She insisted he was the key.

I had some water and sat for a few minutes collecting myself. I then tentatively walked out into the main room of the holistic center. The lectures were finished and everyone was standing around drinking tea and coffee. I noticed the dark-haired man at the other side of the room. I went over to him and haltingly told him my story. As I did I watched his eyes start to widen and his jaw drop open. When I was finished, he jumped in and proclaimed, "That's exactly what happened to me!" Stunned, I listened to him describe how his rib cage had collapsed, cracked, and led to surgery. He offered to show me his scar. I declined. I had had enough revelations for the day.

I had been brought up in a middle-class Protestant family with Scandinavian and Pennsylvania Dutch ancestors. No nonsense. No soda pop in the refrigerator. Nothing bubbly. Keep it calm. Don't make waves. And here I was making trembling, uncontrollable waves with someone else's pain in my body. How did it get there? What did this mean?

I went to see a woman who was described to me by a close friend as psychic. Psychic? This didn't fit in with my background. Gypsies are psychic; Protestants are not. I hesitated. What was I getting involved in? My friend told me that the psychic could be helpful, so I decided to give her a try. I went to the address written on the piece of paper and walked into an elegant doorman building on East Seventy-second Street in Manhattan. When I got to the apartment a friendly woman in her early forties with reddish brown hair opened the door and welcomed me in. Her apartment was clean and neat—normal. She invited me to sit in a chair in front of her in the living room. She then proceeded accurately to describe my mother and father, my childhood, and my tendency to be a "psychic sponge." She told me that I had always been sensitive to other people's energies and that I absorbed them without realizing it. I became other people. I felt what they felt, both emotionally and physically. This phenomenon is what had happened to me the previous week at the holistic center when the dark-haired man was speaking.

She invited me to a healing circle. A place where people do healing with other people. Although her main gift was intuition, she had studied with a healer for several years. I did not really understand what she meant by a healing circle, but I agreed to go. The following week I walked into a loft space where about thirty people were gathered in a circle. The psychic talked about healing and how we could all help one another by sending loving thoughts through our hands. She then invited someone to volunteer. An older woman with deep emotional pain from the loss of a loved one sat in the middle of the circle. Several people went up to her and put their hands on different parts of her body. I remained seated, observing. Less than one minute into the healing I started to feel very sad. The sadness deepened until I started to feel pain in my chest and tears came to my eyes. I had trouble breathing. I felt as though I were going to lose control of myself, and I got up and walked quickly downstairs and out of the building. I walked to the nearest phone booth and broke down sobbing. I called a friend and told him what had happened. He suggested I speak to the psychic the next day and tell her.

When I phoned the following day she told me she had watched what had happened to me, and noted that it was a good example of how I took on other people's feelings. I had absorbed the loss and grief of the woman in the center of the circle. She told me I would have to learn how to control this permeability, separating my feelings from those of other people, something that had never been taught to me in childhood.

My personal awakening had begun. God had smacked me on the cheek and challenged me to wake up to a new life. I had no idea I would open a Pandora's box. I had no idea I would become a healer. I had no clue that the next twenty years of my life would test my strength and my sanity, my love and my hope to the limit of what is endurable to the human spirit. If I had known what it would take to become resurrected, I would probably have kept sleeping.

The next six months became a Herculean challenge. Everywhere I went I sponged up people's feelings. On the subway, in buses, at parties, walking down the street. It was as though the boundaries between me and the rest of the world disappeared, and I merged with everything and everyone. The noises on the street and in the subway were too much for me. If I stood too close to people, I could feel what was going on inside them. Even if they were across the room at a party, all I had to do was to look at them and I would know what they were feeling and thinking. Once I was standing in line waiting for a table in a restaurant when I heard the front door open and close in back of me. I felt an instant pain in my head. I turned around to see a woman standing in back of me. I asked her if she had a headache. Startled, she admitted she did. How did I know? I had just gotten it.

Any shrink would have looked up my condition in the *Diagnostic and Statistical Manual,* the standard guide to various types of emotional and mental disorders. But I fit none of the categories. I had complete use of my faculties. I was working full-time, having normal relationships, sleeping and eating well, and in all other ways functioning normally. I was in the middle of a spiritual and emotional break*through* not breakdown. But twenty years ago, there was no category for such a state. Now we know better. Now I can help my students and patients deal with their intuitive sensitivities without being drugged into a stupor to make them appear more "normal." After all, as Plato said, we're already in the stupor. We're trying to wake up.

One day I was simply walking down the street to my bank and I could see the past lives of everyone who walked by me. That was it. That was too much for me, and I simply decided it had to stop. I was not going to merge with everyone anymore. I began practicing what I called "Psychic Self-Defense." I didn't really know how to do this, so I just began saying to myself "That's their pain, not mine." "That's their headache, not mine." I went through my entire day doing this. It helped. I began to be able to separate out what were my feelings and what were the feelings of others. Often I would imagine a wall of white light between myself and the other person. Sometimes I would have to walk away or move my seat on the subway. But I kept working at it, and in about four months I felt better protected. I began telling my friends what I was doing. I told them I was practicing "Psychic Self-Defense." Nobody knew what I was talking about. Nobody had ever heard of such a thing, but almost everyone I spoke to admitted feeling, at least at times, like a sponge for other people's pain.

As I've traveled around the world in the last twenty years, everywhere I go, people want to know about "Psychic Self-Defense." It became my most popular workshop. I remember being in Washington, D.C., at a conference of scientists and healers, and hearing for the first and only time the great healer Olga Worrall. She was on a panel with the researcher Thelma Moss. They were describing a man who had been seriously injured and was in a hospital bed. I later learned this was Mitchell May, who is now a healer in his own right. They described how he experienced pain in his severely broken leg every time a nurse or doctor even approached his bed. His leg wasn't healing and no one knew why. Then one day a healer came to visit him. The man stopped for a few seconds before entering the room, and then carefully walked around the outside edge of the wall until he got to the opposite side of the room from Mitchell's broken leg. Only then did he approach the bed. For the first time in weeks Mitchell felt no pain. The healer came every day and Mitchell's leg quickly began to heal.

Someone in the audience stood up and asked Dr. Moss about how healers could protect themselves from absorbing the pain of the people they worked with. She said she didn't know. She asked Olga Worrall. She said just to pray. She asked the audience if anyone knew any additional techniques. No one raised a hand. My husband nudged me to raise mine. I couldn't. I was too timid. I felt that I would be deluged with questions and people, and I felt I wasn't strong enough yet to handle it. I sometimes wonder how my life would have been different if I'd raised my hand at that moment. But I kept my secret to myself and tried to just work on my own boundaries.

As I became stronger, I noticed that my hands became warm, sometimes even hot, when I was in the presence of someone who was ill or in pain. Instead of absorbing their physical or emotional distress, I recognized it, defined it as "not mine" and found my hands getting hot. I didn't know what this meant. A friend of mine thought that I was getting healing abilities. No, I said, not me. I'm Protestant. But it kept happening. More and more often my hands became hot with no conscious control on my part. One day a friend had an earache. I spontaneously reached out in a gesture of care and put my hand over his ear. His earache disappeared. I was more surprised than he was. See! he proclaimed, you are getting healing abilities! I thought he was playing a joke on me, but in fact, his earache had disappeared completely and permanently. A few days later he gave me a beautiful leather-bound diary with gold-leafed edges to keep as my first healing journal. Before he let me write in it, he took it back and insisted on scribing a title page. He wrote "Confessions of a Reluctant Healer."

Healing opportunities started happening more often. It became known among my small circle of friends that if they had a headache or backache, they should ask me to put my hands over the area. The results were always positive. Instantaneously, whatever it was would go away. I remembered the vision I had that day at the conference when I saw myself reaching out to touch my mother's forehead. Was that a premonition of healing abilities? At first I was very hesitant to think so. What would this mean to my life? I was working a normal nine to five job in an office. I had no intention of becoming a healer. When I received my undergraduate degree in Comparative Religion people kept asking me what I was going to do. Become a minister? That's the only thing anyone could think of that I was qualified to do. No, I stated emphatically, I'm going to live. Where that line came from, I don't know. The arrogance of youth combined with the wisdom of an old soul voice echoing up from a chamber of my heart?

So I lived with hot hands placed reluctantly upon injured flesh and aching hearts, and I became what is known as a spiritual healer. And for the first time in my life, I felt as though I had come home.

It took only a year and a half before I had a full-time private practice in spiritual healing and could give up my job at one of Manhattan's most prestigious museums. You're going to do what? my friends would ask, astonished. Become a full-time healer? No

✳

one did that. Not in New York City, anyway. California maybe. But New York? We could count on one hand the spiritual healers we knew in New York. It was the mid-seventies and the "new age" and "alternative medicine" were still in their infancy. The phrase "holistic healing" would not enter into our language until the eighties. It was a little anxiety producing, giving up a secure income, moving out of a shared apartment and into one by myself at twice the rent. But I knew it was the right move. I felt I had come to the place in my life where I was meant to be, and everything was falling into place.

When at first I couldn't find the right apartment, I sat down and pictured exactly what I wanted. Big casement windows, old-fashioned tiled bathroom, lots of closets, and a swimming pool in the building. My mother thought I was pushing the envelope a little with a swimming pool. But within a few days of doing the imagery exercise, I found exactly what I wanted. I remember the man in the real estate office taking me upstairs with the key. He opened the front door of the apartment. I wasn't three steps through the door when I said out loud "I'll take it." I remember his stammering "But you haven't seen it yet." Yes I had. And it looked exactly as I had imagined. Later this process of visualization, creating the energy of reality within the mind and the psyche as a way of aligning with external reality, was to become a cornerstone of my healing practice, along with laying-on-of-hands, prayer, meditation, and spiritual counseling.

Friends sent friends to see me. Word got around and strangers started coming. At first everyone I touched seemed to get well. Headaches would magically disappear, and I could feel them rising up and out through the top of someone's head as I pulled upward with my hands. Neck and back problems would ease. Emotional heartaches would improve. My intuitive abilities and my psychic sponge qualities seemed to tie in nicely with the healing. I could often diagnose a problem by feeling it within myself. I had gotten good enough at letting go of other people's pain, so that I could allow myself to feel it for a few seconds and then release it without damage to myself. Once in a while I got stuck with something, and I would have to try to figure out what unresolved wound it had touched in me before I could release it. Once I realized what it was, I could release whatever I had taken on from the other person. I washed my hands after every healing. I prayed before and during the healings and said a word of thanks to God afterward.

I felt like a kid with a new toy. Healing gave me great joy. It was thrilling to be able to help someone in pain. I came from a family with a tremendous amount of physical illness. As I look back on my development as a healer, I am sure I chose my parents and my family so I could be immersed in that suffering and develop a desire to help and heal, to love and care for others. I firmly believe that past lives form our souls, and that as souls we choose each lifetime to learn and to heal the wounds of previous lifetimes. In fact, the belief in reincarnation was accepted in Christianity until 543 A.D., when Justinian decided to forbid the idea. There are still a few references to reincarnation in the New Testament that the Church missed when it deleted all the others. In one, it is questioned whether Jesus is Elijah reincarnated. In Judaism a place is set at the Passover table for Elijah, should he return. All Eastern religions refer to past lives, and the cycles of death and rebirth are seen as the "eternal return."

It doesn't really matter if one believes in past lives. After all, this is the lifetime that really counts, because any previous lives have led up to this life. But past life visions have come to me spontaneously and have given me tremendous insight into myself and others, and so they are an experiential reality for me.

My first past life vision occurred quite unsolicited and very early in my awakening as a healer. A past life vision has a very different feel to it than a dream. It can occur when one is awake or half awake and is very clear. Sometimes past lives enter our dream state as well. I remember hearing of a woman who dreamed every night of living another life with another family. Considering what we are now beginning to understand from physics about time, space, and the possibility of parallel realities, such concurrent lives do not seem impossible.

I lay down on my bed to take a nap one afternoon. As I was drifting off into what I now know is a hynogogic state, that is, an altered state of consciousness between waking reality and sleep, I had a lucid vision. A heavyset Native American woman, middle-aged, with dark hair pulled back behind her head, seemed to float above me. Somehow I knew this was me, another me, from a past life. I watched as a scene unfolded behind my closed eyelids. It seemed to unfold off to my right above me, as though I were watching a movie that someone was projecting into the air. I saw my father as a young Native American brave in his early twenties or late teens. He was going through an initiation involving a poisonous snake. He was in the center of a circle with the snake and I was his mother, this dark-haired woman, watching the ceremony from outside the circle. The snake lunged at my father and bit him. He became ill from the poison. I sat by his side and nursed him, feeding him spoonfuls of something from a bowl. Corn? He died. He failed the initiation. Recovering from the poison would have been a successful initiation. The vision ended as abruptly as it had begun, and I was left to ponder its meaning. I wondered if I felt I had failed as a mother. I wondered whether becoming a healer was my unconscious attempt to heal my father and my wounded soul from that lifetime. In this lifetime my father had been bitten by the poison of alcohol, and his soul had never fully recovered its life force. I also considered that the vision might just be imaginary, but why would my psyche create something so lucid and painful? I had not been studying Native American culture, and if I were to make up a vision, it certainly would have been more pleasant. I was to discover many years later that such a Native American ceremony actually exists.

This vision explained to me why I felt such guilt about my father's illness. It is well known that small children go through a stage where they believe they cause everything. They have no feeling of separation from people and the world around them. From a psychological point of view, as a child I probably felt that I had caused my father to become ill and then couldn't save him. From a past life perspective, I had to go through the grief, shame, and guilt of being mother to a young man who failed his spiritual initiation, and the terrible death and loss of the son I loved. This vision gave me new insight into the path of healing that seemed to be unfolding before me, and insight into why I felt such a deep need to understand the mysteries of initiation, illness, failure, death, grief, and love. As I look back on this vision now, I realize that it has also taught me to accept death and failed initiations as learning experiences for everyone involved and not to experience such intense guilt when a patient dies. Death is not in my control. It is a great mystery and something between God and the other person's soul. I am not everyone's savior.

This insight was to become painfully clear to me many years later when I chose to do a past life regression with Pamela Oline, a New York City psychotherapist with many years of training in past life therapy. I found myself once again in a Native American lifetime. This time I was a medicine man. My tribe was at war with another tribe, and I was asked to intervene and do ceremonial magic that would give my tribe power over the enemy. I went into an altered state and saw that it was my tribe's fate to be killed. I felt tremendous grief in knowing that all my people would die. I knew that the chief and the tribe would not accept this fate, and they would hate and kill me for delivering this message. I felt terrible inner conflict, grief, and guilt. I loved my people and wanted to save them. Instead of obeying my inner vision, I performed the required ceremonial magic. The braves of my tribe had killed a member of the other tribe and brought him to me. I ate his entrails. I can remember the horror and nausea I felt during this part of the past life regression. Eating poison, eating death as a way to save life. I had disobeyed the vision the Great Spirit had given me. I misused my medicine and my powers to save my people and myself. When Pamela asked me what I needed to do to be freed from the horror and suffering of this life, I heard the word "forgiveness." I need to forgive myself. I felt a powerful wave of forgiveness, tears, and healing flow through me. I cried from the depth of my soul and felt the tears wash clean the pain of that life. When I arose from the regression I became aware of how, in this present life, I have kept eating other people's pain, death, and negative energies. No more. I could no longer betray what I knew, saw, heard, and felt. I could no longer ingest poison in an effort to save life—mine or anyone else's. I would have to speak the truth even if I betrayed those I loved. I could not save everyone by betraying God.

It took me years to understand and accept these profound insights. In the early days I think God decided to give me a pregnancy period—about nine months of healing everyone I touched. I look back on this magical time as one of confidence building. Then slowly, one by one, I began getting more complex cases, more people in chronic pain, with deeper emotional problems. I don't remember who the first one was who didn't feel better, but I began to notice that instantaneous healings did not always happen. It was confusing at first. I had gotten so used to being able to heal instantaneously, that it hadn't occurred to me that it might be a honeymoon period until I had to deal with the rough stuff. When people didn't improve, I wondered how much of it had to do with me and how much with them. I had read the stories of all the great healers: Olga Worrall, Harry Edwards, Agnes Sanford, and Gordon Turner. Dean Kraft was just beginning his work in New York then, and my dear friend Bryce Bond had been a healer for years. The books were full of success stories, very few failures. These were the days of what I would call "power healing." The healers had the power and bestowed it on the person in need. Sometimes, we would talk with them about their emotional, mental, and spiritual pain, but the assumption, at first, was that the healer could cure the problem if he or she were powerful enough—if God had chosen to work through them.

So I began by believing in all the same assumptions that my role models believed in. But I was to find during the next few years that the very fabric, the very meaning of healing was on the cutting edge of changing from power healing to empowered healing—from the healer's power, to the healing power within the person in need. One after another, as people appeared in my living room for private sessions, I noticed deep emotional and spiritual wounds that seemed to be having a direct effect on their physical conditions. The more questions I asked and the more intuitive insights I gently offered, the more I became convinced of the essential connection between the mind, the heart, and the body; and between someone's relationship with God and the experience of meaning in someone's life. Between intimate relationships and health. One by one, like foundation stones in a cathedral, each person who offered himself or herself up to me for healing was laying down a stone of wisdom in my spiritual growth as a healer. I have always been grateful to the people who allowed me to build a sacred site from their offerings. They have allowed me to be a healer in this lifetime, so I could learn to surrender to my own healing. There is no greater gift.

Toward the end of my museum work, as I was deciding to leave to become a healer in New York, I walked into the museum cafeteria for lunch. Across the room I noticed a tall man with his hair done up in a topknot. I recognized him at once, although I had never met him. I didn't really understand much about past lives back then, but I *knew* him. I did something I have never done before or since. I walked directly over to his table, where he was sitting alone, and asked if I could join him. He looked up at me surprised, but with a knowing smile on his face, as though he recognized me too. This was the start of a long and fruitful friendship, one that led me down the path to becoming a teacher of healing, traveling to India and Nepal, and studying Tibetan Buddhism and its goddesses of healing.

My new friend was a Tibetan Buddhist yogi, one of the first Americans to be so ordained. John had devoted his entire life to Tibetan Buddhism and had spent long hours translating sacred manuscripts into English. He spent six months of every year in the United States and six months in Kathmandu, Nepal, where much of the exiled Tibetan community was located. He told me that he remembered having a vision at the age of three of one of the Tibetan goddesses. He didn't understand it until many years later, when he saw her picture in a book. At that moment of recognition, his vision made sense to him. He felt that he belonged in the Tibetan Buddhist community, and he felt uncomfortable and out of place having been born into a white, middle-class, Protestant family in New Jersey.

He was the first person to speak with me of past lives. He *knew* he had lived before. Most three-year-old children do not have spontaneous visions of Tibetan goddesses. When he finally found his way to India and Nepal, he said he felt as though he had come home. I knew what he meant.

The following winter we spent a month together in India and Nepal. I remember my first experience after getting off the plane in Delhi. I saw a beautiful Indian woman and, like a typical tourist, wanted to take her photograph. I asked her permission and she shook her head from side to side. I lowered my camera. She stood there, as though waiting, yet when I asked her again, she shook her head no. She finally walked away. I turned to my friend, who was getting the luggage and told him what had happened. He laughed. He told me that in India shaking the head from side to side means yes. Truly, I was on new ground.

India was both fascinating and frightening. The bus ride from the airport passed by poor shacks with dirty and diseased children in torn clothes. There were flies and stray cats and dogs. I had never seen such poverty. My middle-class background had not prepared me for this. I felt saddened by what I saw. With my intense ability to empathize, even merge with people, I wondered how I would survive a month amid such suffering. But I trusted my friend and knew he would guide me safely through what was familiar territory to him. We stayed in small, cheap pensiones wherever we traveled, which was usually by bus and train while we were still in India. We could get to Nepal only by plane.

We traveled through Delhi, Bombay, and down the southwestern coast of Goa, where John had friends he knew well. We arrived in the afternoon after a long, hot bus trip. There were miles of beaches and small houses stretched out along the sand. We walked into a low-ceilinged white house with dirt floors. After the initial introductions, I asked where the bathroom was. John and his friend looked at each other and smiled. Out back. I walked to the back of the house and outside, where I saw a double outhouse. I hadn't used one since camp, which was a distant memory. I summoned my courage and walked in. A few seconds later I heard thundering hoofs and a bloodcurdling scream. Mine. There was a large brown wild pig staring up at me through the seat. Upon reentering the house, I learned that this was the way things were disposed of on the beach. And the way everyone was introduced to Goa.

I slept that night on a thin mat that had been laid on the dirt floor. I awoke to find a scorpion staring me in the face. I bolted upright, and the scorpion went on his way. Mother Nature was present in India in abundance. There was no way to be a "space case" and stay alive. Being grounded, in touch with physical reality was a prerequisite. And I found it hard. I could not eat spicy food, the norm in India. I subsisted on eggs, made into omelets with a few vegetables, and fresh fish while we were in Goa. We would wake up every morning at sunrise, walk out onto the tan sand, and watch the first catch of the day come in at 6 A.M. The boats were multicolored, with big fishnets. The Indian men would lay the nets on the sand in the bright sunlight, and we would watch the fish jump. We knew we would be eating those fish for lunch or dinner that night.

I had heard about Rajneesh's ashram in Poona, and John agreed to go. This guru and his books were just beginning to become popular. Most people probably recognize his name from the commune he founded years later in Oregon. A small newsletter asked me to do an article about my trip to India, and I had brought along a camera. When we arrived, we found a front office that everyone had to pass through before they could walk the grounds. I explained that I wanted to do a news article and asked if I could take photographs. They said that they did not usually allow them, but to walk around the grounds and see how I felt afterward. In other words, use my own judgment.

I saw mostly white Westerners in their twenties and thirties, scurrying here and there, and dressed in orange, the color of the sexual energy center. One woman was angrily shouting, another running. The energy seemed chaotic. I kept looking for some sense of tranquility, but I felt none. Most ashrams are places to find peace through meditation. We walked for an hour or so, and I took no photographs. On the way out, I turned and pointed my camera up at the front gate to get one photo of the entrance. Out of nowhere a woman descended upon me screaming at the top of her lungs "No photos! No photos!" She tried to grab my camera, but I pulled away from her. I explained that I had permission if I wished to take photographs. She told me that was not true. She ushered me into the front office, where I was confronted by the woman who had told me to use my own judgment. The woman insisted that I had been told not to take photos. I repeated to her exactly what she had said. She tried to weasel out of it by saying that she meant I should take none. But that is not what she said, I pointed out. I refused to hand over my film or camera and left.

I was furious. Insulted. Confused. I had gone to an ashram expecting to find tranquillity, clarity, and compassion. I suppose I was looking for an oasis of healing in the midst of India's suffering. What I found was more suffering, rampant confusion, and anger. Everyone wearing orange. Everyone with their sexual centers blasted wide open. No wonder there was chaos. I was to learn later from people who had lived there that there was violence and sometimes sexual assault, all in the name of "letting it all hang out." When the lid is taken off repressed emotions, all the unhealed wounds and primal energies get acted out. In the West, most of this is done within the safety of a psychotherapeutic relationship, a safe container, over time. In most Hindu and Buddhist spiritual practices, such energies are confronted within the safety of the guru-disciple relationship, and through certain meditations, also over a period of years. In Poona there seemed to be no safe container, except maybe the ashram itself, which kept the outside world safe from most of the internal chaos.

Disappointed, and vowing never to wear all orange, we left

Poona. We boarded a train for a long journey whose destination escapes me now. But I remember in vivid detail what happened at one of the stops. Alone in the car while John went to find the conductor, I was looking out of the window when a half-dozen teenage Indian boys lept up and onto the partially opened window. Shouting excitedly in words I could not understand, they tried to force their way through the window and into the compartment. I was terrified. The train whistle blew and the train began to move. The boys fell back and I lept toward the window to close it. The heavy pane of glass fell with full force upon my fingers. The pain was so intense that my whole life passed before my eyes. My fingers crushed, I would never again be able to play the piano. I couldn't lift up my hands. I was trapped. John had insisted I lock the compartment door behind him when he went out. Now he could not get back in to help me. I must have screamed because I heard him pounding on the door. He finally got the conductor to open the door and he lifted the window off my fingers. I looked down at them. They were flat, as though crushed, and beginning to turn blue. The conductor ran for ice. I sat down, nauseated, almost fainting from the pain. Blue. "Use blue," I heard inside myself. My rational mind thought this didn't make any sense, since my fingers were blue, but then I remembered that blue light was the color used for pain relief in imagery healing. I lay down and as they placed ice over my fingers, I kept imaging blue light flowing down through my hands and fingers. The ice was agonizing but necessary. I lost track of time and lay there for a long time sending blue light through my fingers. The pain almost disappeared. The conductor finally brought a doctor into the compartment. He looked at my hands gently and carefully. When he lifted them in his I could feel the healing in his hands. I looked into this Indian doctor's eyes and smiled. I knew a true healer when I felt one. The pain disappeared completely. By the time he left, I was pain free and resting comfortably. Several hours later, at the next train stop, they brought another doctor on to examine my hands. He was brusque and rough. By the time he finished examining me I was in pain again. He was not a healer. I lay awake all night in agony trying to send blue light through my fingers and regain the healing that this man had taken away.

My fingers recovered with my own healing attention to them, and we continued on our trip. One of the last memories I have of India was of a little girl and her mother. The child could not have been more than three years old. She had only one eye. The other was injured or diseased. Her mother was standing off to the side, motioning at her to beg from me. She put out her small hand but then dropped it to her side. She looked up into my eyes and just stood there. I looked into hers, mine filling with tears, and smiled. She smiled back. We stood there for a long time. Maybe time stood still. Somewhere off in the distance I heard her mother encouraging her to beg and John trying to pull me away. We ignored them. Our souls saw each other, clearly and joyfully, with love. A moment in eternity. I wished healing for her eye. I don't know what happened to her, but she lives in my memory as a smiling face of love in the midst of suffering. A true goddess of healing.

From India we flew to Kathmandu, Nepal, where John would live for the next six months. There is a magnificent Bodhi Stupa, or shrine, just outside Kathmandu. The Tibetans circumambulate it several times daily, and a community has grown up around it. The snow-covered mountains can be seen in the background, as well as the monastery. John took me up to his scholar's room in an old house. It was a tiny single room where he lived six months of the year. So tiny, that I imagined him to have been one of the ascetics who lived in a cave in a previous lifetime. As we walked around the Stupa and I looked into the beautiful dark faces of the Tibetan people, with turquoise and coral hanging from their necks, and their soft and gentle dispositions, I could understand his need to get away from the United States. I could appreciate his choice to find sanctuary in his own soul amid his wisdom books.

I left Kathmandu with a small statue of Tara, the Tibetan Buddhist goddess of compassion and healing. The name Tara, according to scholar of myth Joseph Campbell, has two distinct meanings: savior and star. The first relates to "liberation from suffering," the second to "spreading out as light." She sits on my meditation altar to this day.

When John returned from India at the beginning of the following summer, in 1977, we went to Amherst, Massachusetts, to the American Institute for Buddhist Studies. The Tibetan Buddhist scholar Robert Thurman, father of actress Uma Thurman, was holding his first summer institute, and had invited John to give a class. I went with him. At one point Bob started asking me about my healing work. He seemed interested and inquired whether there were any healers in New York who could come up to teach a seminar on healing. Excited by the idea, I said I would inquire. I was just getting started, and had never taught a class before, so I turned to Bryce Bond and to the psychic with reddish brown hair. They agreed to come up for the weekend, talk about spiritual healing, and demonstrate techniques. We picked a day, announced it at the institute, and posted fliers. About twenty people signed up. We had the room all ready and the participants registered, and my friends called the night before and said they weren't coming. I was floored. They gave me the simple reason that it didn't "feel right." As I look back on it twenty years later, I wonder if they knew exactly what they were doing.

Chagrined, I had to tell Bob Thurman. He responded by informing me that *I* had to give the class. I stopped breathing. I had never taught a class before. John smiled and told me not to worry. He would help. I raced for my books about healers and healing, put together an opening talk, and decided to teach people how to open their heart centers and do the laying-on-of-hands. I never considered the possibility that it might not work.

The next day I dressed all in white to protect myself and to symbolize white light, the purest level of the light spectrum and the one that contains all color rays within it. I took my notes and sat at the front of my first workshop. I practically read all my material, talking about the history of healing in Great Britain, the great British healers Harry Edwards and Gordon Turner, and how healers are welcome in hospitals there. I talked of the beloved American healers Olga and Ambrose Worrall, and of the great Agnes

Sanford. The entire time John stood at the back of the room and kept smiling and nodding at me. Then, a funny thing happened. My nervousness disappeared, I forgot that I had never given a class, and I found myself feeling a strange sense of familiarity up there. People often ask me, to this day, if I am nervous in front of an audience. I always say no. They think it's strange, maybe even arrogant of me, but they don't understand that once again, as a teacher of healing, I felt as though I had found a home.

When it came time to do the laying-on-of-hands, I divided the audience into pairs, one person sitting, the other standing behind with hands over the other person's shoulders. I told those standing to take a deep breath, close their eyes, and deeply relax. I suggested they imagine God's love and energy as a white light coming down from the heavens, through the top of their heads, and into their hearts and hands. As they did, I could see that this imagery was helping them get in touch with the love and compassion in their hearts. I encouraged the people seated to think of something they wanted healed, and to open to the light and energy coming through the healer standing behind them. I had the healer first place his or her hands on the person's shoulders, then the heart chakra, the center of love and compassion, emotional empathy. I stood at the front of the room guiding the process and watching.

And then it happened. People started crying. Tears rolled down cheeks, faces filled with light, smiles turned blissful, and I watched as people laid down love in each others' hearts and rested in the presence of God. The wave of emotional healing was profound. Individuals let go of pent-up feelings they had buried for years. Physical conditions and pain began to ease under the touch of trusting inexperience, and light filled the room. I had never seen anything like it, but I would experience it again and again during the next twenty years, like a thousand-petaled lotus opening before my eyes.

At the end of the day, after everyone had left, I walked over to John. He smiled and said "You're a natural teacher. You have done this many times before. You will do it many more."

2
Gifts

The phone rang. It was Apple Skills Exchange, one of the first New York City teaching cooperatives. They wanted to know if I would give a four-week class on healing in Manhattan. How did they get my name? They couldn't remember. I said yes.

One evening a week for four weeks, a small group of students filled my living room in Chelsea. I had looked in all kinds of books for things to talk about and for healing meditations I could try out on people. It hadn't occurred to me to trust myself yet, despite the success of the workshop in Amherst. I guided students through chakra opening meditations that my friend taught me from Tibetan Buddhism, and anything else I could find. They worked, they always worked. I was amazed. The petals of the lotus just kept opening in front of my eyes. People responded. More students came. The Exchange called at the end of four weeks and asked whether I could give another class. I said yes. So many students signed up that I had to break the class up into two groups and give two evenings a week. Then three evenings. Then the students wondered whether there was a way they could continue to study with me. I finally gave an all-day workshop on a Saturday.

What they didn't understand was that I wasn't quite sure how I did what I did. I had never had a teacher or a guru. I had never studied with anyone. I took one or two classes with one or two people here and there, but what I did had happened *to me*. I had no idea how to teach others to heal. The only experience I had was that one workshop in Amherst.

I tried to analyze how the healing happened. Were there steps? What if people placed their hands above the body instead of on the body? What about using color instead of white light? I knew that healing really happened because people opened to God's presence, not because of any particular technique. I kept telling the students, just trust the process. Open to God. Open to love. But that is easier said than done sometimes, for some people, and students kept asking for more and more effective and advanced ways of opening, trusting, and surrendering to the healing process.

At the time I was seeing private clients for various kinds of illnesses and physical symptoms. I worked intuitively. I decided to try to understand what I did in a private session and describe the process to the students who wanted to learn. Most healers at that time, including Olga Worrall, believed healing was a gift that couldn't be taught. As I look back, I realize that I was going against tradition. I was going against the voice of authority. Frankly, it never occurred to me that healing couldn't be taught. Despite knowing only a handful of healers, I never thought that I was only one of an elite group of people who could perform this miraculous act. In fact, I was always startled when people would ask me later in magazine and television interviews whether healing could really be taught. Of course, why not? I never understood the concept of "a chosen people." Aren't we all chosen? Isn't that why we're here? Isn't that what Jesus and Buddha were trying to tell us? You're already chosen. God already loves you. Now love God. Love yourself. Love others.

So I set out to teach what I could already do. I set out to help people awaken the healer within. I have always called my introductory self-healing workshop "Awakening the Healer Within." I have never changed it. It is as true and valid today as it was twenty years ago. Healing is about awakening the inner healer. It is about the empowerment of our inner relationship with God, and, thereby, with our own soul. It is definitely *not* about empowering somebody else to do it for us. Many people do not want to be empowered. Years later, my husband gave me a gift to use in my healing practice: a silver magic wand. He told me I would need it. I told him I wouldn't. He was right. Many people have come to me looking for the magic wand to be waved over their heads. No matter how many times I emphasize the need for people to participate in their own healing process, I always find myself sensationalized into the healer who can perform miraculous healings. The word *miracle* means *a wonder* in Old French. That's all, a wonder.

All of us have a desire for someone else to be the idealized healer, the good parent. The all-knowing, all-loving, all-protective, all-healing parent we never had. We look to healers, gurus, spouses, even our own children to give us what we should have gotten in infancy but never did. We want it to be easy. We want to nestle back into the warmth and comfort of the breast and allow someone else to be responsible for our well-being. The hardest bullet to bite is that once that chance is gone, it's gone forever, and no one can ever give us a new childhood in quite the same way.

But I knew that I could help my students and patients become their own healers. The first step was to discover the place of the wound. That seemed to be what my sensitivities allowed me to do in private sessions. My intuition and psychic sponginess were so great that I could sense people's pain when they made their appointment on the phone. When I opened my front door, I received another set of impressions from their presence, their energies, their face, body language, and clothes. I still remember a young man in his thirties coming to the door of my apartment in Chelsea. I opened the door and heard the word "death" inside my mind. I got scared. Did this mean he was going to die? No, I didn't sense that. Had someone else around him died? Yes, that felt right. He must have noticed my expression because he asked me why I looked so startled. I hesitated to answer, but I asked if someone around him had passed away. He told me his father had just died. He had not told me this on the phone, and in fact, as I recall, his father had just died a day or two before his appointment, but after he had scheduled it. We spent the entire session talking about his relationship with his father. The healing experience for him was emotionally profound. It allowed him to grieve and to begin to forgive the past and his father.

I tried to help people get in touch with their own sensitivities. I guided them through chakra opening meditations, so they could feel their inner energies. The word *chakra* comes from the Sanskrit for "wheel" and refers to the centers of light and subtle energies that we hold in our etheric body, our subtle energy body. Kundalini energy is the movement of these energies through our spine, our chakras, and the nadis, the internal channels on each side of our spine. The subtle energy body is invisible to most people, but it is the configuration of light energy that supplies our physical body with life force. It is the energizing substance of which we are composed. Subtle energies form the life field in and around the body. Without this grid, or network, of interlacing life energy, we would die. It is the astral body, or soul body, which unlike the etheric body, can separate from the physical body during sleep, surgery, or traumatic events, such as car accidents. People often report experiences of looking down at their own physical bodies during such occurrences.

John had initially introduced me to the chakras through guided meditation. The Hindus and Buddhists have used chakras for thousands of years in meditation and yogic practice. The chakras are centers of light energy, rising from the root chakra at the base of the spine, which is a denser, warmer, heavier vibration and more connected to earth; to the crown chakra at the top of the head, which is a lighter, finer, faster frequency, and more connected to the heavens. Each chakra has a particular color, quality, body area or organ, animal, food, gemstone, and planet associated with it. The colors range from red to violet, just as in the light spectrum in physics. The most thorough books on the chakras to date are by Anodea Judith, *Wheels of Life,* and *The Sevenfold Journey,* which she co-wrote with Selene Vega. There is a simple description of the seven major chakras, from my own work:

	color	qualities, energies	body location affected
1	red	survival, grounding, safety	coccyx bone, legs, knees, ankles, feet, skin, colon, bones
2	orange	sexuality, clairsentience, creative life force	reproductive organs, lower back, bladder
3	yellow	will, motivation, vitality	digestion, stomach, liver, gall bladder, pancreas, spleen, middle spine, kidneys, adrenal glands, intestines
4	green	love, compassion, emotional empathy	heart, thymus gland, breasts, lungs, upper back, shoulders, arms, hands
5	blue	self-expression, power, clairaudience	throat, thyroid gland, neck, jaw, teeth, ears
6	indigo	vision, psychic sight, clairvoyance, telepathy	third eye between eyebrows, pineal and pituitary glands, eyes
7	violet	spiritual consciousness	crown of head, brain, scalp, hair

When the chakras are open and balanced relative to each other, they allow the free flow of subtle energies throughout the body. In Chinese acupuncture, now being accepted by Western medicine, there are energy meridians that connect all the organs, nerves, and muscles. They cannot be seen with the eyes, but their energies can be felt by taking a person's pulses and noting the responses when acupuncture needles are placed at certain designated points. In much the same way, the energies of the chakras create an energy system throughout the physical body that can be sensed and felt with the hands and seen with the intuitive senses. Although more centered through the torso than the meridians, which run vertically through the limbs as well as the torso, these spiraling wheels of energy have effects through all the muscles, nerves, and organs.

The chakras rotate in the center of the physical body, opening to the outside world through both the front and back of the body. The first chakra, the center of survival, safety, and grounding, also opens straight down into the earth and connects us with it. The more I worked with scanning the chakras, the more aware I became of the energies at the back of the body holding both the energies of the past and the supporting energies of the body and soul. In fact, if we think about it, the past, including past lives, usually *is* the supporting energy of the body and soul. The energies moving in and out of the chakras through the front of the body are the forward moving energies that keep us connected with the present and future, as well as with the people and events taking place in our lives now.

When a chakra is closed, shut down, or blocked in some way by a repressed emotion or memory, it can lead to physical symptoms. In the process of doing laying-on-of-hands, I began to feel different energies emanating from people's bodies. I noticed that some were warm, others cold, some pleasant, others painful. I could feel pricking, tingling, and stabbing where there was pain; I could feel warmth, gentle swirling, and an even flow where the body was healthy. I also noticed that I could feel a distinctive flow of circular movement over the chakras. When my hands were over such an area, I began not only to feel sensations in my hands, but also to notice emotions, words, and images in my mind and awareness.

Being the psychic sponge that I was, my main sensitivity was in *clairsentience,* which means "clear feeling." In Great Britain, psychics are called "sensitives." This means that I would feel the physical and emotional energies of the person with whom I was working. I could feel an individual's subtle and physical energies in my hands, and I would feel the person's emotional energies within me. Whatever emotion was being stored in that chakra or in a location of the body would blow through me like a breeze. It was as though I would become that person for a moment and experience what the person was experiencing, or refusing to experience. Sometimes I would feel things that people were not aware of at a conscious level, such as repressed emotions and memories. If it was something psychologically traumatic, such as sexual abuse, I would observe the insight but not voice it until given a sign that the person was aware of it as well. If it was less traumatic, such as unspoken anger at a boss, I would express what I was feeling and allow the patient to give me feedback on the validity of my information.

During my early years teaching at Esalen Institute in Big Sur, California, a particularly dramatic example of clairsentience occurred in one of the workshops. We were doing laying-on-of-hands in pairs, and I was moving around to all of the tables, adding some additional healing energy where I felt it was needed. I moved to one table on which rested an Asian woman in her forties. I placed my hands instinctively over her heart chakra, took a deep breath, and dropped down into my own heart to fill with love. I began to feel terrible sadness emanating from her heart and body. I felt myself going down into a deep well of darkness and despair, and I knew that I was merging with her at a very deep level. I grounded my legs and feet into the floor. I could feel my legs becoming like pillars. My whole body began to shake, and before I realized what was happening I could hear myself making a strange sound. I listened to my own voice. Keening. It sounded like keening. I allowed myself to continue, knowing something very important was taking place. A few minutes later I heard another voice keening. It was coming from the woman on the table. She was matching my note. I lost track of time. All I could hear was the keening of deep loss and grief in her voice. It became louder and louder. We were down at the baths using the massage tables for the healings, and one of the Esalen staff noticed what was happening. He came over and stood behind me for support, as my body was beginning to weaken under the power of the energy and grief moving through me. At one point I began to collapse, and he had to hold me up. When it was all over the woman on the table lay very still, resting, with several other students standing guard to see if she needed anything. The Esalen staff member took me outside to one of the baths overlooking the ocean and sat with me until I felt strong enough to get up.

That night in the workshop everyone gasped when the woman walked in the room. She had a new face: open, soft, full of light. It was one of the most extraordinary examples of emotional healing I would ever see. She told us the story behind the loss and grief, a story I have now forgotten. She said that when she heard my wailing, something inside her opened and the same sound forced its way up from a deep recess inside her heart, where she had been keeping it buried. Gone were the twenty years of grief she had been carrying in her face and body, and in front of us had blossomed a new face with new life. It was a true resurrection of heart, soul, and body.

Another area of sensitivity that I had developed to some degree and continue to develop is *clairaudience,* which means "clear hearing." I am able to hear words, names, even whole sentences in my mind as I work with someone, just as when I heard the word "death" as I opened the door to the patient whose father had died. Admittedly, sometimes what I hear is not pleasant. I remember scanning one woman and clairsentiently feeling a strong male presence trying to interfere and to take control. I mentally asked him what he wanted. He said that they had known each other when he was alive, and he wanted to be a part of her life and energy again. I silently told him that I would tell her of his presence, but I would not allow him to take control of her energy field. When the scan was done I did what I promised. She admitted that she knew who he was and that when he had been alive, he was very domineering, very controlling. She had trouble breaking away from him, and no longer wished him to control her life. I gave her some "Psychic Self-Defense" techniques to use so that she could protect herself.

In another case, a woman came to see me for some emotional and spiritual problems. When I placed my hands over her head I felt a dark evil presence and heard a voice say "We have her now.

We have control." I was startled and afraid. I mentally asked who "they" were but could not get an answer. It was very early in my work as a healer. I said a prayer and asked that God's light and healing be with her. I suggested that she go for a medical checkup. The following week she returned to tell me that the doctors had diagnosed cancer. The dark evil force was probably her shadow, the unhealed aspects of herself that were deeply hidden away and had turned destructive in the form of the cancer. Sometimes there are multiple aspects to the shadow, which may account for the "we" that I heard clairaudiently.

When a person's shadow is large, it attracts other negative energies from other people and even from disembodied spirits, and continues to grow. The destructive shadow does not always turn into physical illness. It can turn into emotional and mental illness, such as in the "Son of Sam" murderer who heard voices, or in Timothy McVeigh, charged with the Oklahoma City bombing. In the latter case, from what I have culled from the media, Mr. McVeigh had been abandoned by his mother in childhood and failed his dream of entering the special Green Beret forces. If this is true, his shadow is probably an emotionally starved child looking for love and acceptance. When he couldn't find it, his shadow become enraged and destructive. If he is guilty as charged, he destroyed innocent mothers and children and, thereby, symbolically, his mother and himself.

Clairaudience was not always so frightening for me, however. I heard the nickname "Cookie" during one of my early sessions when I was trying to tune into a deceased family member of a patient. I asked the patient if that name meant anything to her and she said no. But she turned white as a sheet and admitted to me the following week that Cookie was the nickname the woman had called her. She was so startled at the possibility that I had actually made contact with someone who had died that she couldn't admit the truth.

Sometimes I also experienced myself communicating with a positive aspect of a patient's soul. Often this aspect was the Higher Self, which knows much more than the rational mind and can lend wisdom and compassion to the healing process. It is as if each of us has a wiser, more loving observer ready to lend support if only we will pay attention. In Christianity we might think of this Higher Self as the Holy Spirit, or even an inner living Christ. If we are Buddhist, we might consider this Higher Self an inner living Buddha. I would actually hear an entire sentence, such as "What I need for healing is self-love." I remember one young woman with cancer. I heard her Higher Self say to me "You can't heal me. Just love me." I knew at that moment that she would die, but the healing would occur in the form of love.

A beautiful and moving example of clairaudience occurred in one of my early workshops. I had asked my students to bring photographs of loved ones who had passed on. I then instructed them to pick a partner and, one at a time, bring out a photograph. Together they would close their eyes and try to open to the person's presence. A few minutes later I heard faint singing. I went over to one of the pairs and noticed that one woman was singing lullaby after lullaby, while the other sat with her eyes closed and tears running down her cheeks. When the process was over, I asked them what had taken place. The partner doing the singing said she had been asked to tune into her partner's uncle. As soon as she did, she clairaudiently heard lullabies and his voice asking her to sing them to his niece. The niece confirmed that her uncle used to put her to sleep each night by singing the same lullabies to her. She had not heard them in all these years, and this sign, more than anything else, was evidence to her of his presence, and, thereby, of life after death.

Clairaudience can also involve *telepathy,* or mind-to-mind communication of thoughts or feelings. Most of us are naturally telepathic, especially with people we are close to, such as family, friends, and lovers. The phone rings and you know who it is; or you pick up the phone *before* it rings. You could have sworn you heard it ring, but then realize it didn't actually ring. How many times have you been thinking about someone who calls a few seconds later and you say, "I was just thinking about you!" You think of a friend you haven't seen in years; later that day there is a letter waiting in your mailbox. We all have these experiences. It is as though there are telepathic lines of communication between people who have emotional empathy with each other. Just as we cannot see radio waves in the air, these lines of telepathy are invisible.

I found that I had been telepathic my whole life. The kinds of thoughts and feelings I was experiencing early in my practice were like the ones I had experienced as a child. I would look at someone and be able to tell what they were thinking or, at least, have a general idea of it. I remember a friend of mine bringing a boyfriend with her to my apartment for a party. I took one look at him and felt something dark and sinister in his thoughts. He looked straight into my eyes, and I could see that he was aware I knew his true nature. As with most love relationships, friends are afraid to interfere, and most people in love won't listen anyway. I will always regret not telling my friend what I telepathically picked up from this man, because six months later he stole her possessions and burned down her loft.

Most young children are very telepathic. The original telepathic bond is between mother and child. Some mothers facilitate telepathy by attempting to communicate with their child in utero. From the beginning of my healing work, I found myself working with many pregnant and wanting-to-be pregnant women. Women who had exhausted the medical possibilities for pregnancy would come to see me, and after a few healings, would become pregnant. Some of these women continued to see me during their pregnancies, and I found that I could telepathically communicate with the child in the womb. There were times when I could not feel a soul present until several months into the pregnancy. I have since discovered that the Sufis believe a soul does not enter the fetus until it is 120 days old. I think that it is probably different for each pregnancy, though, because I have felt the soul of the child earlier in some pregnancies, and later in others.

The first woman I was aware of helping to become pregnant was a radiologist's wife. He was the first physician to take some classes with me, and when his wife could not get pregnant, he suggested she see me. She did, once, and immediately became pregnant. I did not see her throughout her pregnancy, but years later I worked with several women who not only became pregnant easily after laying-on-of-hands, but came back weekly throughout their pregnancy. One of the most memorable was a woman who came to me from Marble Collegiate Church. After she had become pregnant, she asked me to tune into whether the child was a girl or a boy, something I was 90 percent accurate at doing. At first I got girl, then boy. I couldn't understand why. She desperately wanted a girl, and during the first stages of pregnancy all fetuses are female. So I decided to wait several months and try again. When she went for the sonogram, the baby's leg covered the genitals, and even the doctors couldn't distinguish its sex. We joked together that this baby wanted to keep us guessing. During one session my patient was lying on her side, since she was more comfortable that way. I was sitting in front of her with my hands gently placed over her round abdomen. I started to smile. I could feel the baby. Wherever my hands went, the baby followed with little taps of its body, gently kicking or banging. At one point I clairaudiently heard "Hi! I'm a boy!" We had telepathically made contact and I responded "Hi! I'm so glad to meet you!" I could feel the most beautiful light and love coming from this child's soul. I was overwhelmed with the feeling of being blessed by his presence. I was not the one doing the healing. He was. I could feel my eyes well up with tears, and I sat for a long time feeling extremely humbled by being in the presence of this divine child. At that moment I understood what it must have felt like to sit in the presence of Mary when she was pregnant with Jesus. It was one of the most extraordinary experiences of my life, and I remember it today as though it were yesterday. The telepathic link between us was so strong throughout the pregnancy that he told me what names his mother should choose between. She picked one of them for his middle name. He was, of course, a boy.

Another example of telepathy, and also premonition, happened in regard to another pregnant woman. Premonition means the ability to feel, see, hear, or experience something that has not yet happened. Sometimes premonitions come in dreams, but they also occur in waking reality. I was working with a woman who was pregnant with her first child and had an intestinal condition called Crohn's disease. She was due to go for an amniocentesis. During the laying-on-of-hands I had a terrible feeling of darkness and death. I became concerned and a little frightened. I tried to tune in more deeply to what I was feeling, and I had a sense that the baby was trying to tell me it was afraid. I said a prayer, asking that God's light and love protect this child from all harm. When the healing was over, I tried to tell her as gently as I could what had happened. In one of the only times I have ever suggested that someone not get a medical procedure, I discouraged her from getting the amniocentesis. I had a feeling that it would be dangerous to the baby. She listened to what I said and admitted that she had felt something dark and strange during the healing as well. But she was frightened that her first child might not be perfect because of her own health, and so she went for the procedure. Her doctor, a woman, was just about to insert the needle when she dropped it on the floor. She began again with a clean needle and proceeded to drop that one on the floor. Flustered and confused, her doctor told her to get up and get dressed. She had never before dropped a needle, and she decided my patient was not supposed to have the procedure. The baby, a little boy, was born perfect. He was several months old when I finally met him. The first time our eyes met he held his arms out to me and laughed.

During these twenty years of being a healer, I have always stated that I did *not* have a natural gift of *clairvoyance,* which means "clear seeing." As I began to write this statement here in the book, I remembered one of my earliest experiences of clairvoyance and why I shut down this ability for a long time. It was a few months after I had the experience of picking up the physical pain that I described at the beginning of the book. One evening I had a meeting with one of the heads of the center. He wanted me to write for their newsletter. As I recall, there was a reason that I was hesitant to do so. He tried to pressure me into working there in a much broader way than I wanted. I declined. I could tell he would not easily take no for an answer, but I held my ground. I left that night and went back to my apartment, got ready for bed, crawled under the sheets, and turned off the light. I closed my eyes for a moment and then opened them. Floating above me six feet in the air was a gray astral projection of this man's head. I gasped, sat bolt upright in bed, and turned on the light. Nothing like this had ever happened to me. I ran for the telephone and called a friend of mine who did public relations work for the center. He was surprised but not unbelieving. He called a friend of his, a woman, who he knew had been intimately involved with both the center and this man, and we had a three-way phone conversation. She told me that this man was extremely adept at astral projection and mind-control techniques and that when he didn't get what he wanted, he used them on people. He was a master at power and fear games. He would project his astral, or soul, body to any location he wanted by using telepathy to connect with someone's mind. She said he had done his tricks on her many times.

The three of us discussed what to do about this situation, going back and forth from direct confrontation, which she said he would deny, to performing a little trick of our own. Since it would cause no harm, while letting him know we were aware of his games and could counter them, we decided on the latter. The three of us got off the phone and closed our eyes. We connected telepathically by imaging one another in a circle, so we would be working together, and then visualized the man who had tried to manipulate me. We placed him in the center of the telepathic circle we had formed, and each took a different part of his body to mentally pinch. To be honest, I don't remember what part I took. I only remember what part my male friend took, his backside. Then, I went back to bed. I remember being afraid to close my eyes and telling myself "I don't want to see things like this," referring to the gray astral face. In that moment I closed down my clairvoyance. I found out the next day what effect our telepathic pinches had had on this man. My friend told me that he had gone over to the center, sneaked up behind him, and gently patted his backside. The man jumped three feet in the air and let out a yelp. Our point had gotten through. To my knowledge, he never bothered me again, although his behavior led me to close down my clairvoyance.

Clairvoyance means seeing clearly what there is to be seen, without the veils of illusion, need, fear, and expectation blocking the way. This seeing can involve three-dimensional reality, such as physical objects and people's faces and bodies; it can involve other usually invisible dimensions, such as astral projections, the chakras in the etheric body, or life after death. According to both the Kabalah and superstring theory in physics, there are ten dimensions, only three of which are visible to the naked eye. Michio Kaku, a theoretical physicist at the forefront of the revolution in modern physics, writes in his book *Hyperspace:*

> If all our common-sense notions about the universe were correct then science would have solved the secrets of the universe thousands of years ago. The purpose of science is to peel back the layer of the appearance of objects to reveal their underlying nature. In fact, if appearance and essence were the same thing, there would be no need for science.
>
> Perhaps the most deeply entrenched common-sense notion about our world is that it is three dimensional.

Kaku goes on to describe the theory of hyperspace, or higher dimensional space, and its newest and most advanced formulation called superstring theory. He examines the possibilities of ten dimensions, time warps, black holes, and multiple universes. By examining these possibilities, he is also opening questions of parallel universes, changing the past, time travel, and life after death; from my perspective, maybe even the idea that there is no death at all, but a continuing transition and resurrection of life. Religion has been discussing these higher dimensions for thousands of year. Mystics and healers, including myself, have been experiencing them for even longer. As usual, science takes a while to catch up.

What is so simple and so beautiful in Kaku's statement is his acknowledgment that science's purpose is to peel back the appearance of things to reveal their underlying nature, their essence. So is mine. Any healer or empath worth his or her salt is not concerned about telling someone how much money he or she is going to earn in the stock market, or when the perfect relationship is going to come along. The purpose of these sensitivities is to hold up a mirror to a person and reveal his or her true nature, the soul essence, the place where the heart connects with God. And to reveal the wounds that may be standing in the way of this connection, so these wounds can begin to heal.

Clairvoyance means seeing into the true nature, the essence of a person, and using this sight to help in the healing process. My initial fright at seeing a gray astral face floating in the air above my bed was enough to close down my clear seeing for years. It took great attention, practice, and a willingness to see what was dark and frightening about people before I could open it again. I therefore found myself dependent on my clairsentient sensitivity to give me information, because I did not develop clairaudience until several years later.

I remember sitting in one of the only classes I ever took in developing intuitive skills. I was paired with a man, a total stranger. He gave me his watch to do a psychometry exercise. I was supposed to close my eyes and through the watch, tune into him. The teacher asked the group what we saw. Nothing. She asked us to look for colors, symbols, images. I saw nothing. Blackness. Finally, she came over to me and asked what I saw. Nothing. She had the good intuitive sense then to ask what I felt: a pain in my right arm that was holding the watch. With my eyes still closed, I could hear the man say, "I've had that pain in my arm all day." I couldn't see anything, but I could feel. Clairsentience.

With practice, I began to reopen my clairvoyance. I sat in front of candles, plants, and other objects and practiced looking at them for several seconds, closing my eyes, and then remembering the image. This exercise helps to concentrate the mind on the internal image-making process. We all image all the time but don't realize it. If you think about what you had for breakfast, what happens?

Doesn't your mind go to an image of your breakfast? That is what clairvoyance is like. It is not usually as dramatically clear as a big screen color movie. It is more subtle. If we decide to pick up a pen sitting on our desk, the first thing that happens is that we form an image of the action in our brain. This image sends chemical messengers from our brain into nerve impulses in the spinal cord, then into the nerves in our shoulder, arm, and hand. We pick up the pen. It all began with an image.

In one of my early classes for Apple Skills Exchange, a woman was having trouble with a psychometry exercise. She kept insisting that she was getting "nothing" from her partner's object, even after I asked her what she felt and heard. Still nothing. Finally, in frustration, she admitted that she saw a loaf of bread in her mind but had discarded it as meaningless. I had her focus on the loaf of bread. What did it look like? What kind of bread? Where was it sitting? What kind of table was it on? This woman went on to describe, detail by detail, her partner's entire apartment. Everyone was flabbergasted, especially her partner, who had been a total stranger to her at the beginning of the exercise. It is in those moments that I wish every skeptic in the universe could be a fly on the wall and experience the reality of these sensitivities.

As my third eye began to reopen, I had a number of strange experiences. I would lie down in bed to go to sleep, close my eyes, and visions of faces and unknown places would pass before my closed lids. Past lives? I began to see auras around and in front of people, as though emanating from their entire bodies. For about six months, all the scanning work I did with patients was conducted by sitting in front of them and looking at the colors emanating from their bodies. I didn't even have to use my hands. I could tell what condition certain organs were in by examining the colors emanating from them. One morning I awoke to find that my ability had shifted to being able to see inside people's bodies like an X-ray machine.

These empathic sensitivities and insights led me to develop a technique of "scanning" people's energies. I would begin by positioning my hands over a person's shoulders, as though I were going to do a healing. But I would refocus my intention on receiving impressions rather than sending energy. I found that my hands became like dowsing rods, vibrating and moving with the various flows of energy they encountered in someone's body or energy field. At the shoulders I could very often feel a difference between the right and left sides of the body. Always beginning several feet above the shoulders, I would lower my hands slowly until I could feel heat or cold, tingling or pain in my hands, and then, stop. Usually, my right and left hands were at different distances from the person's shoulders. Sometimes the difference felt very physical, as when I experienced a sharp pain in one hand. This pain usually meant that there was a physical problem in the shoulder. But sometimes the difference seemed more subtle, more amorphous. At times I would get a feeling of my hand's meeting up with a wall of stone, and I couldn't lower it any farther. At other times I would feel shaking in my hand, an emotion like anger, or even hear the word *mother* or *father.* When I would ask the patients or students about my impressions, they would usually confirm that they did, indeed, have several physical symptoms on their left side, and their relationship with their mother had always been very difficult. Over and over, I noticed connections between the mother issues in someone's life and the left side of the body, and between father issues and the right side of the body. The left side of the brain controls the right side of the body and many linear or "masculine" functions; the right side of the brain controls the left side of the body and many nonlinear imaging, or "feminine," functions. Once in a while this pattern would reverse itself in a left-handed person. I would later learn that brain dominance is reversed in 50 percent of left-handed people.

From standing in back of the person with my hands above the shoulders, I would move around to the person's side. I placed my hands above the top of the person's head, where the seventh chakra of spiritual consciousness is located. Always beginning several feet above the chakra, I would slowly lower and pay attention to what I felt in my hands, as well as in my own body and in my awareness. If the person had not yet opened his or her spiritual consciousness, I usually felt nothing, or my hands would lower until almost at the top of the head and remain still. If the person was actively engaged in the process of a spiritual awakening, I would feel the movement of energy flowing in and out of the head. If the person was open and needed healing energy, my hands would be drawn down to the head like a magnet. Sometimes I would see, in my inner eye, light or a symbol of religious importance to the person. I might hear a voice of someone who had passed on and wanted to communicate with the person. I would hold these insights until the end of the scan, unless there were so many that I was concerned about forgetting them. I trained myself to store them in my memory, much as on a floppy disk, and then recall them when the scan was finished.

From the seventh chakra, I moved down to the third eye, the sixth chakra of vision and psychic sight. As I slowly moved my hands, I directed my attention to physical areas of the body that were affected by these chakras. I scanned the head, brain, eyes, and sinuses before focusing on the third eye between the eyebrows. I held my right hand at the forehead and my left hand at the back of the head, as far out as I could reach. If the person had a vivid dream life, I would often see images from a dream or two. If the person had nightmares, my hands would shake violently and I would see dark unpleasant visions, which were confirmed later. If the person had problems with his or her eyesight, there was usually a corresponding blockage in the third eye. As I would move my hands in, I often felt as though I were hitting a stone wall. Sometimes my right hand would move freely in a flowing motion, while my left hand would stop short. Usually, this meant that the person could see what was in front of him or her. The person had forward-moving vision, so to speak, while being unaware of the past and the contents of the unconscious. Sometimes it was reversed, and I would feel tremendous activity at the back of the head, while nothing seemed to be happening in the front. It would turn out that the person was engaged in dealing with the past, but had no vision of the future and what he or she wanted it to look like.

From the third eye, I slowly moved my hands down through the face, jaw, teeth, ears, and into the neck and throat, where the thyroid gland is located. This gland regulates metabolism and is sometimes affected if a person suppresses the fifth chakra of self-expression. Placing my hands in front of the throat and in back of the neck, I would scan for any disturbance. If the person was open in his or her self-expression, my hands would move freely. If closed, I would hear clairaudiently in my mind what he or she was saying. If the person was suppressing a strong emotion like anger, my hands would shake violently. If the person had tension or pain in the neck, I could feel it in my left hand as a dull ache or stabbing pain.

From the throat, I moved my hands down to the heart chakra, the center of love and emotional empathy, or compassion. I would scan down through the thymus gland, part of the immune system below the collarbone, and down into the chest, through the lungs and bronchial tubes, and across the breasts. My left hand would be scanning through the shoulders and upper back and spine. If the lungs and bronchial tubes were congested, I would often feel sadness in the heart chakra. I later learned that the lungs are the organs of grief in Chinese medicine. I also seemed to have an ability to scan my hands down the spine and feel exactly which vertebrae were injured or out of alignment. This diagnosis would always be confirmed by the person, his or her X rays, or the doctor. Many people told me after their healing that my hands always came to rest on exactly the spinal location that was hurting them. It was as though my hands had minds of their own and could home in on where the pain was located.

From the heart chakra, my hands moved down through the middle torso to the third chakra at the solar plexus, the center of will, motivation, and vitality. It controls the physical vitality of the body, because the lower three chakras are physical energies. My hands would scan the stomach, then the liver and gall bladder under the right rib cage, the pancreas and spleen under the left rib cage, the transverse colon, and finally, the kidneys and adrenal glands at the middle back. If the person's vitality was low, I would feel only a faint and slow wheel of movement at the third chakra. I remember scanning one woman, who seemed to have no will energy at all. I couldn't even find the chakra. When I asked her about it later, she admitted that she had given over her will to her guru.

From the solar plexus, my hands moved down to the second chakra just below the navel in the center of the pelvis, the center of sexuality, clairsentience, and creative life force. In women the second chakra is located in the middle of the uterus, in men, the prostate. Certain areas of the intestines and colon are also in the area of the second chakra. I would scan across the colon and intestines, the hips, the sacrum, and through the bladder and reproductive organs. In someone with an open second chakra, the area would feel warm, flowing easily in a circular motion. When women were menstruating, I would notice a slight cramping in my hand and feel mild to severe congestion in the energy emanating from their pelvis. I would be able to distinguish this nearly 100 percent of the time. If a woman or a man had been sexually abused, I would feel a wall at the second chakra, followed by violent shaking of my hands and a feeling of fear. Sometimes I would clairaudiently hear "No!" over and over again or get an image of the abuse. One woman came to see me with what she thought was an ovarian cyst. My hand kept being drawn down to her bladder. I suggested that she see her physician. It turned out she had a bladder infection. I always sent people back to their doctor, never wanting to be responsible for diagnosing something without a medical license or, heaven forbid, being in conflict with their physician. My goal was to be working with the medical profession, not against it. I liked the idea of the British healers being welcomed into hospitals. I still do.

From the second chakra I moved my hands down to the first chakra at the base of the spine and below the pubic bone. This center of survival, grounding, and safety is our connection to Mother Earth. By scanning the energy in a person's legs, ankles and feet, I would be able to tell how much the person was in touch with his or her physical nature. The first chakra reveals how well mothered a person is and how able the individual is able to mother himself or herself. If an individual was not well mothered as an infant and child, the person had no role model for self-mothering. Mothering ourselves means providing for our needs: food, shelter, warmth, safety, play, exercise, rest, sleep, touch, affection, and love. When someone is not fully in his or her body, the person usually ignores some or many of these needs, and instead, substitutes mental or "power over" accomplishments such as success, money, control, work, sex without love, and other kinds of addictions. These are disembodied, nonorganic experiences in someone who is not grounded. There is nothing wrong with success, money, work, or sex, as long as the organic self-mothering needs are given a priority. When they are not, people can easily become more and more removed from their organic needs until only a crisis of illness, loss, injury, or accident stops them long enough to force them to pay attention.

I noticed that many of the people who came to see me had very little energy in their first chakra and legs. Even dancers, who I thought would be the most grounded, had little organic flow down through their legs, into their feet, and into the ground. I often felt restricted energy in their legs, and a very strong will chakra. Over and over again I would notice this pattern, and I began to conclude that many dancers forced their bodies into doing what they wanted, rather than allowing an organic process to take place while they were dancing. This resulted in many stress injuries. One dancer had an ankle sprain and was supposed to dance the night she came to see me. I did a laying-on-of-hands and the swelling and pain disappeared. She was able to dance that night, but the real problem of overstressing her body had not disappeared. Another dancer who came to see me more recently had been so demanding of her body over the years that it completely stopped functioning. She had terrible pain in her knees and legs and could no longer dance. When I scanned her body and all her chakras, I felt a tortured child trying to please her mother. We discussed this, and she confirmed that she had spent her whole life trying to please a mother who only loved her when she was "performing" perfectly. She could no longer perform perfectly. Her body had made sure of that, and her soul was trying to help her get in touch with a much deeper sense of self-worth and self-love than her mother had provided for her.

In classes, when I led my students through a self-opening meditation I entitled "Opening the Chakras with White Light," they could actually feel these flows of energy in their own bodies. In the locations of imbalance, they felt disturbance, pain, or nothing at all. As we began to discuss the results of each meditation, we all noticed that there was a direct correspondence between illnesses and physical symptoms and the chakras where the flow felt imbalanced. I asked people what emotions they were aware of at that location, or if they had any memories, images, or words come to mind. They usually did, and once we discussed what they were, we could see what past events and emotions might be tied in with the development of their illness. We looked for clues to help each person heal. I sometimes felt as though I were Sherlock Holmes.

As my students and patients grew more familiar with their chakras and more comfortable delving into the deep wheels of life within them, their intuitive abilities blossomed. Opening the chakras stimulates flows of energy that have sometimes lain dormant for many years. As children we are all psychic, meaning that we are all aware of what is going on around us. When this awareness and sensitivity is too painful, we cut it off or block it out. It usually takes guidance and a safe space or container to help the psychic awareness reopen.

I consciously tried to provide this space for my patients and students. I kept my heart open with love, so that whatever insights, no matter how painful, were elicited by the healing work, people would feel safe enough to experience them. I developed a guided process that I called "Communicating with Your Body" (*see* "Healing Meditations"). I still use it today with every first-time client who comes to me with a physical complaint. It allows people to drop into a deeply relaxed and unconscious place in which they can communicate with the illness, pain, or condition that is bothering them. Some very profound messages come from the body when it is respected and given attention. One of my early students was a man who smoked cigarettes. He wanted to quit, but every time he tried, he failed. When he focused on his throat chakra, the center of self-expression, he felt tightness and constriction. When he got in touch with the emotion there he felt anger. When he spoke with his throat, and then switched roles and became his throat, he got in touch with some deeply repressed anger toward his mother that had never been resolved. His freedom of expression had been suppressed when he was a child, and he continued to suppress it with his cigarettes. When he realized that he was doing to himself what his mother had done, and allowed himself to feel the anger, his self-expression began to open. Soon thereafter he quit for good.

During the meditations I would walk around the small circle of students and place my hands over the afflicted area. I would wait patiently until I could feel something release. Sometimes I would feel a tug, heat, or pain push out against my hands. At other times I could feel the person's body drawing the energy from my hands into the area, and my hands would become very hot and "charged." People receiving healing would usually feel the heat even if my hands were a few inches away from their bodies. And then they would either feel instantaneous relief or a gradual lessening of pain or symptomology over the next few days. The most profound feeling I experienced during each laying-on-of-hands was an opening of my own heart, my own center of love and compassion. I felt as though I was spiritually falling in love with each person I touched. I felt as though I could touch the place inside them beyond personality, beyond pain, beyond difficulty. I could feel within each person the place where God rested in his or her soul. At the end of every day, I felt more happy and energized than when I began. I felt grateful to be alive, profoundly grateful that God had given me the gift of service.

Watching students and clients heal before my eyes and feeling them heal under my hands was a thrilling experience. I felt as though I had been waiting my whole life for the opportunity to do what I was doing. I felt in the deepest place in my heart a sense of God's grace in my daily life and God's love for humanity. What I didn't realize at that time was that I was taking care of everyone else better than I was of myself. My attention was focused outward, on "the other." I had been brought up that way. My mother took care of my father when he became ill, and she took care of her mother and sisters when they became ill, as well as taking care of me, her only child. I followed in her footsteps like a good daughter, a good Christian, a good healer. I would find out many years later what a terrible price I had paid for being so good.

3
Doves

✳

Each person came to me with a story. Each person entered my life with his or her life. I listened with my body and took the individual's essence into my soul, and sometimes I was able to hand back a whole picture of who the person was.

One of the first astrologers I ever consulted told me: You are a doorkeeper. You hold open the door and people will walk through. What about me? I asked. Do I ever get to walk through? He didn't answer.

For the first two years, I would always jump when the doorbell rang or when I heard a knock at my apartment door. I loved and feared that moment when I would open the door and face another person in need. The moment of truth, when I would be presented with another human being, a stranger, who would ask me to see into his or her soul, heal the body, and want to be told that everything was going to be all right, as my mother has always done for me. But what if it wasn't?

More than that, I feared that some day I would see nothing, feel nothing: Like the day of my first piano recital, when I was seven years old. I had practiced and practiced, and the applause was deafening, and I sat on the bench and stared at the keys, and it all went blank.

I smiled and welcomed into my living room a young woman in her early twenties, slightly younger than I was. She told me that there had been a fire in her apartment building, and her two beloved doves had died in their cage. She had been at work. She cried. She was full of heart grief and didn't know how to heal it. She told me the whole story and kept crying. She was sitting with her back to my large casement window, the one that took up the whole wall and looked out into the courtyard and garden between the two buildings of the complex I lived in. I sat in front of her in another chair, listening, her sadness touching my heart.

I saw a flutter out of the corner of my eye over her right shoulder. I hesitated to take my eyes away from her, not wanting to break away from the empathy I was feeling with her. I saw another flutter. I looked directly over her shoulder and saw two mourning doves sitting on the outside ledge in the middle of my window. I couldn't believe my eyes at first. I sat there stunned with awe. I expected them to fly away any second. I expected the illusion to disappear. But they remained. I waited until she was finished telling me the whole story. I didn't want to interrupt her. When she paused for a second, I whispered, "Turn around." She looked at me quizzically. I repeated my words. She turned and saw the doves. We sat there together, mesmerized, both our eyes filled with tears, as we imagined the spirits of her two birds resurrected in these cooing New York City doves. They remained there throughout the entire hour of her session, and only when she stood up to leave did they fly away. I had never seen them before and I never saw them again, despite living in that apartment for four years.

Journal Entry, late August
I finish writing the above two pages of the book, close the computer and go downstairs to have a second breakfast. I sit outside in

the gentle sun and listen to the chipmunks chirping and the crows cawing. Four poems flow through me and I write them down on a piece of scrap paper, deciding to leave them outside so as to keep away from the computer for a few hours. For some reason I come back upstairs anyway, without the poetry. I look around and my eye catches a book I bought several months ago after seeing it in a friend's apartment: *Women in Praise of the Sacred*, edited by Jane Hirshfield. It is a collection of "43 centuries of spiritual poetry by women." I open it haphazardly and find that I have turned to poems written by Christina Georgina Rossetti. I read one. I don't particularly like it, but I keep mindlessly reading the rest of her poetry. I stop breathing when I reach the bottom two lines to the final poem:

> *Tread softly! all the earth is holy ground*
> *It may be, could we look with seeing eyes,*
> *This spot we stand on is a Paradise*
> *Where dead have come to life and lost been found,*
> *Where Faith has triumphed, Martyrdom been crowned,*
> *Where fools have foiled the wisdom of the wise;*
> *From this same spot the dust of saints may rise*
> *And the King's prisoners come to light unbound.*
> *O earth, earth, earth, hear thou thy Maker's Word:*
> *"Thy dead thou shalt give up, nor hide thy slain"—*
> *Some who went weeping forth shall come again*
> *Rejoicing from the east or from the west,*
> *As doves fly to their windows, love's own bird*
> *Contented and desirous to the nest.*

—Later Life: A Double Sonnet of Sonnets

✳

4
Moon Light
✳

As word of my healing work spread in the late 1970s, a number of women came to see me who were to become dear and long-time friends. Nancy Azara, then director of the New York Feminist Art Institute and a brilliant and innovative wood sculptor and painter, was among them. She took a number of my classes and workshops and found that her deep connection with her inner artistic psyche allowed her to open to healing and intuitive energies. We felt an immediate and deep bond with each other and decided to work together.

We planned weekend workshops at the Institute that would combine healing and creativity. I would create the meditations and Nancy would develop the ideas for the artistic projects that would allow the women students to create a visual piece in which they could express the emotions and insights they got in touch with during the meditations and discussions. Some of the workshops we created and led were entitled: "Finding the Mythical Goddess"; "Psychic Map Making"; "Masking and Unmasking"; "The Psychic Power of Art Making"; and "The Light and the Shadow: Guardian Sides of the Self."

When the Rockefeller Wing of Primitive Art was installed at the

Metropolitan Museum of Art in Manhattan, Nancy and I went to see the exhibit. We noticed a human figure, swathed in dark pieces of cloth, with some kind of sack hanging over its left shoulder. We talked about the symbolic significance of bags as wombs, how women carry purses and how little girls like to play dress up with them. Nancy said her daughter would place her favorite items in her purses and then hide them away, like stored treasure. We decided to do a workshop where women would have the chance to re-create themselves as this shamanic figure with a womb of treasure. Women brought in boxes and bags of fabric scraps, buttons from grandmothers, jewelry from mothers, sticks and stones from vision quests. They took these bits and pieces of their lives and attached them to the doll-sized figures as clothing, hair, shoes, and adornment. The more meaningful objects were placed inside a small sack, like the sack hanging over the figure's shoulder in the Metropolitan. These women created themselves anew in their dark self-created figures, empowered with healing the past and opening a future of womb treasure.

As each woman described the figure she had created and the meaning of each object attached to it, deep and long-standing emotions rose to the surface and were expressed. It was exciting and moving work, sitting in a circle of twenty or thirty women and seeing and hearing these deeply hidden feelings break through taboos of silence and form into goddesses of creation. I watched, I listened. I was mesmerized by the creative process. I could not participate and I did not know why. Nancy would go home on Sunday night after the workshop and create her own shaman, mask, or goddess figure. I would go home and lovingly remember the weekend and everyone else's creations. I had created the meditations. I had done laying-on-of-hands. I had facilitated the sharing. But I could not put my hands to fabric, wood, paint, or buttons to create something for me. It all had to be for everyone else.

I had a longing to create something. At Columbia University, when I was taking a postgraduate premedical program in the days when I thought I should go to medical school, I had taken a drawing class. Charcoal and paper. I loved it. In college I had minored in sculpture, along with a major in Comparative Religion. In grammar school I had painted a beautiful pear. My teacher didn't like it. I was devastated. My mother tells me that at the age of two I used to hide behind the curtains in the living room and draw on the walls in colored crayons. She washed the walls.

From the age of six I grew up with a piano. My first was a one-hundred-year-old upright from the old actors' home in town. My father got it for me. We painted its dark exterior baby blue. I loved that piano and took lessons. One day there was a thunderous crash of indistinguishable notes, as though heaven itself had dropped its harp. The soundboard inside my blue piano had cracked through the middle and crashed. I needed a new piano.

My father found me another upright, an old Gulbransen made in Chicago in the 1920s. We left the exterior dark. I continued to take lessons, although I was never very talented. I'm not sure if I didn't practice enough or if I was just not musically inclined. It is probably closer to the truth to say that I played the piano to please my father. Actually, he had wanted me to play the accordion. I refused. The violin was his second choice. I was awful. The piano was my choice. He had old sheet music like "Old Man River" and "Danny Boy." I would practice those while he sat in his big chair in the living room. Like every other child learning to play, I made mistakes. He couldn't stand discordant notes. One day he came in as I was playing one of his favorite songs. He picked up the sheet music from the piano and tore it to pieces.

During the time that Nancy Azara and I were giving workshops at the Institute, I met two wonderful women who lived in Westbeth in Greenwich Village. Gabrielle Beard and Patricia Horan decided to form a center for women who wanted to explore spirituality and healing. They called it Women and Wisdom. We became close friends, and they asked me to teach my workshops there. They had a beautiful, spacious loft with large windows available to them, and dozens of women from all over New York City came. I taught "Awakening the Healer Within," "Psychic Self-Defense," "Forgiveness and Letting Go of Judgment," "Reclaiming Your Rights," and "Discovering the Goddess Within You." They had a friend,

Catherine Heriza, who played the guitar and composed beautiful songs. She would sing during the workshops. Soon many of the women from the N.Y. Feminist Art Institute and Women and Wisdom joined together in support of one another, sometimes holding joint workshops at each other's locations. Merlin Stone came to speak on her book on the goddess, *When God Was a Woman.* A community of women. The Goddess was being reborn in the bodies and souls of New York City women and we knew it.

I had grown up in a patriarchal Protestant church where there was no emphasis placed on the divine feminine. Not being Roman Catholic, I didn't even have the Virgin Mary as a model. No one ever talked about the Holy Spirit as feminine, and there was little discussion of the Old Testament and its powerful women. I didn't know that Artemis was the Great Mother goddess in Greece for hundreds of years, and that her temple at Ephesus was one of the Seven Wonders of the World. It would be years before I would discover that her great marble figure with the many breasts had been torn down by Christians who replaced it with a cross. How ironic that the same city of Ephesus would serve as the place where a Roman Catholic patriarchal council would install Mary to her rightful place as the "God bearer" and "Queen of Heaven." I went to college and majored in Comparative Religion. That was the first time, studying Eastern Religions, that I was introduced to gods *and* goddesses. Now I was living among them. Now each of us became a living embodiment of the divine feminine. This was new for me. This was enlightening, like moonlight shining its glow into my soul and awakening sleeping beauties.

I fell in love with the feminine for the first time in my life. I looked in the mirror and began to appreciate and love myself and my friends. All women. I began to see women as something more than just workaholics, caregivers, servants, and mothers. I began to see power, beauty, strength, and healing. More important, I began to feel it.

I was living in London Terrace in Chelsea. Sarah Rentschler had a penthouse in the same building and used it as an art gallery. It was a beautiful wide and open space with windows on all four sides and a terrace. When my apartment on the ninth floor became too small for groups, she invited me to hold my workshops upstairs. One weekend Gabe, Pat, and I planned a combination of workshops and presentations by many different women to give in Sarah's penthouse. I spoke about Tara as the Tibetan goddess of compassion and healing. An actress from Israel named Aviva Davidson enacted the story of Ruth in Hebrew. It was a beautiful Sunday afternoon. Blue sky, bright sun. Her voice rang out as she told the story. I was facing a wall of windows, and as she continued, I noticed the sky darken. It got darker and darker until a huge burst of thunder, lightning, and rain rang out across the sky. Everyone gasped. This woman just went on with her performance as though it was the most natural thing in the world. Instant manifestation. A living Old Testament in a modern New York City. It was one of the most extraordinary occurrences I have ever seen.

One of the women I met at this time was a talented screenwriter involved in film and video production. Judy Parker and I became close friends and decided we wanted to try living in the country. We agreed to share a house, and went looking in Upstate New York where I had gone to camp as a young teenager.

Judy and I rented a small house in Woodstock on Zena Road by the reservoir, and we visited on weekends. I soon began to realize that I could hold weekend retreats at the house. I hired a macrobiotic cook to arrange all the meals, and women came up on Friday nights and returned to New York on Sunday evenings. Between several small extra bedrooms, an extra bath, and sleeping bags, we could house a dozen women. The large living room had a fireplace and served well as a workshop room. Woodstock was a few minutes by car, and the many shops and restaurants provided pleasant diversions for the afternoon breaks.

I gave my introductory workshop on spiritual healing, "Awakening the Healer Within." In addition to the meditations and sharing afterward, I began to add the opportunity to draw after certain meditations, such as "Communicating with the Body." I provided colored crayons and markers, and asked the women present to draw their symptoms and illnesses. Remarkable insights came from the drawings. My work with Nancy Azara had led me to understand some of the emotional meanings represented in visual form, including the use of color. I noticed that chakra colors often showed up in symptoms and illnesses that were directly related to that particular chakra, even though the person drawing was unaware of the connection. Red is often used by people to represent physical pain, especially in jagged, uneven shapes. Red is also the color of the light energy at the first chakra, the center of security, safety, and grounding. When someone used red to represent physical pain in the legs, I would be able to help the person connect to issues of security, or the lack of it, in her life. Years later Judy would develop and produce a color chakra video with Steven Halpern and his music.

I found the country a pleasant break from New York City. I had grown up in the suburbs of New Jersey, so this was my first house and the first time I had lived in the country. I would take long walks down Zena Road by the reservoir, sometimes at dawn, sometimes at dusk. It was here that I began to practice short runs for exercise. I loved to walk down in the evening and watch the moon over the water, especially when it was full.

There was a fireplace in the house. I was fond of big crackling fires. I lit the first fire of the season and sat back to relax. As the fire burned I began to notice a strange shape in the wood. There was a flat piece of wood in the fire, and the flames began to etch a strange design in it. A face. A devil's face. I couldn't believe my eyes. I got up and walked into the other room and came back, thinking my eyes were playing tricks with me. The face was still there, getting more clearly etched by the moment. A minute later I heard an enormous roar, like that of a train. I was terrified. The chimney was on fire. I opened the door to the house and shooed the cats outside. I ran for the phone and called the fire department. When I went outside I could see sparks flying up and onto the trees. The men came and told me not to worry. Many people cleared out their chimneys that way. I was not comforted. Something strange had taken place unlike anything I had ever experienced. I was frightened.

My stay in the country was short—a year and a half. Judy took a job in Los Angeles at a drug rehabilitation center, and I decided that renting the house alone was too much responsibility and cost. I moved back to New York City full-time. The morning I left the house I walked down to the reservoir. In the sky was a double rainbow that stretched from one end to the other over the water. I smiled and took it as a good sign.

I was invited to teach at Ananda Ashram in Monroe, New York, about an hour north of New York City. Years before, I had read *Roots of Consciousness* by Jeffrey Mishlove and had seen a small photo of an Indian guru named Dr. Rammamurti Mishra. As I looked at his picture, I felt chills go through my body. I felt that I *knew* him, much as I felt when I met my friend John. It was the strangest sensation, as though I were looking at a photo of someone I had already met. When I received the invitation to teach at Ananda Ashram, I was intrigued. I don't remember how they had heard of my work, but I drove up one summer afternoon. I met with Vyas Houston, the director of the ashram, who now teaches Sanskrit in workshops around the country. We discussed a conference the ashram would be holding, and he inquired whether I would be interested in teaching there. I agreed, and we made plans for me to present. That evening I stayed for the program after dinner. At the beginning of the evening the guru walked into the room. I felt my breathing stop and my heart leap. This was the man I had seen in the photo. I couldn't believe my eyes. After the most beautiful sitar playing I had ever heard, he spoke to the group. We were all sitting on the floor. We made eye contact at one point, and I could feel my heart open. Yes, I knew this man. From how many lifetimes I didn't know. But I knew him and I would come to know him again.

I spent several years teaching at Ananda Ashram. Sometimes I would teach a weekend workshop on healing or "Psychic Self-Defense." But the summer conferences and festivals were my favorite. They lasted ten days, and we would be in residence for the entire time. They would usually begin with an evening of sitar music and Indian dance. Each day different workshop leaders would

✳

present a variety of healing workshops. Delicious and unusual Indian dishes would be served from the kitchen, and in the evening after dinner there would be sitar music and Dr. Mishra, whom we affectionately called Guruji, would speak. Sometimes I felt he was reading my mind and speaking just to me. Soon after I began teaching there he spoke of opening the "psychic heart." Vyas told me he had never used that phrase before I arrived. Another time he spoke of spiritual pregnancy. He would look straight into my eyes as he spoke. One afternoon I was meditating in Vyas's meditation room and focused on Guruji's picture. I went into a deep state of meditation. Everything else disappeared and I felt as though I were merging with him. Later that afternoon he greeted me with recognition and laughed out loud. "You came to visit me this afternoon! You were in my room!" he said in front of everyone. I hadn't known I could travel astrally.

But more than anything else, I loved the sitar music. The man who played, Roop Verma, had studied with the famous Indian sitarist Ravi Shankar, and he was quite accomplished. There were morning and evening ragas, and we all sat in silence listening to his music. I would close my eyes and drop down into the various rhythms. My body would merge with them, and I could feel kundalini energy rising and falling inside me. At the end of each session I would go up to him and tell him how much I enjoyed the beauty of his playing, and I would describe what I had experienced. His eyes would widen as he listened. Invariably, he would wait until I was finished, and then tell me which raga he had played and the story behind it. It was always the same as what I described. I had merged so perfectly with the music that it had played its story inside my body, where I had felt its purpose and seen its vision.

I met Martin Brofman at Ananda Ashram. He had been diagnosed with a malignant spinal cord tumor several years before. The doctors told him it was inoperable. He went to the Caribbean island of Martinique to solace himself with drink and drugs. While tripping on LSD, he wound up sitting next to a monk at a bar. The monk told him that illness was all in the mind. Marty decided that if that were true, then that's where he had to go to cure himself. He did—on pepperoni pizza and hot dogs. Marty decided that if his illness was all in his mind, it didn't matter what he ate. Not something I would recommend to someone with cancer, who needs all the healthy nutrition he or she can eat, but Marty was very strong-minded. After he was completely healed of cancer, he decided to get rid of his glasses and heal his eyesight. After that he went around teaching others how to use the power of the mind to heal by visualizing themselves as completely healed. He had a fish-bowl of eyeglasses to prove it. We became good friends.

I'll never forget the summer evening we arrived at Ananda Ashram for a festival just as the clouds looked as though they were about to burst. We all sat on the back lawn waiting for the Indian music and dancing to start on the stage that had been constructed by the lake. The sky grew darker and darker. We were all waiting for the rainstorm to ruin the evening but hoping it would hold off for another hour or two. Marty looked up at the sky and stated that we should do something about it. He closed his eyes. When he opened them a few minutes later, he emphatically stated, "There. It won't rain now." It didn't. Not that evening, not for the entire ten days. It remained overcast, however, much to everyone's dismay and confusion. As everyone was getting into their cars and leaving the Ashram on the afternoon of the tenth day, the sky exploded with rain. A drenching downpour that went on for hours. A magician, Marty. And he knew it.

I considered what life would be like if I moved to the Ashram. I decided it was too confining. I thought about a magician's life. It seemed a little too dangerous. So I married a shrink. He was tall, dark, and handsome; intelligent and creative; a marathon runner, a teacher and a poet; strong, wise, and a take-charge man. Everything my father had not been. My women friends didn't like him. They felt he was too harsh, too dominant, and too aggressive. One friend pointed out that he always needed to be the center of attention; another that he seemed threatened by the feminine; a third that he seemed in competition with me and threatened by my success. I couldn't see it. I didn't want to see it. I assumed my women friends were afraid they were going to lose me to a man. They did. I was in love. Or should I say, I was in a complex. My father complex. I needed a hero to love and to love me. I needed to be protected, taken care of, made to feel wanted by the masculine. What I really needed was my own inner masculine animus, my soul male to provide grounding, safety, and security. Instead, I got married. The classical Greek words for *to marry* mean "to tame a woman." I did not know this. I did not know that in Greek mythology women were thought to be so much more powerful than men that they were not allowed to look a man straight in the eyes for fear of possessing him with love and desire; or that at the wedding, the bride was taken by her left wrist by the husband as a sign of abduction. Nor did I know that Amazon warriors were Greek women who liked the company of men but refused to submit to them in marriage. Many of the Greek vases show Amazons being killed by men. The Amazon women, at the moment before death, would look straight into their killer's eyes, so that the men would know they were killing what they had loved most. How often this has been reenacted since ancient Greece. I knew none of this.

Many years later, after my divorce, a woman friend asked me: "What happened to you? You were famous. You were in *US* magazine. Then you just disappeared." My reply: "I got married." The truth is that I would not have been able to withstand the attention and publicity that came with fame. I had no inner soul male to give me aggression, strength, guidance, and self-protection. If I couldn't cope with my very male husband, I certainly would not have been able to cope with a harsh, dominant, and threatening world. I had a lot of inner healing to do.

5

Burning Roots

Peple are like trees. When they catch on fire you can hose them down, assess the damage, put a little salve on their wounds, and think the danger is over. But it's not. If you come back the next day, new fires will have broken out and smoke will appear from the ground. The fire is burning underground, and the roots are smoldering.

When fire has reached the roots of a human being, the damage is deep. The foundation of his or her life support system is in danger. Healers, good healers, look at the roots, as well as the leaves and the bark. The leaves are pretty, colorful, and make a nice noise when swaying in the breeze. But the roots hold up the tree, the roots give life.

My roots were not very deep when I began as a healer. I was a pretty delicate tree. I was like so many other people in the sixties and seventies, who were flower children, leaf children. We didn't know we needed roots. We all thought the blossoms were enough. Give up your ego, be free, be spiritual, love everyone, and the rest will take care of itself. We didn't know that you can't let go of your ego until you have one. We didn't know that houses built without foundations are not very strong.

So I relied on my intuitive sensitivities, my deep compassion, and my heightening (not deepening) sense of spirituality to turn me into a good healer. It worked for a while, a long while, actually. People would come to me with burning roots, withered branches, and damaged leaves. I had the sight and clairsentient compassion to know what the problem was and where it had started. I could see into their childhoods, describe their parents, see their auras, and scan their chakras and bodies with my hands. Once I heard the person's story, took him or her through a "Communicating with Your Body" meditation, and did a chakra and body scan, I had a pretty good idea of which roots were burning and where. I then was ready to do the laying-on-of-hands, to see whether the body and soul would accept some deep healing. When I had first started, it never occurred to me to buy a massage table, so they could lie down and I could easily stand with my back straight. Maybe unconsciously I didn't want to be seen as a masseuse. I remember many years later, after I had bought my first table, so people could be really comfortable, a well-dressed professional woman came in for her first session with me, saw the table, and blurted out "I don't want to lie down on that!" I told her she didn't have to. She seemed relieved but wary. It turned out she had been a sexually abused child and didn't even like to be touched. This was definitely a problem in her marriage and one that I could not help her solve. I suggested therapy.

At the beginning of my private practice I sat people in a chair, fully clothed, with me standing behind, initially to center myself and to pray. The position for laying-on-of-hands began as though I were doing a chakra or body scan, already described earlier in the book. I then moved to the right side, sat in a chair to reach the lower body, or stood to reach the upper body. My right hand seemed to be my strongest healing hand as well as my most sensitive diagnostic hand, although I found I could use my left hand for both diagnosis and healing as well. Most healers use one hand for scanning and the other for healing.

I would start the session by standing behind the person with my eyes closed, deeply relax, and clear my mind. I also always prayed. Sometimes I said the Lord's Prayer, sometimes I just asked for help and truth and the ability to open my heart with love. I would start with my hands over the person's shoulders to balance the body, and then move to the right side, placing my hands above the head where the crown chakra, or spiritual center, is located. I would then slowly work my way down through the entire body, right hand at the front and left hand at the back along the spine. As I slowly moved I could feel the areas that needed healing, the areas with burning roots. They were too hot or too cold, painful, agitated, or lacked energy all together. I would rest there, breathing deeply, remaining neutral, waiting for something to happen. Usually this meant the healing energy in my hands would meet up with the disturbance in the body, and, like a weather front, a confrontation would occur. If the disturbance was severe enough, I was pushed back and had to rely on pulling out the negative energy before I could put any healing energy into the area. If the disturbance was minor or malleable, it seemed to melt under my hands and I could move in closer and eventually rest my hands on the afflicted area. Then, the heat from my hands would get stronger and permeate the tissue with healing energy. Many people could feel the heat and imprint of my hands long after I had removed them. Some people became a little disoriented when they opened their eyes and realized I had left the room already to go wash my hands. They thought I was still there with my hands on their body. I resorted to telling them when I was finished.

Healing energy leaves a deep lasting imprint. It sends life force through the leaves and bark into the core circles of the tree and all the way into the roots. It touches the whole person: physical, emotional, mental, psychic, and spiritual. The word *psychic* comes from the Greek "psyche" meaning "soul." I never understood why people are so wary of the word *psychic* except that it has been so misused and abused in this culture. To be psychic is to see into someone's soul with your soul. It is a beautiful concept, a beautiful word. To be healed at a deep psychic level is to be healed in one's soul.

And then there is "energy." I remember the first book proposal

I ever sent to an editor. I had worked very hard on it, and I was rather pleased with what I had written. The reply came back: "What is this thing called energy? This all sounds rather grandiose. Your material is thin." I was crushed. To me there is nothing more natural than the reality of energy. Not even science can really define it, but our entire universe is made of it. We live in a gigantic field of God's energy. It is the most tangible thing in the world to me. I touch it every day. I feel it with my hands. I am a realist. A Taurus. A Protestant. Put me in front of a computer and I have no idea how it works, where all those pages are stored. How does all that material wind up being in one little piece of metal? It's a fantastic magical realm to me. I can't touch it. I never understood mathematics. A bunch of numbers on a page. How can there be a conclusion when there are no feelings to feel, no body to *touch*. It's all too abstract to me. Give me a live flesh-and-blood human being in front of me, and I can look into the person's body and soul and tell you which roots are burning and how much love it will take to heal the person. *That* is reality.

She told me she was dying. A woman of twenty-five with lymphoma had come to see me after two years of resisting her psychotherapist's prodding to do so and after radiation and chemotherapy had failed. "There was nothing else to do," she said. They had given her six months to live. "I don't want to be here. I don't believe in this hocus-pocus." She sat in front of me with her arms crossed, staring at me defiantly. Thanks a lot, God, why did you send this one to me? I thought. I was soon to find out.

I told her she had nothing to lose. She didn't reply. I told her how I worked and asked her to tell me when the illness had been diagnosed and what had been going on in her life for the two years leading up to the diagnosis. She had been divorced, and when she talked about it I could see how hurt and angry she was. She felt betrayed, and after the divorce she decided she was a lesbian. She was overweight and very angry. I decided to dispense with the initial meditation and scan. She was too resistant to close her eyes or to allow me near her. I don't think I even did a healing during the initial session, but I can't remember for sure. I suggested she come twice a week, and we would see how things went. I also suggested she start drinking carrot juice, which I knew was filled with beta-carotene and was good for the immune system.

A few days later she came for another session, and we did a chakra and body scan and a laying-on-of-hands. A few days after that I got a phone call. She had a fever. What should she do? She told me she had been drinking carrot juice. My intuition told me that this was a cleansing reaction from the carrot juice and a healing response to the laying-on-of-hands. I told her that if the fever continued she would have to consult her doctor, but that for the time being she could just ride it out, drink a lot of water and carrot juice, and see what happened. Coincidentally, I had just been reading articles on artificially induced fevers as an experimental treatment for cancer. I told her this on the phone. She let the fever work Mother Nature's healing power on her. At the end of the three days the fever broke by itself and she felt fine.

We worked together for six more weeks, doing healing for her body and talking about her feelings of anger, fear, and grief. At the end of that time she went into Sloan-Kettering for her routine blood work. The doctor was so stunned by the results that he ordered it redone. He thought her blood might have been mixed up with someone else's. He had it done three times. He called her into his office and told her he wasn't supposed to tell a patient such a thing, but he couldn't find any cancer in any of the test results. Her blood work was completely normal. She came the next day and told me. She was scared. The hocus-pocus had worked, and it shattered all her defenses. She admitted to me that she had spent two years getting used to being ill and expecting to die, and now she didn't know how to live, how to be a healthy person with a life in front of her. I told her we would work on it.

The next session she came in with a lump in her right breast. It was a Friday. She told me she had made an appointment with her doctor on Monday to have it checked out. We talked about why she might have developed this right after her healthy diagnosis. Dangerous territory. She told me that when she was born her mother had been in prison. She didn't know why, or said she didn't. But she did say that she wasn't sure she had a right to be alive, to be healthy and happy. I made a silent decision. I decided to go for her anger, for her rage to live. To see if I could uproot it and let it burn out flaming across the space between us. I verbally challenged her, I poked and prodded her with my words. She got angry, enraged. She threatened to leave. I told her she could if she wanted, but she would have to sit down first and let me do a healing on the lump in her breast. She did. I placed my hands over it and didn't feel anything. She stormed out. I got a phone call three hours later. The lump had disappeared. Again, she was scared. Should she try to re-create it by Monday so her doctor could check it out? Of course not, I said. What would she tell him? Just tell him the truth. Never be afraid of the truth. She did. The doctor later called me to see what I was doing. He told me he wanted to invite me to Sloan-Kettering to talk with some other doctors. He too got scared and never did. That woman and I worked together for nine more months, giving birth to her new life. Now almost fifteen years later, she is alive and well.

I look back on myself in those early days and wonder where I got the courage to take such a risk. Most psychotherapists do not butt heads so blatantly with first-year patients, much less first-month patients. Build trust, be conservative, wait it out. Waiting was not a luxury she or I had. I had not had spontaneous risk schooled out of me by years of training. When I began my work as a healer, I only had a bachelor's degree in Comparative Religion from Hobart and William Smith Colleges and no formal training in counseling. That was to come ten years later, when I went to graduate school at Iona College in New Rochelle, New York, and received my master's in Pastoral Counseling. I had only one year of Freudian analysis under my belt. I really didn't know what I was doing. But I followed my instincts, and they were good, they were God-given, and sometimes they worked. We should all be more tolerant of beginners. They have a spark in their soul, and sometimes it jumps across great deserts and comes to rest in the oasis of someone's heart and wellsprings bubble up new life.

There were failures too. Plenty of them. I remember the great healer, Olga Worrall, having been asked why she never talked about the failures. She said because they don't do anyone any good. That's not true. They would have done me a lot of good. I needed someone to tell me that life is full of failures, everyone has them, and not every healing will work. No one did. People came with deafness, gall bladder problems, lung disease, and back pain. They didn't heal, at least not instantaneously while they were in my office. It broke my heart. A man brought in a wheelchair with Lou Gehrig's disease. Nothing. A composer who had suffered a stroke and had lost most of his speech struggled through telling me his story. After the healing his speech was worse. I didn't realize in those early days that sometimes the healing obliterates all the defenses and compensations first so it can sink deeply into the origin of the wound. I should have told him, as I tell people now, to rest for the remainder of the day and not try to talk, but I didn't know. Sometimes beginners are ignorant, too.

Many people were so desperate that they expected me to wave the magic wand of my hands over their body and make their pain and illness go away. Publicity didn't help this illusion. I had already been written up in the local Amherst paper after I taught my first class there. But that was just a local paper. I wasn't prepared when a *Daily News* reporter came calling. Big full-page article with photo. Phone calls poured in until there were hundreds. I couldn't schedule people for more than one healing, and I was booked for months in advance. When the one and only healing didn't work, people left feeling discouraged and so did I. I was trapped. I could no longer see people twice a week for a year until they got well. I didn't know what to do. I had been given this gift of healing, and who was I to turn people away. I thought I should take everyone who came to me. As I look back on it now, with many years of analysis under my belt, I think it was a combination of inflation and dedication, insecurity, and lack of ego boundaries. I had never been taught to say no. I had never been taught to consider myself, my needs, my health, and my protection first. My mother tells me that she grew up with the adage "You are your brother's keeper." Sounds like a jail term to me, now.

I also hesitated to turn people away because sometimes one healing was enough. I remember the woman with a neck problem. I placed my hands on her neck and a few minutes later she was able to turn it for the first time in two years. In one of my workshops I was using a man as a demonstration model for scanning, not even for healing. I focused on his neck. As usual, it's impossible to totally separate a scanning from a healing, and I guess my hands were putting out more healing energy than I thought. At the end of the twenty minute demonstration he turned to look at me and then a stunned expression came over his face. He turned his neck back and forth, up and down, in all directions. He announced to the group that he hadn't been able to do that in twenty years. His neck stayed healed.

I started healing circles to help with the overflow of people and to give them more opportunities to receive laying-on-of-hands. Once I started giving weekend workshops instead of weeknight classes, I had evenings free to contain small two-hour healing circles. We discussed different aspects of healing, and each person had a chance to tell an abbreviated version of his or her story, go through a "Communicating with Your Body" meditation, and receive laying-on-of-hands. I would then give each person feedback after the meditation, since by then I had a number of intuitive impressions I could offer them. The results were usually very good, especially if the person continued to come week after week.

Healing builds over time. The healing energy creates a lasting imprint in the physical tissue, the subtle energy field, the unconscious and the emotional "body" of each person. But this healing imprint first has to fight for its territory, like an animal that finds itself in another animal's den. If the illness, heartache, or imbalance has been there for a long time, it has settled down into a fixed position, a pattern that is sometimes hard to break. The healing imprint from the healer's hands lays down a healthy imprint in the same area, but sometimes this energy cannot hold its position for

more than a few hours or a few days. If the roots of a tree are burning underground, the firefighter can douse the tree with water, but
the fire springs up again. I have patients call me three days after
their sessions to tell me how they are feeling. Usually first-timers
will say they felt great for a day or two after the healing, but then
their symptoms come back. They need another healing to rein-
force the healthy imprint, and they need to continue to explore
their burning roots, the origins of the illness. This is why I began
to create healing meditation tapes, so people would have my
voice, my energy imprint, and a guided imagery process to take
home with them on audio. These meditations keep the healing energy flowing through the body much like an electrical cord
plugged into the wall socket. As Agnes Sanford wrote in her
lovely book *The Healing Light,* "If your iron doesn't work, don't
rant and rave at the iron. Check to see if it's plugged in."

That's what we all need to be . . . plugged in. But how? To
whom, and where? Isn't that the question we're all asking? How
do we experience healing in body, mind, and soul? How do we
live a healed life? Most people who come to me know that they
come to heal more than their body, although the body is important.
After all, if the body isn't healed, we won't be around long enough
to work on the heart, mind, and soul. When I started healing
twenty years ago most people didn't realize there were emotional,
mental, and spiritual components to physical illness. Certainly the
medical profession didn't, despite the fact that the Nobel Prize in
medicine was won in 1977 by Guillemin and Schally for the
placebo effect. Most people don't believe in healing until they experience it directly. I always tell people: Don't believe anything I
say. I only want to offer you the opportunity to have a personal experience of healing. Experience creates belief just as powerfully
as belief creates experience. They go hand in hand. When we are
children, everything we experience molds our sense of reality, our
beliefs. Who our parents are and what they believe, affect our experience of our childhoods as well. Children, like cats, are observational learners. As we all know, children don't really listen to
what we say, they observe what we do. They mimic. That's how

humans learn, we mimic. If we are born into a family in which everyone wears glasses, we want glasses too. We think glasses are a good thing. In the 1980's the *New York Times* published a story about a behavioral study on a group of mothers and their children. The mothers were told to pretend to be in pain or to be ill and see how their children would respond. I remember one mother pretended she had a terrible headache. Her four-year-old daughter's immediate response? "Me too, Mommy, me too."

Illness can be a learned response, a mimicked response. There is physiological genetics, but there is also psychological genetics. Most of the time it's not as conscious a process as it was with that little girl. Most of the time the osmosis takes place at an unconscious level. One of the reasons we mimic is love. That little girl loved her mother. When we love someone we identify with that person. We want to be as much like that person as possible. And we want the person to love us. If we experience other person's love, he or she will know, and we will be loved in return. This type of loving takes place in families all the time. I'll never forget the young man in a workshop of mine at the New York Open Center. He told of growing up in a large Italian family. He was his mother's first son, and she expected him to feel everything she felt. When she was sad, he was supposed to be sad with her. When she was angry, he was supposed to agree and validate her anger. He had no emotional reality of his own. Her reality had taken over his life. This realization was very painful for him. So painful, in fact, that he didn't return for the second day of the workshop. It was too much for him. To come back would have meant to choose a new individuated life for himself, to begin the process of separating from his mother.

The fear of separation, abandonment, and lack of love is so devastating, so potentially death-producing, that we will do anything to avoid it. After all, as babies if we are separated from our mothers, it can mean death. If we are not loved, it is emotional death. The famous study of the orphanage in Canada showed that the babies who were not picked up and *touched* while they were being fed, died. Love and touch are life-producing. Jan Goodwin, author of "The Power of Touch," published in the *Ladies Home Journal* in April 1995, writes that touch is the first sense to develop in a human embryo, and that even when other senses, such as vision and hearing, become impaired with age, the ability to give and receive touch usually does not. She notes that the Office of Alternative Medicine at the National Institutes of Health in Bethesda, Maryland, has awarded four research grants to study massage, which in other studies has already shown the ability to speed the healing of wounds, improve the functioning of the immune system, and reduce depression and physical pain. She cites Lynda Harrison, R.N., Ph.D., a researcher at the University of Alabama working with premature babies, as saying that preemies who were regularly massaged gained 47 percent more weight than other babies fed the same diet. I believe that loving, healing, human touch is more nurturing than food.

We all have some vague memory, in our collective unconscious, of being thrown out of the Garden of Eden. Every religion, every culture has an Eden story, as Joseph Campbell has so beautifully reminded us. And we would all like to get back there, either in this lifetime or after it in heaven. If you are Tibetan Buddhist and have taken Bodhisattva vows, as I did, you have agreed to stick around lifetime after lifetime until all sentient beings experience enlightenment, until we all experience Paradise together. There have been many times I wished I could take those vows back and do it now.

I know what it's like to be sick. As a newborn I was allergic to every formula my mother tried to feed me. I developed pneumonia. I spent the first twenty years of my life fighting off one respiratory infection after another. I almost died of double kidney infections in college. My entire life has been focused on health and healing. I was born into a family in which every member has been seriously ill at one point or another, and some chronically ill. Whatever knowledge or wisdom I have about illness and healing has been gained from years of personal suffering, pain, and heartache. I have lived what I teach.

Whatever physiological genetics I was born with does not explain all those years of suffering and how they molded my experience and beliefs. My entire childhood did that. My family did that—the relationships, words, actions, love, ethics, and levels of meaning I learned from my parents and others I encountered. I think the unhealed wounds I brought with me into this life from past lives also contributed. Each lifetime is an opportunity to heal the wounds of previous lives. Each lifetime is an opportunity to raise the generational tree of our ancestors. The sins of the fathers and mothers and grandfathers and grandmothers *are* handed down to subsequent generations. The word *sin* is an archery term meaning "to miss the mark." All the ways that our ancestors have missed the mark, have failed to love and to forgive, have failed to individuate into a whole healed life, we feel the effects of here and now. Each of us is healing generations of pain, illness, and suffering in our one life here and now. We are digging up the burning roots of our tree, trying to understand how the fire started, and pouring the waters of love and healing into the wounds.

Which brings us back to the original question of who and what do we connect with to experience healing if our original identification with our families has led to much of the suffering we experience? Most of us want to connect with God the Creator, who we believe loves us and gives us life.

Most people think they can go up and out, take a "flight into light" as the Jungians call it, to find God. Most people think that if they think positively, pray positively, experience everything positively and stay away from anything negative and dark, they'll be saved, healed. This was one of the greatest illusions perpetrated by the early New Age movement and, unfortunately, by much of Christianity. Stay away from the dark, the dirty, the ground. Go up and out into the light. Well, as we've discovered from "up and out" preachers like Jimmy Swaggert and Jim Baker, the higher you go, the longer the fall.

God is everywhere, not just at the treetops. Healing begins at the roots. Good homes are built on solid foundations. We have to be able to heal from the ground up and that means having the courage to face the dark soul self that Carl Jung called the "shadow." Whenever there is an emotion, thought, or impulse that we judge as bad, "not me" material, often of an aggressive or sexual nature, we push it into the closet, slam the door, lock it, and hope never to see it again. We all do it. No one is immune. In fact, the more righteous and "holy" someone thinks he or she is the bigger the shadow. This is as true for countries, for example, Nazi Germany, as it is for you and me. It is also true for religions and converted religious fanatics who think their way is the only way. BIG shadows. As long as we can admit to our shadow side and keep it in our awareness, it cannot consume us and we do not fall into the trap of projecting it onto other people. Some of the greatest saints and sages of all time have struggled terribly with this dark self. Jesus experienced his confrontation with Satan. The Hindu sage and teacher Krishnamurti talked of the Hitler within each of us. The people who believe they don't have a dark side are the ones who scare me most. I know they have hidden it more deeply than the rest of us because I used to be one of those people.

My mother had always told me that love heals everything. She had a copy of I Corinthians 13 on the wall of the kitchen: Love bears all things, love is patient, love is kind, and so forth. I grew up believing that if I was just loving enough, good enough, everything would be fine. She never told me *what kind* of love heals everything. She didn't know. It would take me half a lifetime to find out.

Six years into my healing work, my father died and I got married. My father's death put me in touch with my denied grief around his emotional absence in my life. Most of it was due to alcoholism when I was a young child, and later on after the drinking stopped, to the emotional illness existing beneath it. I had so detached my feelings from him, for survival's sake, that I was surprised at how much grief there seemed to be inside me when he died. There were moments when I felt four years old again, grieving the acute pain of that life-filled child who wanted her daddy.

Several months later, as already planned before my father's death, I got married. As Joseph Campbell was fond of saying, marriage is the ultimate caldron of alchemical transformation.

Combining your life and life force with another human being really puts you in touch with the roots that are still burning. I had quite a few. The trouble is, I didn't know how many. I was better at helping others find their burning roots and healing them than I was at discovering my own. I didn't realize it is not something you can do alone. Like innocent Persephone, I was still up in the top branches playing in the leaves and looking at the sky.

Persephone was a young maiden, a virgin in Greek myth. She was beautiful and desirable, and Hades, the god of the underworld, wanted her for his wife. He went to Zeus and demanded Persephone. Zeus refused, so Hades kidnapped Persephone while she was playing among the flowers, oblivious to any danger. She was innocent. Her mother had never warned her of the underworld or Hades, although both were right under her feet. She wasn't prepared to deal with the dark forces of life. She wasn't prepared to protect herself. Neither was I.

Both my father's death and my new marriage had a profound impact on me. I hit the ground suddenly and with full force. It knocked the wind out of me. I was especially unprepared for marriage. I was used to being independent, doing things my way, and so was my husband. It was a tug of war almost immediately. It was like being dragged down into the underworld by Hades and realizing I couldn't find my way back up to the light. Being homeless is a terrible thing. It is very disorienting, and puts us in touch with the deep shadows of loss, abandonment, fear, anger, confusion, and grief that we experienced but repressed as children. For some people, the trigger is marriage, for others it is illness, accident, abuse, assault, or death of a loved one. Some people lose their innocence very young.

When human beings are afraid, they develop defenses, like animals. Except that ours are much more complex. We don't just fight or flee on a rush of adrenaline. We've become too civilized, too genteel, too spiritual for that. We become paralyzed. After all, we are taught not to be too aggressive, especially women. It's not ladylike to punch someone in the jaw even if they're harassing you, although I must say this has changed for women since I was in high school and college. Men have become too civilized as well, but at least they are encouraged, not just allowed, to participate in aggressive sports and high-level competition in other arenas. On the other hand, aggression often takes a less physical form for men. They go from sports in high school and college to sitting behind a desk trying to slash the throat of their business competitors. Not good for the blood pressure.

Human beings have gotten so civilized that we have lost touch with our natural, inherent, self-protective instincts. Instead, we substitute defense mechanisms like projection: the other guy is the enemy, the evil one, we are the victim. Or denial: I'm not angry; I feel fine. This is very hard on the body. It keeps getting mixed signals. When we are afraid or angry, the adrenal glands pour out adrenaline in huge quantities. That gives us the ability to flee or fight for our lives. If we don't, the body and emotions get confused. We mentally tell ourselves to calm down, but the body is posed for immediate action. When we are trapped in a job we hate, an unhappy marriage, an abusive childhood, our natural instincts want us to flee or fight for our lives. If we don't, our bodies continuously pour out this adrenaline until they are exhausted and we don't have the strength to fight or flee. Then the rest of our body's systems begin to break down. The body loses strength, energy, life force. The immune system becomes depressed, weakened. As Candace Pert, the famous immunologist, stated when she was interviewed for Bill Moyers's "Healing and the Mind": when we have a "gut reaction" to something, our gut really *is* feeling our feelings. The stomach has immune cells. Our whole body has immune cells. We now know that the immune system is not localized, as we used to think. It permeates our entire body, and it feels all the emotions we are feeling. Every thought we are thinking has a neuro-chemical component in the brain that is sent throughout the body. Our whole body is thinking what we believe only our mind is thinking. When we are afraid, our whole body is afraid. When we are angry, our whole body is angry. When we are sad, our whole body is sad.

You would think that this means we should only think and feel positive things. But that is not true. Margaret Kenemy, another immunologist, did a study with actors that showed that *whatever* the emotion, if it was felt strongly and fully, for a limited amount of time, strengthened the immune system. It is when prolonged negative emotions, like grief, are left unresolved, that they lead to a weakened immune system, thereby, leaving the doorway open to illness. And I had an ocean of unresolved grief.

Like Persephone, I was dragged kicking and screaming down into the darkness of my unconscious. I didn't like being taken against my will. Imprisonment did not seem like a pleasant prospect. Hades? Not me. I couldn't possibly have such a dark figure inside me. After all, my mother never told me. Carl Jung calls a woman's inner dark male the "negative animus." So unaware was I of this dark inner man, this Bluebeard, as Clarissa Pinkola Estes calls him in her book *Women Who Run with the Wolves,* that I found a man who embodied this dark energy for me and married him. There is something very seductive about this dark male energy. It is aggressive, powerful, courageous, strong, and virile. In all appearances, a true hero. I had never had a hero in my life. My father's emotional collapse and alcoholism looked nothing like the hero every little girl needs to look up to for protection and strength. I saw this hero in my husband, and in many ways he was a hero, having overcome tremendous adversity in his own life. But every hero has a shadow side. When I saw beneath the idealization to the threatening shadow side, the Hades, I could always push it away, because it was outside of me. It was "the other."

Faced with being married to the embodiment of my inner Hades, I could not possibly protect myself. I was being attacked from the inside and the outside. One by one, as my good, loving, Protestant personality's defenses and compensations failed, my shadow asserted itself. I started to get sick again as I had in childhood, with recurrent upper respiratory infections. I was in a car accident and hit my head, resulting in a concussion. My car was stolen. My tooth broke. I found myself full of fear and anger. No matter what I did, said, believed, thought, or wished for, I could not stop this onslaught—all the ways that the external world mirrors the internal world when Hades decides to steal Persephone.

Somehow, my healing work remained relatively untouched in the midst of this tidal wave. It was the one area of my life in which I felt I was safe and valuable. I could go into my office, leave my personal pain aside, and do healing for other people. What I did not realize was that such a dissociated split between my personal life and my work life was not healthy. I went back into psychotherapy, but for the wrong reasons and with the wrong person. As with many people who go into therapy, I wanted someone to support my reality, my goodness, my self-image. I wanted someone to help me rebuild my healthy ego, thinking that my self-image was the same thing. Self-image, or persona, is usually our idealization of how we see ourselves. A healthy ego is a strong structure, like a house, that can withstand the winds of change. It can tolerate anxiety, protect itself from assault and lies, and make healthy choices that support life. It has a deep and strong foundation laid down by years of parental love, strong boundaries, patience, and training in how to cope with life. It is supported by self-knowledge and exploration. I had been dragged underground so I could build a new foundation; I wanted to get back to the treetops in the light.

The therapist I chose was chosen for me again for all the wrong reasons—a friend of my husband. He probably thought she would help mold me according to his reality. A triangle, once again, just as in childhood. She did support my self-image, my good Protestant personality. I let Persephone complain about being dragged into the underworld and raped. But since she was not analytically trained, my therapist could not go down into the underworld with me and help build healing ground from the foundation up. She did not understand that my own inner negative male and my shadow were devouring me in front of her face, and no amount of sympathizing with Persephone would build enough strength to save her.

Years went by and I felt like a mouse in a maze, going around and around and winding up in the same place—unhappy, ex-

✳

hausted, frightened, and angry. I compensated by trying to find value in external things. I bought clothes, jewelry, things for the house, books, a new car. I was the perfect 1980s consumer. All the while my inner psyche, my soul, was sending me night dreams of real gems: inner pearls, rubies, diamonds. It was trying to tell me "You are beautiful and valuable *inside*. Don't be concerned about the outside. Look within."

I started to meditate. I had spent many hours by then in meditation with my students, but my own was haphazard. So I chose a secluded corner of the house and tried to sit down every day. I remember one meditation session in particular. As I went down into my heart grief it seemed as though I went back to the beginning of time, the origins of Creation, when God was One. Then it all exploded, shattered, separated. And the question formed in my altered state of consciousness: *Why would God want to separate from God?* I began to cry uncontrollably. Deep sobs seemed to come up from the core of my being. Why would God or any of us want to become separate when to be One is ultimate peace and love? Was that what we were trying to get back to? Oneness with God? I could not reconcile the question.

Just as I could not reconcile my unhappiness in my marriage. I wanted to leave but kept choosing to stay. I felt love and hate all in the same day. I could not bring myself to separate out. Some deep wound in me from my childhood had been touched, and I clung to my marriage and my husband the way I had clung to my father as a baby when I was sick. I remember having a bad winter chest cold. I curled up in my husband's arms against his chest the way I had against my father's, when I would not stop crying and he would rock me in the rocking chair and sing lullabies to me. I felt his heartbeat against mine, and I was safe and warm and loved. Bliss. The idea, the reality, of separation and abandonment was too painful for me. I could not choose it until years later.

When I finally decided to leave my marriage, I was gone for six months, returning only to pack my things. During the days I was at the house to pack, my husband and I talked. We talked for hours, days, about everything. We cried in each other's arms and forgave each other. We decided to remain together. I fell into the same good, Christian, love-heals-everything trance in which I had grown up. Forgiveness would heal all wounds. Everything would be light and loving and good and all right.

I stayed with the illusion, I realized years later, so that I would not have to be separate, abandoned, alone. And I loved my husband. I could not understand how loving someone so much could be so interwoven with so much suffering. I kept thinking that if I just loved enough, forgave enough, was good enough, and prayed enough, all darkness would vanish and light would win. I forgot about self-love. I was never taught self-love. No one had modeled it for me. Loving the other person was always more important. Self-love was selfish. And lonely.

When my husband and I built an addition onto the house, I had a beautiful round window installed that looked out onto a willow tree. I lined up my statues of Tara and Buddha, small crystals, a Christian cross, a crystal ball and other meaningful things on my meditation altar. I sat and went into my pain. It was enormous. Such grief. An ocean of lifetimes of grief. I prayed for healing for myself, my marriage, and my husband. I was racked with guilt that I was not a good enough wife, and angry that the demands on me were so enormous. I felt overwhelmed by taking care of a marriage, a house, dozens of patients, and hundreds of students. It was too much, but I could not admit that. Being Protestant meant having a work ethic that never quits. There was no such thing as too much. None of the women in my family had ever called it quits—only my father. And giving up frightened me because he had given up on himself, on life, and on me. Or so it seemed to a child. I would never do that. I would never give up.

So I stayed in my marriage another two years until the pain became unbearable and I felt that I was dying. I felt as though my soul was dying. I had a strange sign from my body—a toothache—a terrible toothache that would require a root canal. Every time I went to my favorite Chinese restaurant, I would get the same fortune in my fortune cookie: "A good friend is like a good tooth. It doesn't wear out." I awoke in the middle of the night and went to the kitchen to get something to drink. The pain in my tooth hit me like a tidal wave. So enormous that I passed out. As I was passing out I heard the words "Get out. Get out." When I came to I realized what I had to do. The despair I felt at having to leave once again was almost too much for me. It took every ounce of my strength. It was the most painful thing I have ever done. Leaving the love of someone else to find self-love. Leaving the old life in hopes of new life. Leaving the unsafe familiar in hopes of healing my soul. I could choose death or life. It was that simple, and that awful. I chose life. It has been said that choosing death is easier, life harder. It's true. Choosing life is much harder.

Demeter was Persephone's mother. When she could not find her daughter, she went looking everywhere, stricken with grief. Since Demeter, the good mother, was the goddess of abundance and fertility, all the flowers, trees, and waters dried up. The earth became barren. Hecate, "the old seer 'who knows her people' and has about her the smell of humus and the breath of God," according to Clarissa Pinkola Estes, took pity on Demeter, as did the belly goddess Baubo, a dancing lewd body without a head. Together they convinced Zeus to force Hades to give her back. Zeus agreed on one condition. Only if Persephone had not eaten any food while she was in the underworld would she be allowed to return to the world above. Unfortunately, she had eaten three pomegranate seeds, so she was only allowed to come back up into the light for nine months of the year. The other three, winter, she had to return to Hades in the underworld, where she was a faithful wife. Persephone was never the same. She came back up into the light changed, forever. She had lost her innocence, but she had gained a great gift—the ability to see in the dark.

There is nothing more important in the healing process than learning to see in the dark. It is the most frightening thing in the world. None of us wants to do it. But without this ability, we live in a world of illusory light. We are never prepared for the darkness underneath our own feet, and it can swallow us whole and kill us. There are many people who lost their Persephone-like innocence when Hades came and stole them away and, because they did not have a strong ego or a good inner mother, like Demeter, they per-ished. But if we put aside our rational mind for a while and have the help of our body to give advice, like Baubo and Hecate, we may be able to rise again into the light with new gifts, inner strength, and a whole soul. We may even be able to accept that our underground journey is a necessary crucifixion on the way to res-urrection.

6
Dark Eye

I awoke at 4 A.M. and walked out into the living room. I was in the middle of getting divorced. I sat on the floor, put my back against the couch, and began to cry. My whole body was crying, keening, and my chest felt like it would crack open. I could hear my voice wailing, and I knew once again there was nothing I could do but surrender.

There were moments, months really, when I thought that my life would be one long experience of grief. A whole life of sadness. I believed for a while that I would never be happy again. I wondered why and what I had done wrong that I should carry such pain inside me. My life was supposed to be about healing, relief from pain, light, and compassion. How was it that I could help many other people to experience what was so illusive to me?

And then I died. I just gave up. My mind decided it had nothing else to live for and it stopped fighting. What a blessing. My heart cracked open and a wave of forgiveness flooded me. Not the kind of sweet, blissful, smiling forgiveness that many Christians think of as being a good Christian, but the kind that tears your guts out and makes you rent your garments and lie down on the floor because you can't sit up. The kind that could stop wars if only the people fighting them would allow themselves to be that vulnerable, not to one another, but to God.

I forgave my husband and myself. I forgave my life, my mistakes, his mistakes, my parents, my ancestors, and even God. I forgave everything and everyone. There was nothing else to do, really. There was nothing else to resist, fight for, fight against, defy, defend. There was nothing else.

Finally when I got up hours later I felt empty. I assumed that the waters of forgiveness had ripped through me, cleansed me, and the past had healed. I did not expect the rage—the crackling, enormous, flaming rage that raced and burned through me several days later. It was like a forest fire that tears through everything in its path with the wind at its back. A hot, huge heat reached down to my fingertips and toes. I was angry, really angry. But at what?—everything it seemed, and no one in particular. Forgiveness still held, so the rage was confusing. It seemed to have a life of its own. I took a deep breath and let go into it as well.

You can't put icing on a burned cake. I was fond of saying that to students who took my "Forgiveness and Letting Go of Judgment" workshop. I wanted them to realize that forgiveness is not a sugary sweet emotion that can be used to cover their pain, fear, and anger. So many people try to forgive before they have ever dealt with their darker feelings. I would always recommend to my students that they deal with their darkness first, and then forgive. And yet here I was experiencing profound forgiveness and then going into incredible rage. I didn't expect it, and it was just as well. I realized that I had been brought up such a good Protestant girl, seen and not heard, never expressing rage or saying no when it really counted, that I had to forgive first before I could give myself permission to be openly enraged.

The guilt was too enormous to do it the other way around. Being enraged meant possible loss and abandonment. If I got angry, someone could get angry back at me. They could hate me, stop loving me. Think I was a mean bitch and too aggressive. It meant smashing ideals of how I was supposed to act and present myself to the world. I remember being ten years old and on a weekend

*

trip to a lake with my mother. We were at dinner and somehow got talking with a woman my mother's age. I sat silent, well-behaved, bored but attentive. At the end of the conversation we all got up to leave, and I can still recall hearing this stranger whisper to my mother, "She will make some man a good wife someday." I felt insulted, angry. This woman knew nothing about me. How in the world could she presume to know I would make a good wife? Because I was so passive? pretty? silent?

I had kept my anger hidden inside me, where it got pushed into my shadow and ate away at my self-esteem and life force through guilt. Now that I could experience forgiveness, I could finally feel the power of Kali, the Tibetan Buddhist goddess of death and destruction who clears the path for rebirth. I realized something about how guilt holds down rage. It not only holds down the destructive, murderous rage that we all feel at moments in our lives, but it suffocates the rage to live as well. The screaming, crying rage and pain the newborn feels when it flails its arms and legs, clenches its tiny fists and feet, and howls for the breast. This is God's creation of life screaming out in need of staying alive. This is life force needing to be loved and cared for *in order to stay alive.* This is rage that needs to have its voice and keep it, with no guilt whatsoever. Forgive a miracle? Who presumes to judge moments of grace?

I cut through my days growling. I was angry at people's rudeness, their lies and denial. I was angry when students, patients, and friends projected their negative mother issues onto me. No, I'm not going to accept these projections anymore. You're going to have to take them back, eat them, and deal with your own shadow material. I'm not your garbage dump. I was angry when people didn't keep their promises and when they didn't meet their responsibilities. I was angry when people who professed to love me couldn't hear me, see me, or even be with me. All the denied rage of my life ripped out screaming through the cells of my body. My eyes flashed fire and my words cut truth through the air. I felt like Kali. The rage to live had finally found a home in my body, and I would not lie down and die anymore for anyone except God.

My heart and all my eyes were open, and I realized how much I needed to recommit to my practice of "Psychic Self-Defense." It has become a focus of my life. There is something incredibly clarifying about the rage to live. It's like a feral animal who can see in the dark because its survival depends on it. It's like a mother cat who will defend her newborns to the death if any human or animal threatens them. Protecting ourselves from harm depends on clearly seeing what is real, without the veils of illusion, need, and expectation that most humans put in their way to avoid loss and confrontation.

It means taking a long, hard look at everyone around us and seeing who is potentially dangerous to our survival as a fully alive, unique individual. It means protecting ourselves from people who would invade our physical, emotional, and spiritual boundaries. I very often give the homework assignment to students to go out into a city and take buses and subways, scanning the cars for people who are safe to sit and stand next to, and those whose energy is potentially dangerous. We don't really need buses and subways. Sometimes Thanksgiving dinner with our family is good practice.

When we love and need people, we usually don't see them clearly. Or if we do, we tend to judge them for who they are. It is very difficult to balance clear sight and no judgment, no hatred. It is very hard to be the mother cat protecting our inner newborn life when our own mother is the one standing in front of us. To stand our ground in the face of that kind of confrontation, we need to see clearly with our physical eyes, our third eye (psychic sight), and keep our hearts open. We need to know that we have compassion for the other person, but that we are primarily focused on our own survival and protection.

* * *

I had seen it coming for a year and a half. Her young pretty face had become more and more stressed, exhausted, chalky. It was puffy, as though she were on the verge of tears all the time. There was a deep sadness around her mouth. Her husband had been arrested and jailed for criminal activity. She didn't know what the results would be. She had spent all her money, time, and energy working to get him out and take care of whatever home life she had left. She had thought he might be sent to prison for ten years. They finally let him go, but the toll it had taken on her was enormous. In the morning she would drive an hour and a half to work in a hospital as a nutritionist, taking care of other people's needs, and at night come home to a man who smoked and had no life. I knew she didn't have any time or energy to take care of her own needs. Maybe she didn't even know what they were.

When she thought of dropping out of the training program, I encouraged her to stay in. I knew she would need it; need the support and love of everyone there, including myself. I waited for the inevitable, praying that it would never come. But it did. A lump in the breast. I had thought it might be a recurrence of the lymphoma she had as a child of thirteen, but no, it was breast cancer. She told me on the phone.

I closed my eyes and silently asked my inner voice whether she was going to die. "No. But this is the defining moment of her life. This is the opportunity to choose life and let go of all the death-producing people, situations, and beliefs that are making her sick." I told her. No holds barred, no hedging, no tact. Just the truth. She heard me. She knew. She was scared but not terrified. Better divorce than death. Better leaving a job than a body.

I asked her what she wanted to do with her life. She said she wanted to move out to Sedona, Arizona, live in the desert and mountains, and start a healing center. I told her it sounded like a good idea, but she would have to get well before she began a healing center. First, she would have to find her own inner healing center.

We each have defining moments in our lives. Moments in time, in consciousness, when there is a choice to be made. Moments when reality hits hard, and we have to face a choice about our lives, our bodies, our relationships, our careers. These are the moments that define who we are, what our character is made of, and how much clarity we have. These are the moments that put us at a crossroads, when an angel voice whispers "Choose!" and we can no longer have it all. We have to choose between death and life, waking and sleeping, suffering and healing. Not that these dichotomies are completely separate from each other. They do, after all, interweave all the time. But a defining moment is one in which we choose the road that obeys the healing development of our soul, the deep inner wishes for healing that reside deep in the unconscious.

The inevitable questions arise: How do I know what these wishes are? What do I do? We stay in touch with our soul's wishes by paying attention to the voice that whispers in our inner ear at moments of choice and confrontation. All of us have this inner whispering voice. The voice that tells us: "Don't park your car there" or "This is the wrong man or woman for you." As most of us realize, this voice is usually right, but we don't always pay attention to it. Our conscious mind has its own agenda. The needy child in us also has its own agenda. I remember one morning I was running behind schedule to give a workshop. I drove into Manhattan and down to the New York Open Center where I was teaching. There was an open parking space right in front of the Center. My whispering inner voice said, "Don't park here." My rational mind, combined with my anxiety about being late, told me that it was a busy street with lots of people, the space was right in front of the Center, and no one would break into a car in front of so much activity. I parked the car in the space and went into the Center to give a "Forgiveness" workshop. At the end of the day I came out to find that my trunk had been broken into and emptied of a large bag of clothes that I was going to take to the dry cleaners. All kind of suits, dresses, skirts, blouses, as well as a laundry bag of washing were gone. I was terribly upset, but I knew that I had betrayed myself by ignoring my inner voice. I needed to practice what I preached. I needed to forgive myself and to try to forgive the thieves, who, after all, were just a mirror of my own betrayal. Such psychic thieves.

"Psychic Self-Defense" became a necessary reality in my life. I had helped other people protect themselves from irate bosses and neutralizing pins found in voodoo dolls. But now it had to come home to me. Now I had to protect myself. Once again I had to confront my childhood programming that told me everyone is good at heart. People aren't really bad, just sick. I had never been taught to protect myself. I was not supposed to protect myself. After all, to protect oneself means to *separate out completely.* To separate, to put up a boundary between me and the other person. This was not something we did in my family—too much separation looks like abandonment. To a child's perception, even in an adult body, separation can mean death.

Holding onto the illusion that people are good, that love is the only necessary emotion, and that kindness is the only valuable action means separation is never necessary. Ultimately, when we all attain enlightenment, these options may be true. That is the seduction. That is the real tragedy. These illusions look so much like truth, like desperately hoped for truth, that we get sucked into their glow. In the meantime, we live in a world with thorns where people get crucified. Believe it.

Most people don't want to. I can't tell you how many times people have questioned me over the past twenty years: "Do you really believe in evil?" No matter how many times people watch the news about Bosnia or the Middle East, the Son of Sam, or footage from the concentration camps during Hitler's Germany, the question still comes up. Acknowledging the presence of evil, horror, and destruction in the world is a very bitter pill to swallow. It means that God did not create a perfect universe or that something went terribly wrong somewhere along the way, which is the same thing, not perfect. It means that we have to live with that, face it, and learn how to deal with it. This is not an easy task.

I stared up into a huge blackness in my dream. I looked over for help to my parents playing bridge at a card table. They looked up at me and said: "We couldn't do it. Maybe you can." I stood on shaking legs, knowing that I was not strong enough for this challenge, yet knowing I had to do it. I called out into the black hole: "Come out!" I woke up. I had just called forth the dark shadow in my psyche, the one that had been handed down from generation to generation. The one that I chose to face no matter what the cost. The cost was high.

My marriage was over, and I could no longer project "the other" onto my spouse. There was nowhere to look for "otherness" but in my own soul. Every relationship, every situation is an opportunity to examine ourselves and our projections and the projections of other people toward us. We each have an entire universe taking place within us. We are all multiple personalities. Some of them are inside of us, and some of them are outside of us.

In examining my shadow, the shadows of my parents and ancestors, I was practicing the first step of a four-step process and workshop that I call "Psychic Self-Defense": *recognizing, releasing, repairing,* and *protection and prevention.* The first step is *recognizing* why we are so vulnerable to the negative energies of other people, our environment, and the world around us. Like Persephone, if we don't recognize that there is an underworld containing a rapist and kidnapper under our feet, we are left to play in the flowers with no protection. If we can't see the darkness in our own brother, like Osiris, we willingly lie down in our own death casket with the lid nailed shut.

In ancient Egypt, Osiris was in charge of growth and fertility and was married to his twin sister, Isis. They had a brother, Seth, who was jealous of Osiris, as Cain was of Abel in the Genesis story. So Seth built a beautiful casket and called everyone together. He announced that whoever lay down and fit in the casket might have it as a gift. Everyone lay down, but it fit no one, until Osiris lay down in the casket and it fit him perfectly. All of Seth's dark friends rushed up, sealed the lid to the casket and threw it in the Nile. When Isis couldn't find her husband, much like Demeter, she started mourning and searching everywhere. It so happened the casket had drifted down the Nile, gotten caught in some reeds, and a tree had grown up around it—a beautiful tamarisk tree with a wonderful scent. The king of Byblos had the tree cut down and brought to his palace where it was carved into a pillar. Isis followed the scent to the palace, and when she found the pillar containing Osiris, she flew around it as a swallow. She took up residence as the nurse to the king's son, and finally convinced the queen to give her the pillar with the tree containing Osiris. She opened the tree and the casket, breathed life into Osiris, and conceived a son, Horus.

When Seth got word that Osiris had come back to life, he tracked him down and dismembered him into fourteen pieces. Isis had to locate all the pieces to re–member him. She could find all but the phallus, which had been swallowed by a fish. She had to reconstruct the phallus and once again bring him back to life. Every year the Egyptians celebrate the death and rebirth of the Nile river, their source of life, by celebrating the myth of the rebirth of Osiris. Every year in June the Nile River dries up, then, over the summer, the waters flood back, filling both sides of the Nile with fertile soil, leading to growth and vegetation. For a while Osiris was made both the lord of the underworld and the god of rebirth and fertility. Isis was the goddess of compassion who breathed life back into him. In fact, much like the Christian tradition, in dying and suffering is always the potential for rebirth, resurrection.

Many men confront their shadow in the form of a brother, father, or other male who betrays them. The patriarchal culture has fostered this competition and struggle for power throughout history. God's preference for Abel's offering over Cain's led Cain to become so enraged, he killed his brother. Abraham was willing to sacrifice his only son, Isaac, at God's request. God sacrificed Jesus. It is usually the older men in power that sacrifice the younger men in war. As Freud pointed out, older men circumcise male babies, and the threat of the knife, hanging over their heads as they go through the Oedipal phase of falling in love with their mothers, is a terrifying and intimidating threat. Male against male is a powerful theme running through the collective psyche of all men.

In confronting their shadow, which is always of the same sex according to Carl Jung, men confront the dark inner brother or father within their psyches. The one who would destroy them out of jealousy, hatred, rage, or competition for power. I recall a patient, a man in his thirties, who had come to me with multiple problems.

He originally decided to see me he said because of a groin pull from working out at the gym. It would heal, and then he would reinjure it. He also had trouble with one of his shoulders. We focused on the physical problems, at his request, but as we continued to work together, more and more information came out about his relationships with his family and about his past. His mother had been ill when he was a child, and he took care of her more than she took care of him. His father had preferred his brother. The brother became very successful financially and professionally, while my patient became an addict and went from one job to another. At one point the patient and father had tried to go into business together, and the father had betrayed his son. Despite the betrayal, my patient had always been there for his parents and his brother both emotionally and financially, never wanting to take a look at how much rage he had for all of them. My patient became the caregiver to everyone in his family. When his wealthy and successful brother had an emotional breakdown, my patient listened to his problems hour after hour, the brother refusing to go into therapy. When his father became physically ill, my patient rushed to his side. When his mother needed assistance, he was always there. Year after year, my patient had repressed his real feelings out of fear of losing the only family he ever had and out of fear of confronting what amounted to lethal rage.

Slowly, over several years, the whole story came out and he began to feel the hurt, rage, betrayal, and guilt that he had repressed. His physical symptoms disappeared early in the healing process, while the emotional, mental, and spiritual scars took much longer to heal. His early dreams were full of rage, conflict, confrontation, and death. His later dreams contained women, and at one point he had a dream about stealing a pearl from Aphrodite. This man's soul was trying to work through his shadow material to get back to the original wound, the loss of deep mothering. He needed an Isis of compassion to breathe life back into him. I would provide the external figure until he could find the internal anima, or feminine soul, in himself. Many men these days are searching for their Isis. Unfortunately, most of them don't realize that she exists within them, not in the external world. She will bring them back to life, love them, save them, and give them their own internal son. She will help them integrate into becoming gods of both the underworld and the world above in all its fertile reborn richness. Then, true family is created. A family of the soul. A whole family.

I recognized that all the women in my family were strong, survival-oriented human beings. They had to be. They each had struggled through tremendous adversity and illness. My grandmother was an orphan by age sixteen. My aunt developed multiple sclerosis and spent most of her adult life in a wheelchair, never marrying or having children. My mother was ill her whole childhood. These women learned to put their own needs aside and focus on the needs of their families and children, to make sure everyone survived. There were no luxuries or servants, no wealth or comfort to fall back on. They had to compensate for their own needs by taking care of the needs of others and in some unconscious way, hoped that this would fulfill them. In becoming a healer, I followed in their footsteps, ignoring my own true needs and substituting the needs of others. In doing so, I had left myself open to developing a good mother persona, or image. Many people saw what they wanted to see: a good mother who could feed them in all the ways they had not been fed as a newborn. The danger in this, not only for me, but also for all of us, is that no one person can be a perfect mother. All mothers of newborns make mistakes. Patients and students are not newborns, they are adults. They have needs and expectations that have already been formed by the unmet hunger, sometimes starvation, that has survived from childhood. Accompanying unfulfilled starvation is often rage toward the mother. This is then projected onto the next possible mother substitute to come along, who gets a huge dose of it if the person perceives that he or she is not being fed the right food or enough of it.

This ignorance of my own needs made me vulnerable to the unacknowledged starvation in others. I had to acknowledge my own inner starvation and the persona and self-image that I had acquired. One of the meditations I developed for myself and now use with others is "Sourcing Your Self-Image." This process allows us to get in touch with the people who have most affected, molded and instilled the self-images we have developed. One of my students grew up with an alcoholic mother. Her great fear was of her mother's disintegration or death. My student did everything possible to make sure this didn't happen. When she was a young child she would cook all the meals, clean the house, and take care of errands. All the things a whole mother would have done in the 1950s. My student grew up with an image of herself as a caregiver, having completely repressed her own need for care because her mother couldn't provide it. Her shadow was the needy, angry, starving child. The mirror of her soul was so clouded with this distorted persona and self-image that she could not see her shadow underneath it or the shadow of the person she married. On the outside he was a gifted French chef, his persona being a caregiver, a feeder, a good mother. On the inside he was an alcoholic, drug addict, and womanizer who spent all his free time in bars and pool halls. My student thought she was marrying someone who could feed her, a chef. Instead she married a starving child like herself. At the same time that her marriage was falling apart, her mother died of cancer. Without these two externals, my student was forced to look into the mirror of her own "other" and see her inner shadow. She began taking care of her own needs, feeding herself and gaining a needed twenty pounds.

Another way to recognize why we are vulnerable to the negative energies of others is to look for our "weak link." This is the weak link in our protective chain of self-wholeness. It is usually damaged when we are children. If we grow up in a dysfunctional family where there are no boundaries, where our own ego never has a chance to individuate and become unique, then we are always looking to others for a mirror reflection of who we are. This very often happens in marriages, as it had in mine. One of the major tasks of parenting is to support, encourage, and nurture the unique soul of each child. Many parents, on the other hand, try to mold their children into what they need or want, like the young man whose mother expected him to mirror all her emotions and beliefs. When this kind of parenting takes place, the child develops a weak link in his or her boundary, the integral ego structure that lets a person function as a unique, separate individual. Many people find they then encounter relationships that replicate the same one they had with one of their parents.

One of the students in a "Psychic Self-Defense" workshop described her boss as an angry, explosive man who would lose his temper when anything went wrong. I asked her if she knew anyone in her childhood who had been like this. Oh yes, she replied, her father. We discussed the similarities, and I asked her how she responded to her boss. She admitted she withdrew and felt hurt and rejected by his anger and hostility. She took it personally. She had done the same thing with her father. She was afraid of him and needed his love and approval. The pattern was repeating itself with her boss, and she was responding as if he were her father. Her weak link was her fear of her father and her need for his approval and love. I suggested she work on that issue, and the problem with her boss would begin to heal, at least within her. His personality was another question. I also took her through a guided imagery process in which she saw herself as completely separate from her boss, standing on her own, filled with her own self-love and self-approval. Separation. A good beginning.

Most people think they can come to a workshop with a healer and get magically healed by 5 P.M. on Sunday evening. Workshops are beginnings. They can provide intense insight and sparks of instantaneous transformation. But to keep that transformation alive, one must nurture the spark into a flame that heats the soul and turns dross into gold.

I was much like my female student who was the caregiver, and I realized after my divorce that I had to take care of my own needs. I bought a house of my own and began to get my finances in order. It was a long hard struggle. I had been an only child and thought that being alone would be easy for me, but it wasn't. Right away I got involved in another relationship in which there was a lot of mutual caregiving. Too much. Any kind of separation, especially divorce, is an agonizing, lonely, and frightening process, and most human beings will do anything to ease the pain. Some people go to extremes with alcohol and drugs, others with pain medication, others with people. Forfeiting the love and comfort of another human being is almost impossible when faced with such pain, but very often it is a necessary step in the spiritual practice of mirror-looking. I found I needed to create my own inner home ground. Placing it in another person was being homeless once again.

The second step of "Psychic Self-Defense" for me was *releasing*. It took me a long time after my divorce to *recognize* and *release* all the emotions, beliefs, and thoughts that did not belong to me. It took me a long time to find myself again. This happens to many of us in marriage, in families, in friendships, and even in work situations. We lose ourselves. Our boundaries become blurred, we merge with the other person, we lose track of our authentic feelings and beliefs. Sometimes we even lose track of our own body. We fall under the hypnotic induction of the other person's energy.

The mother's body is the first boundary a child experiences. In utero the fetus is totally protected from the outside world. Once born, the infant usually breast-feeds while being held against the mother's chest, where her heartbeat can permeate the child's body as it did in utero. If the child in not touched and held lovingly by the mother, that sense of security and protection never develops. Likewise, if the infant is handled too often by other people, its sense of integrity and protection is at risk. Most people do not realize this effect, and willingly hand their newborn infants to relatives, friends, and even small children to hold. Everyone who touches a newborn is leaving an imprint of his or her energy on that child's body and nervous system. I have trouble imagining how confusing it must be for a newborn to be in almost total comfort inside the mother's womb, and then come out into a world of harsh clothes, sheets, lights, noise, and a myriad of voices and hands all grabbing for its body. We are often more careful to warn owners of cats and dogs not to overhandle the newborn kittens and puppies than we are to warn human parents. Some experts say that newborns should only be handled by their mother and father during the first three months, as a way of laying down that imprint of protection in their body senses and their psyches. Hospitals are very careful in neonatal intensive care units to avoid overstimulating the premature babies with too much light, sound, and touch. Overstimulating the nervous systems of newborns can leave permanent damage. They need time to rest, eat, grow, and develop a sense of love and protection to become healthy and strong.

A child who has never had that complete and unconditional protection and love remains a starved child for the rest of his or her life, always looking for that nurturing and protection in someone else, a substitute mother. Every time we think we have found that person, we project "mother" onto that person, even if the person is a man. For a spouse, friend, therapist, or healer to remother a starved adult child is an impossible and unfair task. I have found that some of the most ferocious psychic attacks directed at me have been from people so starved that their rage burst forth at me like a wild animal denied its prey. It is misplaced survival instinct, and for that reason, murderous.

We need to release what others direct at us in the way of negative energy. It is a letting go, a separation in which we learn to distinguish what emotions, thoughts, sensations, and beliefs are ours, rather than someone else's. Very often we merge with people without even realizing it, just as I did in the restaurant with the woman who had a headache. We are in a sea of energy all the time, and individuals are concentrations of mass and energy, as Einstein might say. We all have had the experience of sitting on a bus or a subway next to someone and "feeling" their energy, feeling who they are and the "vibes" they are emitting. Many of us can walk into someone's home, an office, or a church and immediately sense the energy in it. Some spaces have more energy than others, and they all have more or less positive and negative energy.

When we are in a relationship with someone, anyone, we are merging with that person's energy whether we like it or not. Most people have auras, or energy fields, that can expand or contract from an inch to three feet all around their body. Sitting next to someone at dinner, or lying next to someone at night while we

✳

sleep, we are in the induction field of the other person's energy. An induction field is a space in which we get hypnotized by the other person's thoughts and feelings if our boundaries are not intact.

I was teaching a workshop at one of the holistic health centers. There were almost one hundred people there for the entire weekend, and I had a faculty member and several student assistants in charge of logistics. I felt rested and energized, happy to be there, and confident about the workshop. As the morning went on, I noticed that little things started to go wrong. At first they were minor logistical problems, but as the day proceeded, they became more pronounced and started to interfere with my concentration. The last thing a speaker needs to worry about when leading a workshop for one hundred people is whether the music tape is wound to the correct side or the microphones are plugged in. I found myself worrying more and more every time another small item wasn't handled correctly. Then, I began to get annoyed and angry with my technician. I became more and more angry with her until finally, I took her aside at one of the breaks and spoke with her. I knew that there was an induction going on. I knew that she was anxious and angry, that her mood was affecting the whole workshop, and that I was absorbing her feelings and enacting the emotions for her because she wouldn't acknowledge them. This is how induction works.

I took her aside and asked her what was wrong. She said "nothing." I pointed out to her that she was not handling her responsibilities as well as she usually did. She had always been very conscientious, and all the workshops she had been in charge of had run quite smoothly. She was in denial. She insisted that "nothing at all" was wrong with her and wanted to know what was wrong with me and why was I so upset. This situation is called projection of shadow material onto another person. I realized that I was getting nowhere at that moment, and we scheduled a supervision session for her the following week. In that session all the anger and fear around her failing marriage and the terminal illness of one of her parents surfaced. It was very painful for her to acknowledge, because it meant that she was needy for once and couldn't adequately fulfill the function of caregiver for me, which was her role at that workshop. She had never failed in that position before, having had a lifetime of experience carrying it out. So instead, she denied her feelings and projected the anger onto me, and before I realized it, I had succumbed to the induction, acted it out, and then had to release it. Fortunately, I caught it quickly, recognized it, and was able to get on with the rest of the workshop without losing too much ground.

If I had any doubt about how I felt that morning of the workshop, if I had been anxious and angry myself, then it would have been much harder for me to titrate out which feelings were mine and which were hers. It would have been almost impossible to know whether it was her anxiety and anger disrupting the logistics, or whether it was mine. But I knew where I stood and how I felt. I saw myself clearly in the mirror and noticed when I began to feel differently, and that allowed me to recognize and release what was not mine.

The technical steps of *releasing* can be done by separating our energy from the other person's or the environment. We can leave a room, sleep in a different bed, give ourselves some time before seeing someone again. We can break the pattern, separate ourselves, and then start to assess the damage. If every time we have lunch with a certain friend, we find ourselves getting indigestion and feeling sad after the meeting, we should begin to recognize that the sadness (as well as the indigestion!) might belong to them. When we return home or to the office, we can sit by ourselves for a few minutes and breathe deeply, imaging the person's voice, eyes, words, and feelings floating out and away from our body. Even saying something as simple as "This isn't mine. This belongs to Susan," can be of help.

Washing our hands is another often overlooked but simple technique. Every time we shake hands with someone we are exchanging energy with them. That is why people shake hands. To show friendly interaction, to make contact. Unfortunately, I am so sensitive from twenty years of working with my hands, that shaking hands for me can be a dangerous action. I can feel the whole person in one handshake. If the person is ill, I feel some of the illness energy in my hand. If I do not wash my hands immediately, sometimes I can feel the energy travel up my arm. It is also dangerous because I have small fragile hands. A man at a conference enthusiastically grabbed my hand so hard that he almost broke it. Actually, I thought he had, and I had to bandage it for the rest of the day to remind myself and everyone around me not to try to shake my hand. After several hours of self-healing, it was fine. But I had learned a valuable lesson: Don't shake hands if your instincts tell you that the person's energy is not safe. In other words, if there is a lot of shadow energy that has not yet healed or if there is illness and you are particularly clairsentient, like I am. Those of us who are clairsentient are more physically and emotionally sensitive to the energies of others, and we should wash our hands as soon as we can after shaking hands with people.

Guided meditations that open and release the energy in the chakras, the subtle energy centers, are good for internal releasing. Checking ourselves before and after each encounter with another person allows us to practice looking in the mirror and then releasing what we took on during the encounter. Even taking a shower and putting on clean clothes can release and cleanse away energies that don't belong to us. Much like cigarette smoke can be held and absorbed, clothing can hold energy. We are all familiar with how clothes can cling together if we don't put an antistatic sheet in the dryer. The emotions, thoughts, and physical energies of another person can cling to us just like static.

Of course, sometimes an encounter does trigger something in us that is not the projected energy or shadow of the other person, as with the woman whose boss was constantly angry. In paying attention to the difference between what is triggered inside of us and what we merge with or take on from someone outside of us, we can accomplish the first two steps of learning how to protect ourselves in a world that is not completely friendly to our needs.

I found that once I had recognized my own needs, I could much more easily recognize them in others before they affected me adversely. *Prevention* is always easier than treatment, something the

✳

medical profession is finally beginning to acknowledge. If I did absorb something I did not want, I found I could release it more quickly, in the moment, rather than waiting for hindsight. I was still faced with the dilemma of repairing the damage that had been done to my vitality. I would feel extremely tired after seeing certain patients, despite practicing the techniques of recognizing and releasing. It seemed not so much dependent on the illness as on the particular person. I had to find a way to replenish my vitality.

I noticed that certain types of people drained my energy more than others. I decided to try to understand the dynamics behind feeling as though all the blood had been drained from my body. I found that people who are compulsive talkers are particularly exhausting for me. They seem to be the ones producing all the energy, but in actuality the nonstop talking is a defense against feeling the emotions underneath. They smother people in words, demanding that the other person listen to them, that way they keep themselves and anyone else from actually getting anywhere near the true feelings lying deep within their soul. Being the empath that I am, I feel as though I am being buried in wet cement.

I remember a young woman in her twenties who came to see me because she could not find any direction in her life. She talked nonstop for most of the first session, and I found myself getting more and more exhausted. My instincts, however, told me to let her talk. I knew I had to find a way to combat drowning in her energy, so I took a deep breath, imaged a wall of white light between my body and hers, and just let her words and energy bounce off this invisible wall. From this vantage point I was able to see and hear the starving child in her and allow her talking to be a release of anxiety that did not bury me. I knew she had booked several appointments and would be coming back. In fact, I let her talk throughout most of the first three sessions. Her anxiety level seemed so high that I was concerned she would not be able to even close her eyes. At one point in her third session I asked her to stop for a moment, close her eyes and take a long deep breath. She immediately burst into tears. This sadness was hidden underneath all her talking, and it took tremendous energy for her to keep it down. Once she allowed herself to feel her sadness and get in touch with the fear of her feelings, the course of our work together shifted. She allowed her soul to open and be nourished by her own truthful feelings. She was able to close her eyes, allow me to do both chakra and body scans, and even several laying-on-of-hands. At the end of every session with her, I had to spend ten to twenty minutes in complete silence in order to revitalize myself.

At one point I saw with my internal sight, my third eye, a vision of her working with food. This idea peaked her interest, and she admitted that she had often thought she might want to go into catering but had been too afraid to try. My mirroring this back to her, a positive mirroring, started her on a new career. She began with cooking a meal or two here and there for her neighbor, and finally branched out into running her own catering business. She became very successful at it and quite well known.

I began to do step 3, *repairing,* after every private session and at the end of every working day, and I still do. I wash my hands in cold water, splash some on my face, and sprinkle some over my hair and sometimes my clothes. I drink a glass of water, and then stand by an open window or go out into the fresh air, recognize any signs that I have absorbed something I don't want from one of my patients, and release it through breathing and imagining it floating up and away from my body. I then repair my own energy and integrity by visualizing a white light flowing down from the sun or moon and filling my entire body, my chakras, connecting me with the earth and heaven, and filling my body and energy field with new life. I complete this process in silence as a balance for the talking that is done in a session. My office manager knows not to talk to me immediately after I have finished a session. After a patient or a group leaves, I take sage or incense, light it, and clear the air. I pass the sage over the healing table and the chairs we have been sitting in. I visualize white light cleansing the entire room and usually leave a candle lit during and for a while after the session. Fire has been used in all religions and cultures for purification and transformation. It is customary to light a candle in the Roman Catholic Church when one is saying a prayer for someone who is ill.

I also discovered the importance of exercise, healthy food, good music, and some kind of spiritual practice, usually prayer and meditation, as essential ways to repair my health and energy. Exercise and healthful food mobilize the immune system, produce brain chemicals that shift mood, and change the rhythm of the body. Science has found that the old adage about eating grandma's chicken soup is good advice. It contains several nutrients that stimulate and strengthen the immune system. If we have been thrown off balance by someone's anger or fear, one of the best ways to ground ourselves, or stabilize our energy, is to eat warm, protein-rich foods. The first chakra at the base of the spine is the security center and controls the energy of the feet and legs. If we feel "spacy" or ungrounded, eating protein-rich foods such as fish, chicken, meat, eggs, or dairy products can help bring us back into our bodies. Early on in my own "Psychic Self-Defense" practice, I remember one evening feeling particularly light-headed and disembodied. I was walking along the street and I could hardly feel my feet on the ground. I went home and cooked a large hamburger for myself, not something I usually did. It immediately brought me back down into my body and connected me through my feet into the ground. When my mother was a young woman in her early twenties, she weighed less than one hundred pounds. Her boss used to tease her each winter by giving her a penny to put in each pocket to keep her from blowing away in the wind. I needed something a little heavier than pennies.

Exercise mobilizes not only the immune system, but also the sense of strength and power that are very often missing in those of us with weak boundaries and a lack of grounding. In building the body's strength, self-image begins to shift from being weak and vulnerable, or only a caregiver to others, to that of a self-caring, self-nurturing individual. A strong body is healthy and vital, with a coherent aura, or field of energy. There are no weak links in the body's defense. It can maintain its own integrity.

Music has a profound effect on the body. It affects our nervous system immediately, calming or energizing it. Studies have shown that Gregorian chanting actually alters the brain waves and produces an altered state of alpha waves, similar to meditation. I now use several Gregorian chanting tapes in my healing sessions with patients, and during the laying-on-of-hands in workshops. I found that classical music like Mozart or Bach would calm and reground me after an upsetting confrontation with someone, whereas rock 'n' roll would energize me if I felt drained.

The same is true for prayer and meditation. The discipline of sitting down every day at the same time to quiet the mind produces profound results. Like everyone else, I resisted the idea at first. Stopping the constant forward motion was anxiety-producing. What if I stopped for meditation and then couldn't get going again? It seems like a simple enough question, but it's not. We are afraid we can't get going again because our instinct tells us there is something so important, so deep within us that we might actually have to devote time and attention to it. Devotion, according to the *World Book Dictionary,* is "the act of devoting or setting apart to a sacred use or purpose; solemn dedication; consecration." We are setting aside *ourselves* to the sacred purpose of our own healing. Another definition of devotion from the same dictionary: "a deep, steady affection; loyalty; faithfulness." I found that sitting in meditation every morning and every evening was one of the most powerful ways I could show steady affection, loyalty, and faithfulness to myself—qualities a good mother shows her child.

"Psychic Self-Defense" is a lifelong spiritual practice, especially step 4: *protection and prevention.* This step requires opening the third eye, the center of clear vision, so that we see what and who is in front of us (and behind us) at all times. Instead of simply *recognizing* (step 1) why we are so vulnerable to other people's energies, and then following through with *releasing* (step 2) and *repairing* (step 3), step 4 requires that we confront life *at every moment* with a dark eye. It does not mean being a pessimist or only seeing the worst in people. But it does mean seeing both the best and the worst in people and in every situation. It means seeing beneath the veneers, smiles, and good intentions, to the shadow. Everyone has his or her shadow hiding underneath the most beautiful face, the biggest smile, the friendliest hello. If you grew up watching Haley Mills and Shirley Temple, you might think that if you're cute and friendly enough, you will always win everyone's heart. You would be wrong. And in great danger. You must learn to develop a dark eye.

In my workshops, I guide participants through an exercise in which they pair up with a stranger and look deeply through all the layers presented into the core of the person. I have people look for emotions, fears, childhood information, talents, gifts, health issues, and the shadow. The shadow is always hardest for people to see.

When we were infants we saw all sides of people. Whatever the energy and the face our mother or father brought to us, we saw. We saw when they were tired, angry, anxious, joyful, and loving. Psychologist Melanie Klein talks about infants probably being unable to distinguish that the angry, negative mother is the same person as the happy, loving mother. We are so fragile at that age, so unable to defend ourselves against our fear of being devoured or destroyed by that negative energy, that we split it off. Most of us chose to see the best, the most idealized so that we could choose life instead of death. Or at least ignore the worst in people.

My inherent sensitivity to my environment has been both a blessing and a curse. Whereas others can blissfully walk down the New York City streets ignoring everyone around them, I have to protect myself with white-gold light before I even leave my home. White light has the full spectrum of color rays, and gold light is the alchemical color of transformation and power. I have to accept myself the way I am and treat myself as a good mother would protect her child from harm. Every morning I have to write down all my dreams to clear them from my mind and to understand the needs of my soul. I exercise to build strength, eat well to fortify my energy, and then meditate to protect my energy field. I mobilize the energy inside me through opening the chakras, and around me through "Strengthening Your Aura" (*see* "Healing Meditations"). By mobilizing and visualizing the life force in and around the body, I am programming my brain and central nervous system to make it so. I am remaining conscious of my needs and setting into action a program to take care of these needs. Intention and consciousness make a very effective and powerful combination in "Psychic Self-Defense."

When I arrive at my office, I turn on the lights, open the windows, light candles and incense, and stand or sit to meditate for a few minutes to set or program the healing energy in the room and on the massage table used for laying-on-of-hands. I make sure to keep my chair to myself, so no one else's energy permeates it. If someone sits in it accidentally, I sprinkle a little water on it, wave some sage over it, light a candle next to it, and say a prayer to clear it. Sage is a powerful herb and cleanser when dried and lit. It has been used by the Native Americans for centuries, sometimes combined with cedar and lavender.

I go through a similar process between patients, clearing their chair and massage table as well, so no one will be affected by anyone else's pain or illness. At the end of the day I clear the room and chairs again. When I return home, I place my clothes in a hamper that is not in the room in which I sleep, take a shower, and sit to meditate and release the day. I briefly focus on each of the day's patients, drop down into myself to check whether I have gotten hooked by any of their issues or pain, and then say a prayer for their healing. In these ways I keep myself protected and do my best to prevent myself from absorbing other people's negative energies.

Before healing circles and workshops, my faculty and student assistants light a candle, put on healing music, clear the room and my chair, and set the energy in the entire room. When we travel, they get to the space at least an hour early to do this procedure. People always comment on how good the energy feels in the workshop space. When I stay in a hotel room, I clear the bed and pillows as well as the room. I do the same thing in cars and airplanes, although I do it mentally. I clear my seat, pillow, and blanket, set a boundary of energy between myself and the person next

✳

to me, and send healing light through the rest of the car or plane. As the plane is taxiing for takeoff, I surround the plane in light and see it taking off, flying, and landing safely. I do all of this mentally, as I am sure they would not appreciate candles, incense, and music in the aisles. Acting appropriately at the right moments can also be good self-defense.

At "Psychic Self-Defense" workshops, someone always comments that these procedures sound as though they take a lot of time. Some people may even think they sound obsessive. When you first begin to practice them, they may take a little time. But after years of daily practice, I find doing them to be automatic, easy, and no more time-consuming than brushing my teeth. It is trying to repair the damage after I have absorbed something unpleasant and harmful that is time-consuming.

One Friday night at the New York Open Center we were not careful enough with our energy preparations. I felt something strange in the room. A strange energy. I looked at the young man sitting directly in front of me: twenties, blond, handsome, stone-faced. A young dark-haired woman a few people over to his right, my left, and a man beside her. Another woman, heavier, a little older toward the back. My eyes kept scanning the room for I knew not what, but I could feel it. I noticed about seven or eight people in the room. My eyes seemed to home in on them. I felt anxious, tense, not something I'm used to feeling in front of a group. The topic was "Forgiveness." I was giving an evening talk to a large group, almost one hundred.

I started the talk. I felt scattered, unfocused. I found myself talking about "Psychic Self-Defense." I had trouble breathing. I kept trying to return to the topic of "Forgiveness," but something kept drawing me back to "Psychic Self-Defense." When it came time to ask if there were any questions, the young man with blond hair directly in front of me raised his hand. He made a preachy statement about how all his relationships were fine, and he didn't feel any anger toward anyone. My gut reaction, something I was still not good at paying attention to when it conflicted with my good-girl Protestant upbringing, was to snap back *Then why are*

you here? But I didn't. Instead, I said something innocuous, like "Well, maybe you don't need forgiveness." I knew it wasn't true, but something told me not to get into an argument with him. The girl with dark hair raised her hand. The other people my eyes had honed in on all raised their hands one by one. The girl with dark hair gave me a particularly hard time. I don't remember what she said, but again my gut reaction was to ask her *Do you come here every Friday night just to give the speaker a hard time or am I targeted for this?* But I restrained myself. I would have seemed too aggressive, too unpleasant, maybe I would have embarrassed myself and people wouldn't have liked me. Heaven forbid. Be nice at all costs was how I had been raised. Even if someone is not nice to you. So I kept quiet.

At the end of the evening, grateful to be finished, I found myself surrounded by four or five of the same people who had given off strange energies and asked particularly hostile questions. They wanted to know what I felt during a laying-on-of-hands. I described it. They asked me to demonstrate one on the young man with the blond hair. I refused. I told him he could make an appointment at my office if he wished. They wanted to know how I felt about digging up the past to heal it, saying they felt it wasn't necessary, and in fact was destructive. Only the present should be focused on. Never the past. They all seemed to be saying these things in unison, agreeing together on each point. I asked how they proposed to heal the past if it was ignored. They said it would heal by ignoring it. I went over to my student assistants and several close friends waiting for me at the back of the room. One of my friends wanted to know why I had talked so much about "Psychic Self-Defense." I said I didn't know. My assistants said they felt "weird vibes" in the room and noticed how hostile some of the people had been. I agreed. One of my students was a volunteer at the center and proceeded to get hold of the registration list. She looked down the list and found that eight people were registered under the name of Smith. No first name, no individual names, just Smith.

I knew then that I had been psychically attacked. Two weeks

later, Christmas week, I received a letter in the mail signed by eight people saying that they had a "teacher" who taught "the only true healing," and since my opinions and methods disagreed with his, I was a fake. They said they were planning on assembling an organization that would seek out all fake healers and take legal action against them and destroy them.

I was, of course, stunned. I knew that this letter was composed and signed by the same people who had been to my talk. This was not the first time I had been psychically attacked, and it would not be the last. I had practiced "Psychic Self-Defense" for years, taught it, and had loving friends around me who were powerful healers in their own right. We recognized the ferocity of the shadow energy of these people and took our own powerful steps to combat it, some of which I have already discussed in this chapter.

Several years after this incident I read an article in one of the New York magazines about this man, his cult, and his followers. He apparently threatened to inflict cancer on anyone who attempted to leave him, and in other ways terrorized and abused his followers. He wound up projecting his shadow onto his own followers. Many people awoke from the trance induction of his power and found the strength to leave; many were pulled down with him into his underworld by the Hades figure he embodied— a Hitler in spiritual clothing.

There are several life-saving lessons to be learned from this kind of incident. The first is that it is easy for people to lose their dark eye and idealize someone who seems powerful but really embodies evil. The second is that the projected shadow has great power to do evil in the world. When we ignore our past, our shadow, our burning roots, we deny who we are and where we come from. Denial is a terrible and powerful force. It both idealizes and demonizes. It cannot be contained for long, and so has to be projected out onto the other. The other is always the one that seems to embody all the qualities that we do not, either godlike goodness or demonic darkness. With the former, we project enormous power onto the other and become a follower. With the latter, we project the qualities we fear to admit onto the other, make him or her the enemy, and, therefore, the one that is bad and worthy of destruction. This projection of the shadow is the cause of all evil in the world.

When we are strong enough, we can choose our sacrifices. Until then, our sacrifices choose us. Most of us don't realize we are in a state of induction most of the time. We are hypnotized, persuaded, led by other people's energies and by past influences. The word *induction* has an interesting etymology. The *World Book Dictionary* states that it begins with the word *induce,* from the Latin *inducere,* which means "to lead." To induce means to lead, influence, or persuade. It is also a physics term meaning "to produce an electric current, electric charge, or magnetic change without direct contact; to bring about radioactivity in an element artificially by bombardment with particles." This is exactly what happens to us. We are bombarded by the energetic particles of other people and of our environment. The definition of energy is the shifting of orbits of the electrons within atoms. This shifting produces heat, electricity, light, electromagnetism. When our energy fields are either so weak, or so merged with people around us that we can't hold our own charge, hold our own energy field autonomously, then we become induced. We fall under the spell of induction. We are hypnotized by the energy of someone else. When we are first born, we are completely open and vulnerable. We are protected by the energy field of the womb, but still very much in our mother's induction field. After we emerge from the womb, our family becomes our induction field. We are exposed to the experience of being tossed out of the Garden of Eden that has been our mother's protective womb. In the external world we are exposed to the harsh realities of jealous and competitive brothers and sisters. I remember one student of mine confiding that she had actually tried to kill her infant sister while she was in the crib. An adult had interrupted the act, but the energy field of danger still remained, and that baby sister most likely grew up in the induction field of a jealous and hateful sister, wondering why she felt so unloved and unwanted.

When we feel something very strongly and that feeling is accompanied by an image in the mind, we set up an induction field. Our electromagnetic field, our aura, becomes filled with the effects of that feeling, thought, and image. It may get pushed deep into the unconscious mind, meaning that we don't consciously think about it all the time, but it is still there. It is like minimizing and maximizing documents on the computer screen. If you minimize the control panel so that you can maximize a document on the screen, the control panel does not disappear. The document just takes up the foreground of the screen. The control panel is still there, hiding underneath and controlling everything. Most of us think that as long as a feeling, thought, or image is out of sight, it has no effect. Not true. It may be the controlling factor running the whole show. Just because someone is smiling at you, doesn't mean he or she doesn't want to kill you. Or as the old adage goes . . . just because you're paranoid doesn't mean they're not after you.

The younger sister of that student of mine probably grew up thinking she *was* paranoid. Her family probably looked fairly normal, so she must have wondered why she felt she was going to be murdered at any moment. Or if not murdered, so unloved and unwanted. She probably thought it was "just in her mind," as many people do. This incident brings us to a very controversial subject: abuse. There is so much debate nowadays over whether an adult who remembers being sexually abused as a child is telling the truth or is having false memories. I have worked with people for twenty years, and I have seen many people who were aware of abuse, as well as those who were not aware of it, but in whose induction field I felt the abuse. I have worked with people who carried the unhealed abuse that their parents suffered as children. The parents had never remembered the abuse, and it had been left unhealed in their unconscious until their children came along and had to carry it for them. Much like the children of holocaust survivors, children of abused parents carry the trauma of their parents in their own souls.

I have seen programs on television about people who accused their fathers and mothers of abuse, only to retract the accusations later. I look at these people with all the intuitive powers that I have, and I usually see people who are so traumatized by having the courage to make the accusation, then having it denied by everyone around them, and then being turned into the victimizer for telling the truth, that they give up. There is no support, no love, no healing in the confrontation. And because their ego structure isn't strong enough to stand alone, they cave in and retract the accusation. The loss of love, the abandonment, the projection of evil onto them is too much for them to handle. They would rather take the blame for creating a false memory, or blame the therapist for planting the idea, than hold their ground and be utterly alone in their own defense.

On the other hand, I also believe there are therapists who are so unhealed in themselves, that their own induction field of childhood abuse influences their patients. Either the therapist projects his or her own trauma onto the patient and suggests that the patient was abused; or the patient feels the therapist's unhealed, abused shadow and identifies with it. That's what patients do when transference develops. A great deal of the healing in a psychotherapeutic relationship is in the transferential relationship. The patient projects his or her feelings for the parents onto the therapist and then works them through. If the transference is positive, the patient identifies with the therapist. This identification then triggers true memories in the patient, or, it can trigger an induction field of false associations. The subject is very complex, and sometimes the media's attempt to paint a picture of sexual abuse memories as either true or false only leads to the confusion. There are both true and false memories, and each case needs to be healed individually. The question I always ask myself when I deal with, see, or hear of someone making accusations of sexual abuse is *What did happen* in this family that this child feels such hatred for his or her parents? What did happen to the Menendez brothers to lead them to kill their parents? Such a thing doesn't happen in a family where children are loved, nurtured, and taught to respect life. *What did happen?* is the most important question any of us can ask. Because whatever the details, *something happened.*

Which brings us to the issue of evil and sanity. Anyone who intentionally, with hatred in his heart, sets out to kill or destroy another human being is evil and, by definition, not sane. As Jesus said on the cross about his executioners, "Forgive them. They know not what they do." Evil may intentionally set out to destroy a life and still not know what it is doing. One of the questions that the courts use in insanity pleas is: Did the perpetrator know what he or she was doing? Does the person know the difference between good and evil? The person can know, rationally, and still be so filled with insane rage, fear, and hatred, that the person does not know his or her own shadow and the power it is exerting. The individual is literally possessed. Hitler thought he was doing the world a favor by killing all but his vision of the most "perfect" people. In truth, Hitler was setting out to try to destroy his own evil inner shadow by projecting it onto the Jews and others who did not meet his standards of "light and pure." There are examples of this thinking today in this country and around the world. Everyone who righteously thinks that everyone unlike them is evil and therefore needs to be destroyed, is a mini-Hitler. Moreover, as the great Indian sage Khrisnamurti once admitted, we all have a Hitler within us. The difference is that some of us are willing to admit it, and some of us aren't. And herein lies the definition of sanity. If we can admit it, we're sane and have a chance of healing the darkness within by reclaiming our power from that Hitler. If we can't admit it, we're still too scared of him to take back our power, and he is always potentially in the control panel behind any new document on the screen of our life.

Evil is that consciousness that does not know God. Evil is that which is so disconnected from love, comfort, safety, and abundance that it will strike out in fear, rage, and hatred at anyone or anything that threatens its concept of itself. If everyone would take responsibility for his or her own shadow, repressed emotions, childhood pain, and ancestral darkness, there would be no need to project it onto anyone else and therefore no need to create enemies from our own fears. Fear attacks. Love protects. Fear destroys. Love heals. Fear hates. Love forgives. What kind of love? Self-love.

Self-love has to be extremely strong to face truth. It is much more powerful than projection for the very reason that we have to love ourselves first to face our own darkness, our own shadows. It is when we hate ourselves that we cannot face it, and therefore must project it outward, fearing that to face the inner darkness would kill us. I remember seeing the movie *The Exorcist* many years ago and paying very careful attention to how the Devil attacked the priest. I also read a book on evil by Malachi Martin. They both seemed to portray the Devil as a force that attacks people with the horror of their weaknesses, their shadow. All the hidden thoughts, feelings, and fantasies that people think have been locked away in the closet permanently are what are flung back in their faces as a way to weaken their egos against Satan. Instead of denying the shadow, what would happen if we admitted it? What would happen if we agreed with Satan? Yes, I do have a dark side to me. Yes, I do have those thoughts, feelings, and fantasies. I *know* them, accept them, and love myself anyway. All of me is loved and forgiven. All of me belongs to God. What then would Satan have as ammunition?

So I sat. I lit my candles, sat on my beautiful rug, and looked into my soul. And I was not turned into a pillar of salt. I called out into the dark hole for all the shadows to emerge, and one by one they did. I placed each one in front of me and looked for the starvation, the grief, the rage, the fear, the abandonment. I looked into the face of everyone who had ever attacked me or drained my energy and saw my shadow. I took deep breaths and at each moment faced possible death with faltering legs and found myself standing with the support of God's grace. And somewhere there had to be a light shining for me to see the shadows in my soul.

✳ ✳ ✳

One of the greatest healing energies is that of forgiveness: self-forgiveness and the forgiveness of others. The patient of mine whose family had such a hold on him has learned to forgive them while protecting himself at the same time. He sees how dangerous and destructive their pain and neediness is to his health. He no longer takes phone calls from his brother, who calls only to get free therapy. He warns his mother and father that if they try to manipulate him with guilt, he will refuse to have any contact with them. After many months of standing strong on his own behalf, they are finally listening and their entire family dynamic is changing for the better. Systems theory in sociology tells us that it only takes one member of a family system to change the entire family. He is also doing other things to protect himself and prevent future vulnerability. He stopped drinking. Every morning he gets up and does yoga and meditation. He has changed his eating patterns and gets daily exercise. At night, for an entire hour before he goes to bed, he goes over a list of all the things in his life that he is grateful for. He counts his blessings. He has become an Osiris, a reborn male who can bridge the underworld and the physical realm of resurrection.

In combining good "Psychic Self-Defense" with self-forgiveness, I found myself being much more careful with my boundaries and the integrity of my energy. When I spoke in front of large numbers of people, I began to have my student assistants move the first row back, farther away from me. Sometimes I had them put coats on the chairs directly in front of me, to keep them clear, knowing that the neediest people always sit there. Unless I felt particularly strong, I sometimes asked people not to attempt to shake hands with me or to hug me. Most people are not aware that they are acting like energy vampires, trying to feed off other people's energy. Some people are quite aware of it, and don't like being confronted with the truth. I'll never forget the evening when I was speaking about "Psychic Self-Defense" and a woman came up to me at the end, after a two-hour talk and a long line of participants posing questions. She asked whether I would read her aura for her, right then and there. I said no but suggested she come to my office for a private session. She persisted, "sweetly" begging me to just give her "an idea of what it looks like." I said no, that if I did it for her, I would have to do it for everyone. Her face became dark and angry and she snapped back at me, "Well, you certainly do have strong boundaries!" I thanked her, knowing full well that she did not intend to compliment me except that it *was* a compliment—a great compliment. Self-love in action.

We have to be willing to risk other people's wrath when we do not give them what they want, which is a full breast all the time whenever they want it. That is what most people are looking for from us, whether we are in the health care profession or a member of a family. For our own protection, our own health, we must learn to assess our strength and availability and say "no" when necessary, or just when we want to. Even wanting to say "no" is enough. We have a right to protect ourselves, to keep our energy to ourselves.

Many years ago a friend of mine told me of an incident that happened to him when he was a student in a zendo, a Zen monastery. It was the middle of the night and everyone was sleeping. He and several other students heard a loud and insistent pounding on the front door. They got up to see who it was and opened the door. A large, burly and drunken man plunged into the front hallway and started screaming for the roshi, the Zen master. All the students, including my friend, tried to politely hush him so he would not disturb their teacher. In whispered voices they conjoled and begged him to leave. The man kept screaming at the top of his lungs that he wanted to see the roshi. A few minutes later the roshi appeared at the top of the stairs and with a thundering clap shouted "Get out!" The drunken man stood quiet for the first time, looked up into the eyes of the teacher, turned, and left. My friend said he learned more from that one interaction than from almost anything else during his three years at the zendo. As they say in rehabilitation programs for addiction, sometimes tough love is the only kind that cuts to the heart of truth.

I was in Hong Kong about ten years ago. I had been invited for two weeks to give two workshops and several dozen private sessions. The workshop that weekend was "Forgiveness and Letting go of Judgment." There were about twenty-five people in front of

*

me, mostly "ex-pats" as they called themselves: citizens of other countries who worked in Hong Kong. A few were Chinese who could speak English.

I announced my name and the title of the workshop. "Forgiveness!!!" a woman screamed out, "I don't want to forgive!!!" I stopped breathing and looked at the woman sitting directly in front of me (they always do). She was gray-haired, early seventies, of medium build and very angry. Yes, I managed to sputter out, that's the subject of the workshop. "My daughter tricked me!" she shot back. "She told me this was a 'learning how to meditate workshop.'" I told her we would learn how to meditate, but by that time she didn't really care.

It turned out that her husband of forty years had left her for a thirty-year-old woman two years before. He had abandoned and betrayed her. She was full of rage and hatred for him, and it was poisoning her life and the lives of her children and grandchildren. She made it very clear to me that she had no intention of forgiving him. I told her she didn't have to and she could still stay. She was silent, staring at me trying to figure out whether I was lying to her. I wasn't. She thought for a few uncomfortable moments and then decided, "Well, I don't have a way to get home and the workshop is already paid for." So she stayed.

That weekend we talked about the meaning of forgiveness and the meaning of the expression "you can't put frosting on a burned cake." We explored feelings of rage, hatred, fear, grief, and love. We did a meditation entitled "Prisons of the Mind," so people could get in touch with all the judgments they have received from others and all their own judgments. We looked into the mirror of our idealized selves and our nonidealized plain and honest selves. We felt the difference between guilt and remorse, and I asked them to have the courage to go home that night and ask someone for forgiveness. We opened our hearts, forgave ourselves, and confessed to one another all the things for which we would like to be forgiven. And we explored why we bother with forgiveness at all: because not to forgive is to hold onto the past and to injure ourselves continually with the pain of the original injury done to us

✳

by someone else—over and over again, like this woman who had once been abandoned, but was abandoning the rest of her own life.

She not only stayed all day Saturday, but also went home with her daughter that night and came back on Sunday. She stayed the entire weekend. By Sunday afternoon at closing, she raised her hand. One very courageous woman told me and the group that she had decided to let go of her husband and the past and to give herself and her family the gift of embracing, with love, the rest of the time she had left. She did, as I found out later, and I've never forgotten her.

Forgiveness is an act of courage. It is not simply a rule that most religions impose on us because it is the nice thing to do. It is a challenging, difficult, painful, and ego-threatening act. It is the decision to let go of the past because it is continuing to injure the present and the future. Letting go of the past threatens the very fabric of our rational mind. The mind is like a chattering monkey, as the Buddhists say, jumping here and there, trying to get our attention. Of the thoughts we think each day 85 percent to 95 percent are the same thoughts we have been thinking the day before. And if the thoughts from the day before are filled with anger, resentment, guilt, sadness, and fear, those are the thoughts and feelings that get reproduced the following day. Every thought and feeling we have is experienced by our entire being, body and soul. There are instances throughout most of our days that have the potential to injure us in some way, to hurt our feelings and threaten our security. There are minor annoyances at work, when people make mistakes and fail to live up to their promises; and there are the huge life-changing betrayals in our personal lives, such as the one experienced by the woman in Hong Kong. If we feel so injured by these experiences that we replay them over and over again in our minds, we can find ourselves living in the past instead of the present. We can find ourselves reproducing the past *in* the present.

A young woman who had been mugged came to see me. She told me the story of how she had been assaulted, not once, but five times within a year. She was angry, frightened. At one point in the session she motioned to her purse and told me she carried a gun with her. A gun in a healing session. I felt the chill of that realization go through my awareness. I tried to talk with her about studies done by sociologists on the criminal mentality that found that most muggers choose similar types of people. They did a study in a prison in which they showed videos of people who were walking down the street to muggers and rapists. They asked them to check off on a sheet the people they would choose to assault. When they tallied the results, the prisoners had all chosen the same people. When asked why, they explained that these people looked frightened and vulnerable. They walked in a way that hinted they did not feel confident or know where they were going. In other words, they looked like weak prey who would not fight back.

I suggested to the woman that the imprint of the first assault had left an energetic impression in her aura, her energy field, that needed to be released. I asked her whether she had gotten any counseling or help after the initial trauma. She said she had not. I told her I believed that with each assault the fear and anger had built up so strongly in her energy field, body, and face that she looked more and more vulnerable to potential attackers. I suggested that the gun may not be the only answer, and she should seek therapy. One session with me might help her energy field, but she needed to rebuild trust over time and to get the support of other people who had suffered similarly. Eventually, she needed to let go of the past even if she did not believe she could forgive her attackers.

Most of us do not realize the power of the unforgiven past to permeate the present. It is like a magnet that pulls like to like. Neurologists tells us that each time we think a thought or have a feeling, it chemically etches a neural pathway in our brain. The more often we think that thought or feel that feeling, the deeper the "groove" in our brain. This woman's fear and anger grooves were very deep. The image of being assaulted was replayed over and over again. Her past was recreating her present and her future. And the only option she thought she had was to become like the muggers: fight weapons with weapons. She was so filled with anger that to let go of the past or forgive the men who mugged her was unthinkable. The most valuable thing for her to do would have been to go into therapy or analysis, where she could heal the negative inner animus, or soul male, who was obviously attacking her in both the external and internal worlds.

The relationship of forgiveness to "Psychic Self-Defense" is that the seeds of shadow energy are inherent in our soul, handed down from generation to generation and lifetime to lifetime. When they are ready to burst forth, if we don't uproot the weed in our own internal garden, we usually have to meet it head on in the external world. The internal shadow gets mirrored in some person or event in the external world. Forgiveness is an act of courage because it means we use the past injury as a way to heal our own soul, forgive ourselves, and forgive the other person. If we experience ourselves only as the victim, we have not learned the lesson of empowerment from the healing of our own soul. We are then forever at the mercy of the external world, which, as we all know, is not always so merciful.

Forgiveness empowers by "unhooking" us from the past and the people in it who have injured us. It releases their power to create pain. It reclaims our control over our own selves and allows us to move into our future with clean energy. Forgiveness does not condone what someone has done to us; on the contrary, it forces us to acknowledge the darkness of the act and its consequences. But it also forces us to acknowledge our participation in both the act and the perpetuation of its injury *within us.* Forgiveness allows us to heal ourselves with our choice to let go. It gives us the opportunity to become our own healers rather than to wait for the other person to correct the injury. The latter position is the one of the child and the victim; the former, the one of the empowered healer.

Sometimes letting go of the past and becoming an empowered healer means having the courage to face the pain that we have caused other people. They are not always the aggressors. No matter how good and blameless we think ourselves to be, we are often the ones that have hurt people close to us, either by omission or commission. In some of us, this produces a deep sense of guilt.

Guilt is a life-threatening disease. It is the self-punishment for judging ourselves as bad, unworthy, and a failure. It is a mental state of reliving the painful memory over and over again, a state of "mental butchery," a phrase that once came to me in meditation.

There is a tremendous difference between guilt and remorse. Guilt is mental cruelty. It is the self-accusatory replaying of the harm we have done to someone else or to ourselves. Month after month and year after year it replays itself in our minds, with no seeming end, like Sartre's *No Exit*. Remorse is the exit. Remorse is the deep admission and feeling of the sadness, the grief, that we have caused ourselves and others. In the "Forgiveness and Letting Go of Judgment" workshop I take people through a "Remorse" meditation in which they look into a mirror and see themselves clearly and without the gilding that so many of us would like to add to our self-image. I have people go deep into their hearts and remember the times in their lives that they have done things they regret. I allow time for grieving over these mistakes, these sins. Sin, as I've mentioned, is an old archery term that means "to miss the mark." We all miss the mark sometimes. It is nothing to feel guilty about, but it is something for which we can feel sad. This deep heart sadness can be healing. Out of this sadness can come the desire to reach out and ask forgiveness. We don't need a special day like the Day of Atonement in Judaism to ask for forgiveness. We don't have to wait until we are on our deathbed to have the remorse to make amends. Every day can be a day of reconciliation, a term familiar to Christians. Every day can be a Day of Atonement, forgiveness, and healing.

Some of the most moving stories of forgiveness have come from workshops I have taught at Esalen Institute in Big Sur, California. I used to teach the "Forgiveness" workshop there during the week between Christmas and New Year's. Sometimes it would fall on New Year's Eve or Day. I remember one man who told the story of his having been in business with his father and three brothers. They were all suing each other. Because homework during a "Forgiveness" workshop is to see, phone, or write someone and ask for forgiveness, that night he wrote four letters, one to his father and one to each of his brothers. The next morning he placed them in the mailbox. He phoned his secretary to ask how things were going with the litigation, and she had a New Year's gift for him: his father and brothers had dropped all the lawsuits against him! He rushed into the workshop to tell us the story, unbelieving of his good fortune. At the end of the story he hesitatingly asked, "Do you think I could still retrieve my letters from the mailbox?" We all laughed. No, I said. Those letters and the intention behind them are what opened up the healing power of forgiveness in your family at a telepathic level. Your father and brothers received your request for forgiveness at a soul level, without even being aware of it consciously. They will be touched even more deeply when they receive the letters. Let them stand. He did.

A man in his sixties came to Esalen one Christmas after having been diagnosed with colon cancer that year and after having been divorced from his wife the year before. The night of the homework assignment, he phoned his ex-wife to ask her for forgiveness. The next day he told us that there was a long pause on the phone line. He didn't think she'd respond. When she finally spoke, she told him that she never thought she would ever hear those words from him. They talked, she forgave him, and the following Thanksgiving she invited him to be with her and their grown children. They started seeing each other again and were remarried the following year. His cancer healed. This man became a student of mine and completed the training program. He and his wife invited me to dinner one night to celebrate their remarriage. It still brings tears to my eyes to write about it. The power of forgiveness is lifesaving. It opens the door to love and healing in mysterious and life-changing ways, and it heals all those in its path.

Self-forgiveness is the ultimate act of healing (*see* "Healing Meditations"). It depends on no one but ourselves. In forgiving others, we can always tell ourselves "they didn't mean to hurt us; they didn't know better." We can forgive them because there is something to gain, like their love or presence in our lives. In asking them for forgiveness, we also have their love to regain. But to forgive ourselves means that we have to take the position of the forgiver and the forgiven, the blesser and the blessed. We have to stand in front of the mirror and look at the truth of our own actions, feel the pain of remorse, and open our hearts to our own woundedness. To forgive ourselves is the choice to put an end to suffering. The choice to stop crucifying ourselves over and over again. With one admission of responsibility and a deep experience of remorse, we choose to heal the wound. Responsibility is the "ability to respond." It is different from obligation, which means "to bind." By having the ability to respond to our sins, our "missing the marks," we unbind ourselves from self-hate, self-loathing, self-shame, and self-abuse. We set ourselves free from the generational possession of self-hatred and shame that began when we were expelled from the Garden of Eden. We choose to see our nakedness and accept it; and we choose to drop down into the grief of our hubris in allowing our false selves, our false egos, to control our lives.

God is the keeper of the Garden within us. The Great Spirit, as the Native Americans say, who tells us when we are ready to know more and when we are not; who tells us when the apple will be poisonous to our undeveloped soul and fragile ego, and when we are ready to bite. The serpent is full-power wisdom, full-power knowing of secrets, which to a child's ego is poisonous, even death-producing. When we bite too soon, we disobey and betray our inner Great Spirit, and our connection with God is broken, severed. The only way to go home again is to suffer the remorse of our actions, the grief of our betrayal, the devastating loss of our home in the Garden and our connection to unconditional love.

✳ ✳ ✳

Across a large room with many windows I looked at faces alive with light. The participants in the "Forgiveness" workshop were in pairs, and each person had written a list of seven items for which they would like to be forgiven. One partner was the mirror of unconditional love and forgiveness for the other; while one partner took each item, one by one, and spoke it out loud by saying "I would like to be forgiven for. . . ," the mirror opened his or her heart, and all the love and light the person could allow flowed from the person's eyes and body, at first silently, and then, in the soft words, "You are forgiven." The partner asking for forgiveness kept asking until finally, the experience of love and forgiveness was absorbed into the person's heart; until the person allowed himself or herself to feel self-forgiveness. Tears streamed down some faces; shame down others. Some people sat frozen with fear; some smiled with anxiety. As the exercise continued and my assistants and I went around slowly and carefully laying hands on people's hearts and helping them open to their inner Garden, a softness began to permeate the room. Eyes began to glow, shoulders relaxed, breathing became full. At one point I stood at the front of the room with tears filling my eyes and deep heat permeating my heart, looking out across a sea of forgiveness and love so powerfully beautiful that I knew, beyond a shadow of a doubt, that if I died right then and there it would be all right.

✳

7

Dreams

I wanted a home. A place I could call my own, where I could continue to grow in self-love, healing, forgiveness, and strength. I wanted an end to the suffering, to all the ways I had given myself away and compromised my soul. I no longer wanted a hero to tell me who I was and what I needed. I needed to find my true value within instead of trying to buy it in a store or find it in someone else's eyes.

One weekend when I was house hunting, my friends Paula Lawrence and Charles Bowden, both well-known in film and theater, came up to Connecticut for a visit. We were driving through the towns that had been hit by the tornado, looking at the damage. The entire town of Bantam, including the church, had been leveled. In Cornwall there were acres of trees felled like matchsticks. Other sections had acres of trees with their tops shorn off. It was a strange, eerie sight. In a way it was as if I were looking at the remains of my marriage. Luckily, except for Bantam, no other houses had been leveled, and only one person had been killed, a camper in the woods.

Charles and Paula must have been good luck charms for me, because as we went through one of the towns, we passed a "for sale"

sign. I barely got a look at it as we went by, and I could hardly see the house from the road. But I scribbled down the real estate number on a scrap of paper. I had already looked at a number of houses. One was in Sharon off a little dirt road. A sweet cottage with more than two acres. The house was large enough for one person and on a lovely piece of property, but the bedroom was underneath the house. I would have had to walk outside and down a steep flight of stairs in the middle of winter to go to bed. This did not seem like a pleasant or safe option. I sat in the living room several times by myself trying to imagine living there, but I couldn't. It didn't feel right. I felt depressed and wanted to cry every time I thought of buying it. I wasn't sure whether I was picking up the owner's energy or whether it was a sign that I shouldn't buy the house. I decided it was the latter and kept looking.

I found a sweet old farmhouse in Lakeville that I fell in love with. It was farther north than I wanted to be, but the town was beautiful and offered much. The house had been fully renovated inside and had three bedrooms, a wood-burning stove, and a modern kitchen. The property was small, and the driveway opened onto a blind curve, but I decided I could deal with those challenges. I wanted it. It was more than I could afford, so I made an offer that I thought was reasonable. The owner didn't. I tried negotiating. She wouldn't come down. I was devastated. My heart had been set on that house, and I could already see myself living there, so I had to change my vision.

A friend of mine reminded me that if I didn't get that house, I was meant to get one that was even better. Have a little faith—like a mustard seed. Oh, yes, Faith. Isn't that what I told everyone else? I took a deep breath, closed my eyes and prayed—hard. I had been praying hard my whole life. When I was ten I wrote a letter to my father telling him that if he just believed in God and Jesus he would be healed. My mother found it in my father's drawer after he died. I wrote it about the time I went to Billy Graham crusades with my mother and aunt, who sang in the choir. I went forward when he called people. I wanted to be saved. When my father was ill, I would sit in the upper balcony of the Trinity

Lutheran Church to pray for his healing. It didn't work. I didn't understand why. Maybe God didn't hear me.

I prayed for the right house for me. I surrendered to the process. I also threw the Motherpeace tarot, a lovely deck designed by women for women. I had found that my unconscious would sometimes work through things like the *I Ching* or the tarot deck. I kept getting the same card over and over again. No matter how many times I shuffled the deck and rearranged the cards, when it came time to pick the card I always pulled the same one. The one with all the maidens jumping off the cliff rather than having to submit to the male warriors. They chose death rather than rape and imprisonment. Oh dear. I hoped this wouldn't be death. Well, at least it showed my commitment to taking a leap.

I called my real estate agent and told her of the house I had driven by. She called the other agent and arranged for me to see it. The house had just gone on the market and the listing was due to come out the next day. I would be the first one to see it. When we arrived, I looked down the property to a little brown house set back from the road. There was a small carriage house on the property. We walked in and I immediately saw a wall of red brick and a large fireplace. I loved a fireplace. Neither of the other houses had had one. But I was sure from the looks of it that this house must be more than I could afford. I walked through the kitchen, living room, hallway, and the second floor. There was one bath and three tiny bedrooms—very tiny. But one of them also had a fireplace. My heart lept. Two fireplaces. There were only two closets in the whole house. I looked out the back bedroom window and saw one of the most beautiful views I had ever seen. It stretched across the back of the property and down toward a large meadow with a line of maple and pine trees. Off to the right was the neighbor's field, and far off in the distance to my left a small house on a hill. I could live here—if I could afford it.

I asked the price. I couldn't believe my ears. I could afford it. I decided to make an offer, contingent on inspection. We went back and forth a little, but finally, the offer was accepted. I had an inspector come look at the house. He pointed out several problems with the foundation and the roof, the barn, and the insulation. I knew it would need some work, but unlike the other houses at least this house had a full basement and an attic for storage.

We set a sale date for the last day of September. Most of my things were still in storage from when I had thought I would get divorced two years previously, so there was not a lot of packing to do. This final wrench from my marriage was difficult, but I was excited about my new house and did not feel the true impact of my leap until after I had moved. I arranged for the house to be cleaned from top to bottom, and I cleared each room with candles, sage, water, and prayer. On the day of the sale and the move, I realized that the king-sized bed would not fit around the corner and into the bedroom. The bedroom that was straight ahead was not large enough. I would have to take down the wall between the two bedrooms. I called my contractor and he came over a few days later. It was an amazing process to watch. As they broke through the wall there appeared layers and layers of different colored wallpaper—pink, blue, and ivory. Lots of paint, probably leaded. I covered my mouth and nose. And horsehair for insulation! My father would have smiled.

It took about a week after the move to get settled enough to spend a night there. Whatever the moving van hadn't brought over, I moved in my car in short trips. I was finally ready to spend my first night in the house. A friend came over to keep me company and slept on the couch in the living room. That night I dreamed a man came to the window to the left of the fireplace in the living room. He was short, old, friendly looking, and peered in the window in curiosity. The next morning I told my friend about the dream. He had had the same dream. We looked at each other in astonishment. Who was this man? We decided he must be the original owner, the caretaker who first lived here when the house was built as a caretaker's cottage for the larger stone house next door. I felt safe, cared for, watched over by a good spirit, a good angel.

A month later my divorce was final. In getting divorced and starting a new life, I thought I was taking myself back, making a home for myself rather than depending on someone else to do it for me. My conscious awareness had all the right intentions. My unconscious was still dealing with a broken foundation, an unstable womb. My house was on a slope with an old drywall foundation where the water poured through the cellar every time it rained hard. The windows leaked cold air, the roof leaked water, the front stoop was crumbling. The plumbing needed fixing, the electrical panel needed replacing, the barn leaned to the right. The day I got divorced it rained so hard the water poured down through the chimneys into both fireplaces and the kitchen window broke, in the open position. My house needed a lot of repairs, but it was all I could afford at the time.

However, it sat on a beautiful piece of property. A little half acre with pear and apple trees, very old, very deeply rooted. Not all the trees were in good condition, but they all produced a lot of fruit. In the autumn they would drop apples all over the ground, sometimes making walking difficult, but putting nutrients back into the earth. There were other trees: cypress, Greek olive, mountain ash, sour cherry, birch, a recently planted tiny evergreen. Unfortunately, I had to cut down an evergreen by the front corner of the house. My contractor said it was pushing into the house and its foundation. It also blocked light from two of the living room windows. I hated to cut it down. The birds seemed to congregate on its branches. But I opted to be reasonable and I liked light. Once the tree was cut down, water poured through that corner of the foundation, having no roots to absorb it. It also exposed the unattractive Con Ed dial. My gardener later told me it was unnecessary because roots always choose the path of least resistance, unlike me. The tree would not have harmed the foundation after all. To this day I am sorry I cut it down.

There were flowers as well. One large lavender lilac bush, a true red climbing rose vine, four peonies, and two holly bushes, one of them huge and protective by my front door. A few perennials were left in the garden, although a neighbor told me the former owners had taken many plants with them. My kitchen and second bedroom windows looked out across a large meadow lined at the back by tall maples that would change to flame and gold every autumn.

But my favorite feature of my property was the birds. Cardinals, robins, yellow finches, wrens, blue jays, and mourning doves. In the spring when I awoke, the singing would fill me with delight. I would look out at my barn and see the pair of mourning doves sitting on the top left corner peak and hear them cooing at each other. The bright red cardinal would announce his search for a mate, and the little brown wrens and robins would nest in the branches by my bedroom window in the summer. I put out a birdbath so that I could watch them flutter, and I hung a feeder that at one time attracted seven yellow finches. The feeder lasted a whole year until I realized that it also attracted mice into my house. The chipmunks were cute, and they would sit on top of my crumbling stoop by the front door and chirp and chirp, drawing attention to all the holes they had dug in my garden and the bulbs of the irises that were being digested in their tummies. Red and gray squirrels raced along the top of the aging wood fence, sometimes carrying small apples in their mouths up to the hollowed-out trunks of the older apple trees. White and yellow butterflies winged their way from plant to plant between the trees.

One morning I stood at the kitchen window and heard elephants. I thought for sure this was a sign that I had totally lost my grip on reality. Elephants in Connecticut. I was doing well. I heard them again. I looked out the window that by now had been fixed and saw something moving off in the distance. I got my binoculars and searched the horizon. Elephants were walking in a circle, and then I remembered: There was a farm that housed circus animals during the off-season not far from my new house. I breathed a deep sigh of relief.

I started repairing my house. I had a new front door handmade to allow more light into the kitchen and to allow me to see out. I had the plumbing and electrical wiring fixed, and put two sump pumps in my cellar. I had the walls painted and added new dampers for the fireplaces and a built-in desk in my study. The following spring I started planting gardens. I added roses and perennials in front of the house and annuals along the borders. I planted herbs in a garden right outside my front door so that I could pick them easily: spearmint, peppermint, rosemary, rue, marjoram, thyme, lemon balm, and lovage. In the sandbox left by the children of the former owners I planted arugula, radichio, parsley, tomatoes, and six kinds of lettuce. I dug my hands into the earth and felt its fertileness under my nails. I talked with the chipmunks and told them their chirping was driving me crazy. I hugged the trees and felt the cool moist strength of standing tall. I felt grateful to be alive and not burning down.

I set about building a safe home for myself. The trouble was that I kept on letting people in the door. Instead of focusing solely on my own healing, I got involved in another relationship. I continued to follow in my mother's footsteps by putting my love, healing, attention and energy into "the other," unconsciously making sure I was loved and not alone. And of course, no matter what I did or didn't do for the other, it was never enough. For someone who has been starved as an infant, the replacement breast is never big enough. And I continued to choose men who had been starved. I needed to learn the hard way. God must have decided to give me the spontaneous gift of healing because She knew that I would be such a slow learner in my personal life.

I broke my foot—I'm still not sure how—something about it getting caught under a rocking chair. My right foot, my male foot, connected with my first chakra of survival, safety, and grounding. I wasn't strong enough to support my own weight yet. I wasn't grounded enough in my own male energy. My connection with my former husband, marriage, and male ground was broken. I awoke at 2 A.M. screaming in agony. In fact, my own screaming woke me. I was alone in the house. Alone, on the second floor, with no one to help me. I called my new friend, who lived several hours away, and he suggested I call an ambulance. I lay there helpless, my foot embodying for me in that moment all the agony of being alone, frightened, and helpless. I cried and cried. Finally, my body was giving me a release valve. The child in me wanted someone to take care of me. I didn't want to call an ambulance. I wasn't sure the front door was unlocked. I was in my pajamas. I was embarrassed. I called the ambulance.

I spent the next month on crutches. I couldn't get up and down the stairs easily, so I moved into the living room. I couldn't work. A new house and I could barely move. It was difficult. But it gave me plenty of time to grieve, meditate, be alone. I found out that my husband had canceled my medical insurance. The company had never sent me a certified letter, as they were required by law, so I didn't even have strangers to take care of me financially. I tried to fight it legally, but I was just too tired. I gave up and paid the bills myself.

As always, in times of crisis, my mother was there for me. She helped me buy the house and even moved in for a week several months later to take care of contractors while I was in California working. Her forte was dealing with crises. Her Scandinavian blood always held up. She always had a light to shine, having come from a good Christian hatred for darkness. It was hard for her to see me suffer.

Once my foot was healed, I began arranging the inside of my house. Box by box I opened my life and put it back together again. I hung Nancy Azara's paintings on my living room wall. The ones she had done of two healing hands and many eyes of clear vision. The small turquoise and gold one in a frame that she had given me for my birthday. It showed many gold feet walking in a spiral. Extra feet in case I needed them, which I did. And the small wood carving of a yoni, in gold and red, the Hindu symbol for female power and magic. Every year in India there is a festival for women celebrating Durga, the Great Mother of fertility and the slayer of demons. Hindus believe the two go together. Fertility, sexual magic, and protection. The temples hang carvings of sexual poses where human meets divine on the wall areas. Through sexual union new life is born in the human soul and body.

I had a wall-to-wall bookcase built in my hallway to house the two thousand books I had acquired over many years of studying religion, mythology, healing, and psychology. I had a used bookseller come in to look over some of them. I couldn't fit them all and decided to relinquish a few hundred. Difficult to let go, but they were only books. If I could let go of a marriage, a whole way of life, I could release a few books.

There were photographs taken by my friend Judy, from my house in Woodstock, and a few of me, one by a fountain; a few artistic photos of nature, broken glass, running horses; hand-carved statues of the Virgin Mary, Jesus, and St. Francis from Italy; a sketch of a beautiful and elderly Native American from my friends Charles and Paula; photographs from my trip to India and Nepal that I had placed in hand-carved wooden frames designed with lotuses; a photo of Tara, the goddess of healing and compassion; yellow and pink water lilies; a plaster of paris of one of my student's faces, also a student of Nancy Azara. She molded flames emanating from her head and painted the creation with red, blue, and yellow gold, the gold bursting forth from the seventh chakra. I placed it at the bottom of the stairs to the second floor. It frightened friends of mine who unexpectedly encountered it. It was like walking into Durga or Kali in Connecticut. I liked that. My male friend suggested I move it. He knocked it and chipped a piece off the breast plate. Interesting. I didn't move it.

I set up my meditation altar in a corner of my bedroom with my statue of Tara from Nepal and various Buddhas from India. I had a packet of sweet-smelling gray ash from the hands of Sai Baba, one of the Indian gurus. A pale blue-gray ceramic blessing bowl with a thousand Buddha faces on it from the artist Nicholas Kirsten in Seattle. I had also acquired two of his other pieces: a Chinese monk standing on the edge of womblike opening symbolizing new life, and a small Buddha-like figurine with a round turquoise disk emanating from his head symbolizing rebirth. I had a dream not long after I'd moved into the house that this figure was growing out of my fingertip. The right index finger that I had cut badly as a child with a knife. Rebirth growing out of old wounds.

On the altar I also placed a pair of milk glass open hands, given to me by a patient who I had helped to heal. She had developed serious liver disease from many years of drinking. The doctors had

told her she had not much time left without a liver transplant. After a week of healing, she was healed. Years later she had a stroke
and insisted on playing my healing tapes in her hospital room
twenty-four hours a day. Much to her doctors' amazement, she began speaking and recovered in record time. Also on the alter I
placed a hand-painted gold and blue box with a small crystal ball
inside and a tiny African brass box that Nancy and I had acquired
in a shop in New York City. The box had birds on the lid, perched
in a row.

In front of the altar I leaned small cards of various angels that
friends had sent. I also placed other cards and photos: a small image of St. Anne; a photo of my mother so I could send her healing
when I sat in meditation; a photo of Guruji, another of Gurumai,
the young and beautiful woman who had succeeded the Indian
guru Muktananda—finally, a woman, a goddess, had succeeded a
guru. And a beauty as well, who seemed to embody the Good
Mother in the depth of her eyes and smile. Muktananda had come
into my healing room once with one of my students, who was his
devotee. He had passed on recently, and she was grieving. I had
never met Muktananda, but I could feel his powerful and loving
presence. I felt blessed in having had such an opportunity. There
are many times that I am healed by the healing I do for others, because the process keeps me in touch with the depth of love and
peace that is available to all of us when we open our hearts.

On the mantel above the fireplace in my bedroom, I placed two
statues of Kwan Yin, the Chinese goddess of compassion. One
was dark; the other white—two faces of the goddess: dark and
light, black and white, yin and yang. I placed a small photo of
Paula Lawrence standing under a carved arch in Mexico with a
tree in back of her in the distance. She was dressed in white, with
black hair, a red flowering bush to the left, bright blue water underneath her feet, and light shining through the arch. One hand
was up, the other down, like a standing Tara emanating all the el-
ements of compassion, fertility, and beauty. In a double frame I
placed the only photo of myself as an infant with red-gold hair,
next to my grandfather, my mother's father who died before I was

born. Another double frame of my grand-niece and grand-nephew, my half-sister's grandchildren. And a photo of me holding the little boy who survived the amniocentesis that never took place.

On the wall next to my meditation altar I placed a canvas bought from my neighbor, Robert Hall, a painter. His paintings mesmerized me. Each one so unique, so full of life and color, movement and power. I was so fond of one hung in his home that he offered to paint a similar one for me. I called it "Angel Kites" when I noticed how the collage of all the chakra colors floated through the canvas like kites. This first painting I placed in my office. The second one I fell in love with was a canvas with raised pieces of wood, painted white, and a glowing gold sun in the middle. The word *resurrection* came into my mind as soon as I laid eyes on it. I knew his wife, Elise, who was to become my close friend, would not give it up easily, although both of them were thinking of placing his paintings on sale in gallery shows. I finally oohed and aahed so much that they sold it to me. It hangs on the wall next to my meditation altar, and it is the first thing I see when I walk into the room. I have since bought several other paintings from him, including a white-and-gold-leaf canvas I call "Choir," which hangs in my counseling room between my chair and that of the patient, and a fabulous expanse of movement and form called "Mood Indigo," which is one of the most beautiful expressions of the third eye, the sixth chakra, imaginable. Robert Hall has a healing soul.

All throughout the house I placed crystals. On the bookshelves, my altar, the mantel above the fireplace. I loved crystals and stones. All kinds and colors. Clear quartz, amethyst, rose quartz, smoky quartz, calcite, topaz, turquoise, citrine. I was especially attached to the clear quartz crystals that I had dug with my own hands in Arkansas. My mother-in-law, Hilda, and I had gone together and sat on top of mounds of clay and dirt, digging our hands deep into Mother Earth and pulling out gems. It was hard to tell what was dross and what was treasure. They were both dark and muddy, until placed in a chemical solution that removed the obstructions to the light. Then the iron and dirt disappeared and pointed facets of hard clear transformation stood up. Alchemy. Just like working the soul.

And I did work my soul. Once the initial excitement of finding and organizing my new home had passed, all the months of suffering, separation, and divorce caught up with me. I crashed. I went into periods of deep depression that might last three days. I would sometimes be unable to physically move. I would have to sleep for two hours after lunch. It was as though my body came to a complete standstill. I now had a home that I felt safe in and I could let go. I grieved for my lost life, marriage, husband, house, and family. He owned a large house that had become mine for almost nine years. I had lost everything. It had been my choice, but that didn't ease the pain. I had even left my dog with him, believing I couldn't take care of him alone.

I sat in meditation and tried to forgive myself and to let go of the past. I worked the sadness, anger, anxiety, and hope. I comforted my broken heart and soothed the child within. I listened to the birds and nestled into stillness. I lay in front of the fireplace and watched the flames. I forgot to open the damper one night and scorched my beautiful soul portrait on the mantel above. It had been painted by a spiritual empath named Marion Wurster, in the form of a mandala, a circular whole, with different areas representing various aspects of my spiritual growth that I was learning to integrate into my soul. I was still dealing with some hot fire energy inside me. I'd better watch out for anger, for my shadow, so it didn't burn me up.

I had to drive one hundred miles each way to get to my office in the City, so I only made the round-trip once a week. While there, I stayed with either my mother or my new friend. I continued to see private patients two or three days a week and to work three out of four weekends a month. I taught at the New York Open Center in Manhattan, Esalen Institute and Mt. Madonna Center in California, Wainwright House in Rye, New York, Omega Institute in Rhinebeck, New York, and Rowe Conference Center in Rowe, Massachusetts. In addition to these centers, I ran my three-year program for healers that I entitled the TOUCHING SPIRIT® Training

Program. I now had a house to take care of, and I had to pay all the bills myself—never give up. Keep on going.

Years later a friend would point out to me that I probably should have moved in with my mother for a year after the divorce and saved some money. But I couldn't. That seemed like going backward. The idea was unimaginable. I needed boundaries and a safe nest to rebirth myself—my own nest, not anyone else's. So all my money, all my energy, went into paying for a house, a car, an office, a secretary, travel, phones, taxes, and all the myriad expenses that go along with supporting a new life.

I started paying closer attention to my dreams. I had always done so, and when I was in college, I had been particularly fascinated by Carl Jung and Joseph Campbell. I had used material from both men in my undergraduate thesis, *Nikos Kazantzakis: Myth, Metaphor, and Reality.* Years later in my master's thesis, I contrasted Carl Jung and Sigmund Freud and pointed out how the antireligious Freud had finally come to admit the reality of telepathy toward the end of his life. He had brought the Western world's attention to dreams as the "royal road to the unconscious," analyzing aggressive and sexual drives. Jung went further and applied personal unconscious dream material to the collective unconscious, with its myriad of symbols and images. He introduced the world to the concepts of shadow, anima and animus, and exploration of dreams as a journey of soul healing. He believed in the parapsychological dimension of dreams, that is, dreams as messages from the soul.

Jung believed that the first and general function of dreams is compensatory, that is, they restore or maintain a psychic equilibrium between the conscious and the unconscious. In this function, he believed that dreams could be premonitions, warning people of dangers, even death. If these warnings are ignored, accidents, illness, and death might ensue. In *Man and His Symbols,* Jung cites just such an example of this warning function of dreams:

> I remember the case of a man who . . . developed an almost morbid passion for dangerous mountain climbing, as a sort

of compensation. He was seeking to "get above himself." In a dream one night, he saw himself stepping off the summit of a high mountain into empty space. When he told me of his dream, I instantly saw the danger and tried to emphasize the warning and persuade him to restrain himself. I even told him that the dream foreshadowed his death in a mountain accident. It was in vain. Six months later he "stepped off into space."

In his paper "The Practical Use of Dream-analysis," Jung describes a second function of dreams—the diagnosis of organic disease. He had been consulted about a seventeen-year-old girl. One doctor had made a diagnosis of progressive muscular atrophy, while another believed it was a case of hysteria. In meeting with the girl, Jung asked her to describe her dreams. She related the following two dreams:

I was coming home at night. Everything is as quiet as death. The door into the living room is half open, and I see my mother hanging from the chandelier, swinging to and fro in the cold wind that blows in through the open windows.

Another time I dreamt that a terrible noise broke out in the house at night. I get up and discover that a frightened horse is tearing through the rooms. At last it finds the door into the hall and jumps through the hall window from the fourth floor and into the street below. I was terrified when I saw it lying there, all mangled.

In commenting on this case, Jung stated: "It is notorious that one often dreams of one's own death, but that it is no serious matter. When it is really a question of death, the dream speaks another language." In elaborating on this other language, Jung noted that he reached his interpretation and prognosis in this case through the symbolic reality of the dreamer, which told him that the girl's unconscious life was destroying itself. He confirmed this second function of the dreams, the diagnosis of organic disease, and was correct in this case.

In addition to dreams functioning as warning and prognosticators of organic disease, Jung acknowledged a third relationship between dreams, illness, and death. He describes the case of a psychiatrist who came to see him with a series of dreams written by his ten-year-old daughter and given to him as a Christmas present. All the dreams began as fairy tales with "Once upon a time" and contained complex religious symbolism to which the girl had never been exposed in daily life. Nine out of the twelve dreams contained allusions to destruction and restoration. Jung felt that none of the themes or symbolism in these dreams pointed toward the normal approach of puberty, but were, instead, the motifs of an aged person approaching death. When he first read the dreams, he "had an uncanny feeling that they suggested impending disaster." Experience shows that the unknown approach of death casts an *adumbratio* (an anticipatory shadow) over the life and dreams of the victim. The girl indeed, died of an infectious disease about a year after the Christmas she gave her father the book of dreams. Jung acknowledged that the girl's dreams "were a preparation for death, expressed through short stories, like the tales told at primitive initiations or the Koans of Zen Buddhism." This function of dreams, the preparation for death, leads directly into what Jung considered a fourth function: the foretelling of the future.

Throughout his autobiography *Memories, Dreams, and Reflections,* Jung reveals dreams and visions that foretold future events. His own near brush with death in 1944 initiated an out of body experience, or vision, in which he foresaw his doctor's death in place of his own. A client of Jung dreamed, about two months before her death, that she visited the afterlife and described it in detail. Several months before Jung's mother died, he had a dream that foretold of it. While riding on a train, he kept imaging a drowning accident and discovered later that one had occurred at the same time that he had been assaulted by its image. These incidents brought Jung to the conclusion that our notions of time, space, and causality are incomplete at best and that part of the psyche may actually exist outside time and space. Jung's conclusions are the same as those now being examined by the foremost minds in physics, including Michio Kaku in his book *Hyperspace,* which I mentioned in the second chapter. In the classic story *Gulliver's Travels,* there is a line: "I've been where you dream." There may be a very thin line, if any, between dreams and reality.

Dreams seem to come from a dimension of life and soul that knows much more than our rational minds. Our higher, or deeper, self that is still connected with God and our body, truth, and healing. John Sanford, Agnes Sanford's son, an Episcopal priest and Jungian analyst, wrote a book entitled *Dreams: God's Forgotten Language.* Spiritual literature, including the Bible, is full of dreams and visions, and the stories of healing that have come out of paying attention to them. Joseph was going to divorce Mary as a harlot until an angel of the Lord came to him in a dream and told him she would give birth to a son, and he was to name him Jesus. In paying attention to our dreams we are acknowledging this dimension of life and death, healing and love. In the Talmud there is a saying that every dream not given attention, not understood, is like a love letter unopened. A love letter from our soul. The Sufis have a similar saying. We dream up to an hour and a half every night: four years of free therapy over the course of a lifetime that most people ignore.

When patients and students come to me, I always ask whether they record their dreams and try to understand them. Nine out of ten times the answer is no, or people tell me they don't remember them, or they don't make sense, or they are "not important" and only about day-to-day small things. Most people have a great resistance to dreams. Many of us are afraid of them. What if they *do* mean something? Then what about all the bad ones, the nightmares? They have to mean something too, and we don't like that idea. After all, they happen to us, without our conscious control.

.No matter how frightening, the dream is always a gift. Like prayer and meditation, dreams are one way that our soul, even God, can communicate with us. They tell us where we need to focus healing so that we can more fully cooperate in creating a new life. Dreams are windows to the soul—like the computer program Windows. Instead of working in DOS, or in words, our dreams are usually in pictures, or images. They give us windows that look into the workings of our body and soul. Doctors have now found a correlation between dreams of loss and death and heart disease. When a friend of mine had a dream of walking down a flight of stairs and being stabbed in the heart with a knife by a woman with long dark hair, I suggested to him that he might want to give consideration to getting a medical checkup. I was concerned about his physical heart and blood pressure as well as about his emotional heart. This dark inner feminine, a negative anima figure, was trying to get through to him, trying to open his heart. And the only way she could do it was to resort to violence, something that was not unknown in my friend's life. This is not the best solution for opening the heart, and it can have a detrimental effect on the physical heart.

Dreams also tell us when we are in conflict, in pain, in love. They tell us when we have Hades running around trying to steal away our Persephone, or when an aspect of our psyche is healing, like an animal giving birth to her young, to new life. I have experienced the healing power of dreams in my own life and have integrated dream interpretation into my healing work with patients. Jung and Freud have influenced me the most, but I also used the Gestalt approach to dreams from my former husband, a Gestalt therapist. I sometimes ask patients and students to become each character and object in their dream, speaking through the narrative of the dream from each of these positions. In the TOUCHING SPIRIT® Training Program, we sometimes take a dream from one of the students and enact it as a psychodrama with everyone in the group. This can bring new insights and deeper levels of meaning to a person's dream. One of my present faculty members, Michael Kaplan, recalled that physically enacting his dream with his training group was emotionally powerful for him in a way that simply discussing it was not. He told me that the psychodrama had a vivid and lasting effect on him and increased his confidence and trust in his fellow students.

We also do group dream work by taking one dream and reading it out loud, while each of us experiences the dream as though it were our own, often helping the dreamer to see new dimensions and interpretations. As Jung did with his patients, we also draw and paint dreams, adding the visual dimension of color and form to understanding dreams.

Working with my own dreams has taught me more about the healing process of the soul than any study of Jung, Freud, or Gestalt psychology. While writing my master's thesis, I decided to create a watercolor of each of my dreams. I would wake up each morning, write down my dreams, and then, try to visually re-create them in color. One morning I had a dream about my father giving me red roses. When I went to paint the roses on paper, they looked wilted, almost dead. I felt sad. The real truth of the dream was not revealed until I tried visually to re-create it. The love, passion, and romantic idealism that every little girl feels for her father does not always last. Sometimes it wilts, fades, and dies as we grow up. It certainly had with me.

When I had decided to go back to my marriage after the six-month separation, my husband and I decided to see a marriage counselor. After a year of working together with this man, I decided to continue alone. I had always been afraid of my husband's anger, yet I could not reconcile my fear along with his other good qualities and the deep love we shared in positive moments. One night I had a dream about a gorilla in a cage. The gorilla was angry, snarling, baring its teeth. I could see and feel the danger of this animal's anger, this primitive rage. A placid anonymous man stood outside the cage and told me that the gorilla was not dangerous. Who should I believe? myself or this man? my own eyes, ears, and instincts? or what this man was telling me? I chose to believe myself. What I did not realize at this time and what had not been pointed out to me by the therapist was that the gorilla was as much a part of me as it was of my husband. I was just as terrified of my own primitive anger at having been imprisoned in a cage as I was of his energy. I chose to let myself out of the cage.

It was also during this period that I had a dream of a lovely young woman with blond hair—a younger version of me, a Persephone, sweet, gentle, and naive. In the dream she completely disappeared in front my eyes, and I knew I would never see her again—ever. I felt the loss and grief as though someone had died. She had. I would never again be that young woman. She was gone forever.

A friend of mine had a similar dream years later about a woman who disappeared in front of his eyes. He said he knew he would never see her again and felt terrible loss and grief. At the time his young wife, a dear friend of mine, was battling cancer, although she had been in and out of remission for many years. But at that point it was not apparent that she would die—not apparent except in his dream. I pointed this out to him. He was beginning to go through the grieving process over her impending death. It was both a premonition of her death as well as the process of his own grieving. And several months later she died. A week before her death, I dreamed that she had died and her husband had not called to tell me. I felt upset and hurt. I somehow made it out to the gathering at their house after the funeral. In the dream I was looking around and feeling her absence. I realized there was no need for me to be there. She was not in the house. A week later one morning her husband called to tell me she had passed away that morning. I was one of the first people he called. I was devastated but prepared. I arranged to go to Seattle for the funeral, but a snowstorm prevented it. I remembered the dream and realized that she was no longer in the house or Seattle. I could commune with her from Connecticut. I did.

One night I had a mandala dream. Mandalas are circular paintings that portray the universe as a whole. Tibetan monks create sand mandalas of brilliant colors for many ceremonies and rituals, including healing. In my dream the mandala was empty save for a small brown house in the lower left-hand corner. I did not understand its meaning because the house I lived in then was natural grayed wood. It was not until a year later, when I was getting divorced and looking for a house, that I would understand this dream as a premonition of my buying my brown house and beginning a new life.

Dreams also can call forth the healer within us to heal our body. One night I had eaten too much dinner and went to bed with a distressed stomach. As I closed my eyes to sleep, I placed my hands over my stomach and prayed for relief of my symptoms. I fell asleep and dreamed that a being of white light stood at the foot of my bed and beamed white light into my stomach. I awoke with a tremendous feeling of heat throughout my body and my stomach felt fine. It is impossible to say whether this being of white light was my own inner healer being projected outside of me or whether a spirit had stood at the foot of my bed and sent me healing. I believe that both scenarios are possible.

One of the more unusual phenomena that takes place concerning my own dream life is my ability sometimes to cross over into another person's dream or find that someone enters mine. As I've mentioned this phenomenon is often called astral travel. It is commonly accepted in shamanic tribal cultures, and the shaman does much of his or her work in dreamtime. I would sometimes find myself having discussions with students or getting information about patients. During one of my dreams I visited a patient in the hospital. I could see the exact layout of the room, the placement of the bed, and a chair at the foot of the bed with an old woman seated in it, who was introduced as my patient's mother. When I arrived at the hospital the next day, the room was laid out exactly as I had seen in the dream, including the chair with the patient's mother-in-law, who the patient introduced to me as having been like a mother to her. This can be explained as soul travel, or as distant viewing, a form of clairvoyance in which the person is able to view, at a distance, a scene or location in great detail. The psychic Ingo Swann is famous for this type of work and has provided researchers and archaeologists with detailed maps of the ocean floor and the ruins that would be found there.

A more common occurrence for me is that my students often tell me that I come to visit them during their dreams. I am usually not aware of this, although at times I do dream of my students. An example that I remember quite vividly concerned a dream of my speaking with a student. I did not remember what I had said during the dream, but the next morning she came to the seminar and told me that I had visited her in a dream. She said that she had been concerned about a particular problem the day before. In the dream she and I discussed her problem and its solution, which, luckily, she remembered.

Often students and patients dream of me as a sign that they have integrated me as a positive feminine figure in their soul life. I become the good mother they never had, or the archetypal healer embodying their own healing potential. This is a very positive sign when it happens and usually signals an opening within their soul of deep healing potential. When I appear as a negative figure in their dreams, then it signals a need to look at what the person is projecting onto me, that is, a negative transference. It also requires me to look at myself and see whether there is something I should examine in my relationship with this person. Maybe the person is seeing something about me that is frightening. What the individual is seeing may or may not be true, depending on how much of his or her own negative mother transference is being projected onto me. But since dreams are compensatory, meaning that they always show us in our sleeping life what we are not seeing in our waking life, they are a good way to remain honest with ourselves.

Over many years of working with cancer patients, some of them have revealed dreams to me in the course of their treatment. One, in particular, stands out as an example of the predictive power of dreams. A woman in her early thirties, married with two small children, was diagnosed as having cancer of the uterus and bowel. She had the following dream:

> I dreamed I was giving half of my chemotherapy to a man I did not know. I told him: "This chemotherapy will either cure me or kill you."

When asked what associations she made with this male figure, she had none. He was obviously an inner animus. When asked to become him and talk through the dream as this figure, she replied: "I don't know why she is giving this chemotherapy to me. I don't need it. I don't understand." Upon hearing this dream, I had, like Jung, a sense of foreboding. Despite the "either . . . or" statement of the dream, I felt that she was really attempting to cure herself by killing this animus figure and, in doing so, would destroy them both. She died several months later.

Another patient, also a woman in her early thirties with a young child, had cancer with bone metastases. The cancer had begun with a small mole on her heel, gone into total remission for seven years and then recurred with a vengeance, speeding rapidly through her body. About two months before she died, she had a dream that it was important for her to give her son a religion and to choose a gravesite for herself. As James Hall notes in his book *Jungian Dream Interpretation*:

> Persons actually approaching organic death have
> dreams . . . that may encourage the waking-ego to focus on
> conscious concerns and responsibilities rather than on the
> approaching death of the physical body. It would seem that
> dreams are much less concerned with the death of the body
> than with the individuation process.

The individuation process is what Jung called the soul's journey of becoming whole. It is when the conscious and unconscious, body and spirit, heart and mind reach a place of healing and wholeness; when the shadow and all the inner figures, positive and negative, anima and animus, are at peace with the ego and the personality. It is a state of balance, peace, and fulfillment.

When someone comes to see me about a physical illness, my goal is to see their soul and the way that it is trying to speak through their body. Illness breaks down the hold of the ego and allows the soul to shine through. This experience is not always pleasant and is often frightening to us. We don't like being out of control. Most of us reach for the remedy that will put us back in control as quickly as possible: pain medication, anti-depressants, antibiotics, cold remedies, surgery. Dr. Gerwin Neumann, who performed the surgery on Larry Bird's back, remarked at a panel for back pain held at Interface Center in Boston that once a dentist had come to him wanting immediate surgery. When Neumann suggested a more conservative, long-term approach, the dentist told him that he couldn't afford to be away from his practice for more than a day or two, and that he preferred to have the surgery done on a Friday so that he could be back to work on Monday. This is an extreme example of the low tolerance that most of us have for pain, illness, or anything that jeopardizes our control over our life. The trouble with this approach is that in putting our ego back in control, we are ignoring what our soul is trying to tell us. Then the soul has to find another way to get us to pay attention. Each time it tries and fails, it becomes more insistent, more forceful. Maybe another illness is created, or an accident takes place, or nightmares occur. The cycle starts all over again, until we can break it by paying attention to the soul.

One of my patients had been sent to me by a neurologist, who told me that he had run every test possible on her and could not settle on a diagnosis. Her symptoms were severe dizziness and weakness in the legs, so that on certain days she could not even walk. Her doctor had considered that she might have multiple sclerosis, epilepsy, migraines, or a brain tumor. But she was not sure she wanted to work with me. She told me that she just wanted the medical profession to find out what was wrong with her so that she could get on with her life. During the first session, I realized that there was an underlying message her soul was trying to get across to her. She was not listening. I took her through the process "Communicating with Your Body." In this guided meditation she was able to get in touch with deep pain about being abandoned by her father when she was young, as well as with her unhappiness about her relationship with her husband. She had thought about leaving the marriage for several years, but had not allowed herself to "walk away." She was too frightened. At the end of the first session she expressed her reluctance to believe that emotions could have anything to do with her illness, because that would mean she was "crazy." I reassured her that this was not the case.

We worked together every week for eight months, exploring her childhood and her marriage, her fears and sadness. During each session I did a healing through the laying-on-of-hands. This energy acted as a catalyst for the healing energies in her own body to begin the healing process. As the weeks went by she made the decision to leave the marriage. As soon as she did, her legs became stronger. Her dizziness, while not disappearing, began to decrease. At one point she became dizzy during a session in which she began to get in touch with strong feelings of anger toward her father for abandoning her in childhood. She reached into her purse for her medication. I asked her to try an experiment with me for five minutes. She was reluctant. She insisted that if she didn't take the medication immediately, she would become so dizzy that she wouldn't be able to drive home. *It had always been like this.* My intuition told me that if I could get her to break that association and focus on her feelings, she would be able to release the dizziness. I did not tell her my plan, however, since I did not want it to influence the outcome. She finally agreed to give the process five minutes. I had her close her eyes and go into her feelings of anger. I asked her to notice where in her body she felt them, and how they were affecting her. I asked her to fully feel them and express them. At the end of five minutes she opened her eyes. When I asked her how she felt, she exclaimed, "I'm not dizzy anymore! This is the first time in two years I haven't had to take medication as soon as a dizzy spell came on!" She was able to finish the session with no dizziness and drive home, and did not need her medication for the rest of the day. Thereafter, with the approval of her physician, she was able to lower the dosage from three pills twice a day to half a pill twice a day. She is now living a normal life. Whenever she begins to feel a little dizzy, she can get in touch with the emotions she is feeling and acknowledge them, and the dizziness disappears.

This woman is a wonderful example of the healing power of suffering. It sounds strange, doesn't it? Suffering has healing power? Yes. In her book, *Gnostic Gospels,* Elaine Pagels reports that Jesus said: "If you bring forth what is within you, what you bring forth will save you. If you do not bring forth what is within you, what you do not bring forth will destroy you." Illness is the soul's message to our conscious ego self that there is something more, something meaningful to be explored down in the center of the suffering. There is a pearl of wisdom, a nugget of gold to be found among the dross, the base metal, or *prima materia* of the body. Like in statues of Kali, there is a small golden goddess of spiritual rebirth in the belly of suffering. This is the alchemical process of healing, as if base metal were being turned to gold. This is the resurrection process that we are all engaged in. Instead of rising above our pain, we need to dive down into the center of it, distill out the true meaning it has for our life, and allow this meaning to heal us.

It is in this alchemical healing process that the physical body becomes a resurrected body. The old patterns and imprints die and make way for new life force to rise again. The body "remembers" wholeness, health, and its connection with God. Rather than relying on the imprints and patterns of the past, we can be nourished by the life force that is released as we reclaim the energy that has been stored away and repressed in unhealed emotions, thoughts, and beliefs. This invisible consciousness then takes on visible form in our bodies. It becomes a healing energy available to us at all times when we pay attention to it. It means that our physical bodies are being born again at every moment, just as our consciousness is being born anew. Together they are "rising again," in a spiral of evolution that is moving all humanity toward complete resurrection, or "enlightenment," as the Buddhists and Hindus call it.

The resurrected body is one that contains all the wisdom, love, healing, consciousness, and enlightenment that our soul has acquired in all its lifetimes, including this one. If we are born again into another lifetime in another physical form, we will carry with us this resurrection into our new body and new life so it can continue to evolve.

Not all the people who come to me arrive with physical symptoms or illness. Some come for spiritual guidance and emotional healing. Examining the dreams of this kind of person is just as essential as when someone has a physical disease. One of my patients kept having hand dreams. They frightened her. After her mother died she had a dream about her mother's hands reaching out to her from a closet. Another was about a bloody hand, ground up like hamburger, lying on the bed next to her. A third was about a free-moving hand, unattached to a body, like the one in the *Addams Family,* running through a graveyard. She would wake in the middle of the night in a cold sweat, standing in the middle of her bedroom, having ripped off her nightgown. Then, someone tried to break into her apartment. Then, she found herself in the subway during a shoot-out. I tried to get her into analysis, but she wouldn't go. Her positive transference onto me was so strong that she told me I was the only person she would talk with about these things. And she was terrified of doing that. She was convinced that dreams "don't mean anything." She didn't want to talk about them. It meant she had to deal with the reality of them. But she was so distressed by waking in the middle of the night standing in her room without her nightgown, that she agreed to discuss them. It turned out that one of the last times her mother touched her before she died, she reached out to grab her daughter's arm and accidentally scratched her. Her mother had long nails that she always kept beautifully polished. Even while her body was deteriorating from alcoholism, she kept her nails perfect. That was the only way my patient remembered her mother taking care of herself. And she did this even after she had abandoned the children to foster care and, finally, to my patient's grandmother. She never saw her mother again.

These dreams gave us a window into my patient's soul. They gave us an entry into discussing her relationship with her mother and all the grief, loss, abandonment, fear, and rage that went with it. The night terrors stopped and she slept through the night for the first time in months. She started having dreams about men, and they gave us a way to explore her relationship with her father and her own inner damaged animus, or male energy. Her soul is healing, slowly, but it is healing. If she had not paid attention to her dreams, they would have continued to get more and more desperate, and so would her life. She might have had a complete nervous breakdown from the stress of her soul's trying to get her attention. She might have been lost to Hades and never found her way back up into the light. But she had the courage to face her underworld, explore her shadows, and learn to see in the dark. She is becoming, as many women are, Persephone resurrected.

In my own efforts to find my inner Persephone and help her rise again into the light, I kept getting lost in the dark. Despite getting divorced and making a new home for myself, my dreams told me that I was still caught in a labyrinth. In some ways I felt like the Sumerian goddess Inanna, hung on a meat hook, waiting for someone to rescue her. She had journeyed into the underworld to pay her respects to her dark sister, Ereshkigal, whose husband had just died. Mad with grief, anger, and jealousy, Ereshkigal took it out on Inanna and made her a prisoner, hanging her on a hook to rot. Inanna was helpless and hung there until she was rescued by grandfather Enki, the God of Wisdom, who arranged for her release. How ironic. I never knew either of my grandfathers.

The relationship I had after my divorce was with a wonderful, kind, and gentle man. But his own shadow and mother complex had never been addressed, and in many ways he was inwardly starving at an emotional level. It was all I could do to take care of myself and my own needs, put a home together, pull my life back together, and work more than full-time. I could not take care of another starving man. In many ways he took care of me, but since he was starving inside, he eventually ran out of energy. We both did. Toward the end I had dreams of being in the air and calling to him for help. In one dream I was on a tightrope strung between two high-rise buildings. I had a magnificent view of the sunrise, the skyline, trees, and airplanes, but I was off the ground, not in my body. I started to slip off the rope and cried out to him for help. He was standing on the top of one of the buildings. I couldn't reach him. I woke up.

I realized that I was depending on men outside of me to take care of me because I had no strong male energy inside of me. No positive animus. My inner male figures were still caught in some

kind of heroic patriarchal ideal of the more power the better. Win
the race. Be the best. Overpower. Dominate. Control. Steal.
Claim. Or as in one of my dreams, caught in the air, in spirit, in
idealism flying through the violet light of the spiritual chakra. Jungians call it spirit animus. We see it in our culture all the time.
Spiritual perfectionism. Holy rollers. Think, pray, stay in the
world of ideas, ideals, goals, words, purity. No body, no feminine,
no ground. Nothing dark, keep it all light. Light, light, light.

I began to wonder why, after twenty years of studying Jung and
fifteen years of teaching dreamwork, I had never gone into formal
analysis. I had begun with a Freudian analyst in my early twenties,
but because of the expense, had not continued. The one dream I remember from that analysis was of a beautiful plant with orange
flowers, delicate flowers like puffs of beauty with air inside. In the
dream I blew on the flowers and they shriveled. The analyst helped
me realize the debilitating sense of inner self-judgment that I carried. It would be many years before I understood the meaning of
the color orange and its relationship to the second chakra of sexuality and creativity. This harsh self-judgment, part of my inner
male animus, was wilting my inner feminine energy. Other therapists I would work with in later years were psychotherapists of
varying modalities, but none analytically trained. I wanted to finally take the leap. I wanted a Jungian. I knew there was an entire
dimension to my soul that was not getting healed and I wanted to
do it. I took the plunge.

I called a female Jungian who had been highly recommended to
me. I made an appointment. She suggested I keep track of my
dreams from that day on, bring them in with me when I came, and
continue to keep track of them through the analysis. Two weeks
later I went to meet her for the first time. She opened the door and
our eyes met. In an instant I knew she was the right person for me.
I *saw* her with all my eyes. Her darkness, her depth. She *knew*. She
had been there. I wanted that. She had been Inanna and Persephone and survived. She would know how to bring me back up
into the light. I walked in.

Little did I know I would have to stick around with Hades in the dark underworld for a while longer. She didn't value the light as much as I did. She was not about to let me up too quickly. I had a dream about my house having a cracked foundation. It did, but I knew that the dream meant my inner foundation was cracked. It leaked water, the emotional element of the psyche. I went to work on healing it. I had a dream of swimming in a large swimming pool, a good sign of my ego structure being able to "hold water." Some of my dreams got worse instead of better, a sign that I was diving deeper into the hidden levels of the unconscious. I had dreams of being psychically attacked. I told her of the group that had psychically attacked me. She suggested we work on who was psychically attacking me from the inside first, and that would strengthen my ability to protect myself from outside attacks.

I had a dream that I was once again walking on a tightrope. I looked down into the mud and didn't want to jump. But I knew I had to do it. I jumped.

It was like spiritual archaeology. I unearthed my mother's shadow, my father's shadow, my grandparent's shadows, the whole Teutonic shadow of despair and rage that I had been handed down from my ancestors in Scandinavia and Germany. The Nordic cosmology is very dark. The gods and goddesses, even heaven, gets destroyed in the end. Defeat and death are certain. The only way to respond is to face the end with heroism. Go into the battle with sword raised and face death without fear. There is only one small mention, a few lines at the very end of the *Elder Edda,* that hints there may be something after total annihilation. A thin thread of hope, not to be depended on.

No wonder, I thought. No wonder there are so many burning roots and fallen trees in my family. I had a dream one night about seeing my grandmother, my mother's mother, standing on top of a mountain against the sky. She had been dead for many years. When I was a child I had loved her very much, and I often wondered whether she watched over me. In the dream I was standing down below the mountain on the ground next to a fallen tree. She was giving me lessons in how to raise the tree—the family tree. I was having trouble doing it, but at least I was standing on the ground.

I also had a dream in which I was helping a physically challenged women run a race. She was partially crippled in the legs and had to sit down in a kind of race car that gets worked with the arms. There are two or three of us helping her complete the race. I wondered why she is so intent on pushing herself to the limit to complete a race she could not win. When I awakened I lay in bed for a long time, allowing myself to feel the emotional impact of this dream. I realized that I had been pushing myself to the limit with an organically challenged body to run a race I could not win. *Surrender to organic reality* is the phrase that came through as I lay there. Surrender. How devastatingly ironic that in surrendering to the body is the real healing. Surrendering into my fear of defeat and death I am reborn to a new life. To resurrection.

My former husband has become a triathlete. I think back to the days he tried to get me to push myself physically, run, become strong. What I had was a crippled body and soul, and what I needed was to feel my weakness. I knew it then, said it to friends of mine, but gave up what I knew for love, for being loved. Love or truth. I chose love. Now I choose truth. My truth.

After writing up some emotionally difficult dreams about death one morning, I turned on *CBS Sunday Morning* with Charles Osgood. There was a piece about Virginia Hamilton, a writer of children's books that contain African American folklore and stories. Her grandparents had been slaves, and she wanted to keep the folk wisdom of those generations alive for children of future generations. I listened to African American women respond with their feelings to her work, and I burst into tears when one of them revealed, "No one told me to listen to my grandmother and now she's gone." I realized that not only had no one told me to listen to my grandmother; no one even suggested I ask her about her stories, her childhood, and her life. No one in my family ever talked about their lives. It was like some silent taboo. I have periodically asked my mother to sit down with me and tell me about herself and our family. She told me that her mother and father never talked of their past, their childhoods, and their parents. She knew very little. She was told almost nothing. There were no stories. It made me think about how bleak a past has to be for someone to bury it so deep that no stories are told. In that moment I missed my grandmother. I wanted to hear her voice resurrected into words of vision that could paint pictures in my third eye, no matter how dark the waters. A mirror, a looking glass of soul. I wanted the dead bodies to be brought to life again in legends of birth and death, love and hope, loss and rebirth. I wanted to hear it all, feel it all, see the meaning of life through my grandmother's eyes.

My friend the storyteller Derek Burrows has such a heritage. He plays music and tells stories from his childhood and family in the Bahamas. The moment I met him I could feel his soul shine out through his voice and countenance and touch mine. He is living organic magic. He told me the story of his avocado tree. When he was small, he desperately wanted an avocado tree. His family planted one, and he waited and waited for it to grow avocados. It didn't. Finally, one day he asked his grandfather why the tree didn't produce fruit. He grandfather took a knife and cut into the tree. He turned to Derek and said: "You'll see. Next year it will produce two or three avocados. The tree will think it is dying and produce fruit." It did. What a heritage. What a grandfather.

As I unearthed my heritage though my dreams, I found them getting more profound. Even with the all the years of therapy and dream work I had done, I found there was plenty more to do. As if I were peeling off layers of an onion, I kept going deeper into my own soul and finding buried treasure. Sometimes the treasure was dark, frightening, angry, disembodied, and unexpressed in my waking life. Personalities that I had buried and needed reintegration. I found inner animi, male soul figures with whom I needed to form relationships. I realized that I could not have a good relationship with an external male until I had good relationship with all my internal males.

I discovered more aspects of my inner shadow, or the dark female figure I had inherited from my mother, grandmother, great-grandmother on down. There were inner figures of different heritage from mine: Italian, Spanish, South American. I had spent years digging through the first few layers; now I was unearthing the cellars of the structures that made up the home of my soul.

I had dreams of lost children, starving children, babies left in the dark. And finally, after much soul work, I had dreams of being pregnant. I had always had dreams over the years of being pregnant, but the baby was either never born, born prematurely, or born dead. I also found animals in my dreams. Some were injured or dying, some healthy. I realized how neglectful I had been of the inner instinctive primal life within me. I had spent years helping others get well; now the inner survival life in me had to be fed and protected. Animals are very instinctive, survival-oriented. They don't rationalize and talk themselves into or out of certain actions. They always act on their own behalf and for the protection of their young. I had a growing child within me. I would have to do the same. *No one* was going to abort this child.

God had tried to impregnate me many times. My womb had not always held the seed. I had not always been a good mother to myself. As soon as I became fertile with love, forgiveness, protection, I would spend it on someone else. I would see them as my child, worthy of all the gifts I held in my womb. I would offer myself up as the sacrifice. After struggling through a few more very brief and wrong relationships, I closed the door to outsiders. I wanted my home for myself. I realized that I had spent my whole adult life in relationship with "the other," and now I would have to go it alone. No more relationships, no more marriages. Just me, pregnant with myself, seeded by God.

I remembered a vision I had many years before. It was before I was married, and I had been at home with a cold and sore throat, like the ones I had when I was a child. My breathing had changed and I had gone into some kind of altered state. I had a vision of Olga Worrall's deceased husband, Ambrose, a powerful spiritual healer, standing near the foot of my bed and telling me, "You'll never be alone again." I assumed it meant that I would have the help of healers from the other side, heaven, to help me in my work. It hadn't occurred to me that maybe they were telling me I wouldn't be alone in my own healing process. I remembered that vision now and it gave me comfort. Alone but not alone. I could handle that.

8

Hunger

She sat on the floor throwing up. A student in my healing workshop who had pancreatic cancer. She had just gotten in touch with the memory of nursing at the breast and her mother's milk was sour.

She spent the rest of the workshop, "Awakening the Healer Within," going back and forth to the rest room and vomiting. All the newborn's sickening fear of being fed poisonous milk while starving for the nourishment of the sweet loving breast had hit her all at once. Terror of dying, grief, loss, rage, hunger, dependency. A whole life of denial had caught up with her in that one moment, and her body wanted that poison *out*. From what she told me later, she spent three days throwing up. She finally subsisted on sips of sweet carrot juice. The cancer disappeared. Ask any oncologist, and they all will tell you that pancreatic cancer doesn't just disappear. It did, and she stayed healed.

The first taste of life is not always sweet. No wonder so many of us would like to go back to the womb, into what Freud called "oceanic bliss." He believed, like Marx, that religion is the opiate of the people. That we all want to get back into the womb and go to sleep, go into unconsciousness. This may be true, but it is certainly not the definition of healing or spirituality, which is a wake-up call to discover where our true hunger is buried and to find a way to feed it whole food.

The first god we have when our souls decide to take physical form is our mother. She is the creative matrix out of which we form. We rest inside her womb for nine months and nurse from the milk of her body's breast for several more. If we are fortunate, the milk is sweet and comes from a healthy body, mind, and soul. If we are not, the breast milk is sour, or we are fed processed baby formula, and we have to swallow it because we will die if we don't. What a choice: death or poison.

The only way to survive such a choice is to repress some of our hunger. I have watched kittens when they are born. Once the mother has licked them dry, they instinctively find the nipple. They are voracious in their breast-feeding, pushing aside any other kittens to get to the milk. They will cry and whine until their mother lies down when they are hungry and nurse as long as they need. If you try to wean them too early and shove other food under their nose, they will refuse it. My cat, when she had kittens, would eat all the food put out for the kittens so they couldn't get at it. She instinctively knew how long to let them nurse. She walked around the entire living room, once they were up on their feet, and tasted the leaves of all the house plants to make sure they weren't poisonous. She had never done this before. She wasn't going to let her babies be poisoned.

Human babies don't spend every waking minute with their mothers, like most kittens. They are not allowed to shove and push and cry, insisting that their mothers lie down whenever they want. They are not allowed to push the breast away, or the bottle, if they don't like the taste. They may try, but many times they are force-fed what they don't want, just as they will find later when they are told to eat what is in front of them or sit there until they do. This winds up translating into eating negative emotions, thoughts, and beliefs, just as much as it does food.

A psychotherapist once told me a true story of a case he had heard about child abuse. Every morning a son would sit at the table and try to pour a glass of milk. And every time, he would spill it. This had been going on for years. The father would stand in back of him with a lit cigarette. "Now drink the milk!" the father would demand. The boy, terrified of spilling it, would lift the glass with shaking hands and, of course, spill the milk. The father would take his lit cigarette and burn it into the boy's back, saying "I'm doing this for your own good. I have to teach you not to spill the milk." This sadistic relationship continued for years until a teacher finally noticed the burns on the boy's back.

Here was a young boy, starving for both food and love, being offered cruelty, sadism, pain, and humiliation. The natural hunger of this child had to be repressed, or it would have killed him or driven him mad. He lived in terror, trying to please his father to get one drop of approval or love from him. Without help, he would have fallen into the same projected cruelty as his father, taking out his rage and grief on another human being, most likely a child, like himself.

Most parents are not so sadistic, and they try to do the best they can when it comes to feeding their children. But if they themselves have been fed poison, or underfed, or overfed, and not confronted these issues, what they have to feed their children will not be healthful food. If, as adults, they are still starving for a good breast, they will try to force-feed their children. In a social situation, I once saw a father shove a bottle of formula into his year-old daughter's mouth every five minutes for an hour, despite the fact that she consistently pushed it away and was obviously not hungry. I watched as she got angrier and angrier, making disgusted faces and being held prisoner on his lap. I gently tried to suggest to him that she was not hungry, but he was so caught up in his own inner unconscious starvation, that he had no control over what he was doing. She wanted to toddle around and play with her bright red ball, so I sat on the floor with her and bounced the ball back and forth, giving her a few moments of freedom and delighted giggles until the father picked her up again. I sat there thinking to myself that already this small radiant goddess had developed rage toward her controlling father, and if this continued, which I had no doubt it would, she would wind up hating men. What a tragedy. Where was the mother? She sat there, attempting at several points to tell him their daughter wasn't hungry, but even she gave up. His grip was too tight, his psyche a prison, for everyone. I wanted to grab that little goddess out of his hands and set her free, permanently, but I knew that for some reason her soul had chosen this family and this karma to learn from, and she would have to struggle with this issue for the rest of her life. I could not change her father's entire history of starvation in one bold grab. Those moments of seeing the suffering of others and having to endure the knowledge with sad patience are torture for me. Better not to see? No. Better to let it crack open my heart a little wider with compassion and send healing and the food of real love to that family in my prayers and meditations over the following days and evenings. And to use it as a mirror to remind me to look within myself at my own issues of starvation.

I went home that evening after playing with the little goddess and the red ball and sat in meditation. I closed my eyes and went deeply in and allowed myself to feel the rage I had at such a controlling parent. I processed all the ways that I felt I had too much shoved down my throat at home, at school, in my marriage, life, and career. I felt the imprisonment of being held in situations against my will, where I didn't have the strength or courage to demand or to take my freedom. I realized most of my childhood was like that. I wonder, sometimes, whether we all experience childhood and adolescence as imprisonment. We are needy and dependent on our caregivers, therefore, trapped and imprisoned by everyone else's reality. No wonder we pretend we don't need people even when we do. It's like giving over part of our souls in return for care and love. I meditated on my marriage and how imprisoned I felt there. Trying to love and be loved, living up to my own and someone else's expectations. Trying to be free and connected at the same time.

I remembered a time when I was twelve and my aunt insisted I needed a new coat for winter. I didn't, but she didn't like the style of the one I had and demanded I replace it. She said she would give it to me for Christmas. I thanked her but told her that I liked the one had. She expected me to succumb to her wishes. I refused. One of the only times I stood up for myself at that age. A controlling, domineering, shove-it-down-your-throat person who didn't seem to care what I wanted or needed but was focused only on what she wanted. A bottle of poison in the guise of a gift.

One of my patients came in one day, upset by her mother's having arrived for a visit the day before. She was upset because they had driven over in the car together for her session with me, and her mother had worn perfume, something to which my patient was highly sensitive. She didn't dare say anything to her mother. I asked her why. The question elicited a memory of when she was younger and her grandmother, mother, and she had gone on a four-hour trip in the car. Her grandmother had doused herself with perfume, and my patient said she was overcome by the fumes. She asked her grandmother to open the window, but she refused, saying she couldn't take the draft. My patient complained that the scent was too much for her, and her grandmother's response was, "What's wrong with you! All women wear perfume!" She had to sit in an unventilated car for four hours breathing in heavy, nauseating perfume. When they reached their destination, she was sick in bed for three days.

We spent the entire hour discussing this poisoning of both her body and psyche. She felt both rage and sadness that she had experienced herself as so helpless that she couldn't take any further action and that her grandmother was so unfeeling toward her needs. I asked her why she didn't demand to be let out of the car so she could take a bus or train, but that had not occurred to her. When we are paralyzed in this kind of negative mother complex, the other options available do not occur to us until much later.

I told her about a time when I was living with a friend who had a male friend visit for a few days. The visitor always doused himself with cologne, and left his toiletries all over the bathroom. Both my friend and I were highly sensitive to scent and never used any. We asked him to put away his toiletries and to avoid using his cologne when he was in our house. He grudgingly did so, although we could see he felt insulted. A month or two later he came for another visit. I woke up one morning on the second floor to smell his cologne floating up from downstairs. I walked down and the whole house reeked of it. I felt rage surge through my body. The protective rage of the good mother in me who didn't want her inner child poisoned by an abusive passive-aggressive male. I told him that he obviously had no respect for our wishes and needs and he would have to move to a hotel.

When we are children we are so hungry for our parents' love and approval that we will do almost anything to get it. If they don't feed us food, we die. If we aren't touched, we die. If we aren't loved and encouraged, we die emotionally. Children live in a life-threatening situation. One moment of disobedience and we can be punished, ignored, abused, or hit by a truck. When human beings are in constant danger, we usually do what is necessary to stay alive even if it means deadening our feelings, thoughts, beliefs, and needs—even if it means denying our true self, our true voice, and our true soul. We are sometimes masters of disguise, finding ways to stay alive while hiding most of our aliveness and hunger for love underground out of harm's way.

But hunger has a way of popping its mouth open at the most re-vealing times. I was teaching a workshop in Boston. On Friday night there was a young woman in the front row in the seat directly in front of me. I imagined she was in her early twenties, although she looked no more than fourteen. She was sweet-looking, pas-sive, sad, thin, and very hungry. I could see that she was only in touch with a small amount of that hunger. During the meditation that night I could see tears roll down her cheeks. After the medita-tion, when people were sharing with one another, I went over to her and commented on her sadness. She burst into tears and told me she heard a voice that told her she didn't want to be alive. I asked whether she was going to be in the workshop over the week-end, and she said yes. I spent the only minute or so I had doing a laying-on-of-hands on her heart and then told her to sit in the same seat directly in front of me over the weekend, and we would talk more then.

The next morning I looked for her just before the workshop was to begin. She was nowhere in sight, and there was another woman sitting in front of me. I had thought to save that seat for her, but I decided to see how much effort she would put into getting there in time to take it for herself. I had a feeling that she was not enough in touch with her hunger to make sure she got the seat, and I was right. About five minutes after the workshop started, she showed up, noticed that the front seat was taken, and took the seat in back of it, where she had a less clear view of me. I smiled at her, and she smiled back.

After the lunch break I noticed her come back into the room. She looked pale, almost gray, as though all the life force had been drained from her. My inner psychic voice said, "Ask her what she had for lunch." I waited until we had done a meditation and it was time to share. Everyone had drawn color pictures of the symptoms bothering them. She volunteered. She walked up to the front of the room and shared her picture. I no longer remember what it was, because I was so focused on this insistent inner voice that kept demanding for me to ask her what she ate for lunch. I did. Her reply: "Nothing." She said she didn't have any money for lunch. I asked whether she didn't have any or whether she had forgotten to bring money with her. She said she hadn't brought any with her and that another group member had offered to loan her a few dollars so she could buy lunch, but she had refused. There it was. The archetype of the starving child who didn't even believe she deserved to eat. I told her that I had seen her come back after lunch and how I had heard my inner voice telling me to ask her what she had eaten. Her eyes widened. Someone had noticed her—finally. She wouldn't have to starve herself into death for someone to notice her suffering. I asked the group if anyone had a piece fruit she could have. One by one group members came up and laid food on my side table: an apple, a banana, an orange, a thick slice of bread, a bottle of juice. I placed my hands over all the food and cleared it of people's energies. I took the picture out of her hands, placed all the food into them, and told her to go back to her seat and eat. She did. The bread, the staff of life, first.

The next morning she was in the parking lot as I got out of my car. I asked how she was. She told me her dog had been hit by a car the night before and had died. I felt terrible for her and wondered whether this was a sign that her inner animal energy, her instinctive life force, was not going to make it. I kept my thoughts to myself and walked in with her. The last few words she said were something about her father's coming to get her and being terrible to her.

I found a free leader's meal ticket on my table for the cafeteria upstairs. Knowing that I had other plans for lunch, I placed it in her hands. She couldn't believe her eyes. "Really? You don't need this?" she inquired. No. I imagined her mother had needed to keep all the emotional food for herself and had none left for her daughter. I didn't. I had more than enough.

I came back after lunch to see her cheeks pink and her face smiling. During the afternoon break I noticed her eating a big cookie at her seat. I pointed this out to one of my assistants, who told me that she had seen her upstairs in the cafeteria eating a large lunch. In that moment I knew she had chosen to live. I realized that her dog had sacrificed itself instead so that she could live. Sometimes animals do that for their owners: take on illnesses and accidents, even death, to protect their owners. I had to turn away for a few minutes so no one would see the tears in my eyes. I felt that I had just seen Lazarus resurrected from his grave. I felt so immensely grateful for the desperate childhood hunger that I had allowed myself to experience again as part of my own healing, so when I looked into the face of starvation in another, I could see its gaping mouth and feed it.

I remember always feeling hungry as a kid. Thinking about food, imagining what my next meal would be. Like many people in the fifties, our family subsisted on a diet of meat, cheese, overcooked vegetables, and sugar. Not that my mother wasn't health conscious. She was, in her own way, making what I called gobbledegook in the blender—a mixture of raw carrots, celery, apples, and raisins. Before the advent of juicers, we would put everything in a regular blender and mash it up until it was almost drinkable. But that was just an addition to an otherwise high-fat and high-sugar diet.

But no matter how much I ate, there was always a deeper hunger, a well of deprivation. I was to learn years later just how hungry I was for love, safety, structure, stability, reality, truth, and clarity. I was hungry for someone to depend on who had a true sense of self and a strong grounding in reality; someone who could help me cope with the harsh realities of life without sweetening the bitter gall with ice cream, sugar, or "Don't worry. Everything will be all right. God is watching over you." Yes, God is watching over all of us, or I prefer to believe, residing within all of us. But that doesn't mean everything will be all right and we should deny our starvation and substitute a Pollyanna outlook on life and a bowl of Häagen-Dazs. Doing that means stuffing our mouths with sugar, drinking alcohol, taking drugs, shopping, gambling, and having compulsive relationships.

The major component of mother's milk is sugar alcohol, predigested milk sugar that goes directly into the bloodstream, as does the bottled alcohol that adults drink. Babies who have just breast-fed fall into a blissful drugged sleep. Is it any wonder that alcoholics often do the same after drinking? Is it a surprise that people who eat a lot of sugar get very excited and high and then crash and collapse, often into sleep or a sugar-induced stupor?

I ate a lot of sugar and milk products, substitutes for the breast-feeding I never received. My mother almost died in three days of childbirth, and I was bruised from being yanked out with forceps. She was too weak to nurse me, and I was allergic to every formula they tried to feed me. The first few weeks of my life must have been lived in semistarvation. Not a pleasant entry into the world. We know now that one of the benefits of breast-feeding is the proper formation of the jaw, throat, and neck muscles. I have had lifelong trouble with my neck and with tightness in my jaw. Many people do.

Breast-fed babies have the advantage of ingesting the colostrum that is secreted during the first two to three days after birth and before the true onset of lactation. Colostrum is a thin yellowish fluid containing a great quantity of proteins and calories, in addition to antibodies and lymphocytes. These cannot be reproduced in man-made formula. Antibodies are protein substances that are produced in the blood and tissues and destroy or weaken attacking invaders, such as bacteria and viruses. Lymphocytes are cells present in the blood and lymphatic tissues that derive from the stem cells, from which all blood cells arise. These begin to form and strengthen our immune system, the basis of lifelong health. Without a strong immune system, we are vulnerable to invasion from external bacteria and viruses and to any mutant cells that may form in our bodies.

Breast-fed babies also have the experience of physical and emotional bonding with the mother. The fetus is protected from the outside world by the mother's womb and is actually fed by her blood, which forms the placenta. The placental barrier filters many toxins, although some get through, such as in fetal alcohol syndrome. Once born, the mother continues to protect the infant with her body. She is responsible for keeping away threatening people, animals, and situations that would assault the baby's well-being. During nursing, her arms, hands, voice, and heartbeat help her bond with the child.

When you can't recognize a gaping mouth opening in front of you, you are at risk of being devoured. Hunger is a powerful force in the world. Maybe the most powerful. Someone who is starving will do almost anything for food, drugs, power, sex, money, love, alcohol, or whatever "food" they perceive as the most filling at that moment. No one wants to walk around announcing "I'm hungry! I'm hungry! Where's my mother?!" It's not only embarrassing, but also means that we actually have to acknowledge our hunger and the strength of its position in our lives. It is much more acceptable to say, "I want to become the president of the company!" or "I want to make ten million dollars!" or "I want a woman who looks like Cindy Crawford!" We substitute many other things to focus on when we are no longer newborns searching out a good breast with sweet milk. In the process of substitution, we repress the original hunger until it is no longer recognizable to our conscious mind. If the original hunger is strong enough, if it was left unrequited and reaches starvation, it turns into addiction or obsessive-compulsive behavior of some kind. This behavior then leads us into repeating over and over again a substitute enactment that, if left unchecked, like alcoholism, can destroy us, kill us. If we admit to the symbolic meaning of the behavior, that it is a search for food to fill a starving body and soul, then we have a chance to touch the original woundedness within us. We can then slowly build a healing relationship that will reformulate an inner good mother who can truly feed our soul needs as well as our body.

This good inner mother that needs to reformulate has to have a role model. Children learn by modeling. If our own mother was not a good role model for self-love, abundance, wholeness, and grounding, then we need to find someone else who can model these qualities. But people also do not want to run around the world questioning everyone they meet, "Are you a good mother I can first feed off of and then model myself after?" Whether we want to admit it or not, that's exactly what most of us are doing.

I spent most of my life not even realizing I was hungry, much less just how hungry I was. I offered myself as a meal for everyone else, and then wondered why I always felt so tired and hungry emotionally and physically. Not only was I feeding people with my own energy, I was merging with and feeling their hunger. As part of my good-mothering process, I changed my eating patterns and cut down on sugar, meat, coffee, and completely eliminated dairy products. I ate more whole grains, vegetables, and fruits. I added miso soup and seaweed for iodine and calcium. I started going to bed earlier. Instead of 11:30 P.M. or midnight, I went to bed at 10 P.M. I found myself getting up earlier in the morning, sometimes at 5 or 6 A.M.

Healing the body and soul is not a linear process. It is more like a spiral. The process keeps circling back around while moving forward at the same time. It doesn't always feel this way, however.

If we are caught in a cycle of devouring hunger and are looking in all the wrong places for food, it can feel as though we are caught in an exercise wheel in a hamster cage circling round and round, never getting anywhere. This is what psychologists call repetition compulsion. Our soul keeps repeating certain patterns until we finally get the lesson and move on to the next grade. This can be a very frustrating experience. It can feel like everyone else in the world has left us in the dust and we are still eating dust.

I felt this way for years. I kept wondering why I was working so hard and never getting ahead. Why was I never able to save enough money to take time off? Why was I always so tired? As soon I would rest and get revitalized, I would spend it all on other people, on work, on things, on running around being successful. In many ways I was too successful. I had too many patients, too many classes, too many workshops, too many planes to catch. People kept asking me, "How do you do it all?" I didn't know. I had always done it all. I had always done five hours of homework a night even in high school. I had always stayed up until 4 A.M. writing papers and studying in college and graduate school. I had always gone for the brass ring. I didn't know any other way to be. I had been brought up to spend it all—spend myself—all of me, so there was nothing left over for me.

What most people don't realize is that the 1980s was not just the decade of decadence. It was also the decade of starvation. Everyone was so starved for soul that they consumed everything they could get their hands on. The government consumed, the consumer consumed, the stock market consumed. If we examine all the horror images in our culture, as well as around the world, we can see that they all represent some form of devouring hunger. The films that scared me the most as I was growing up were *Jaws* and *The Exorcist.* I refused to see either of them until almost tens years after their release, and then only on the small screen. I instinctively knew my psyche was too delicate to handle them at the time, especially on the larger-than-life movie screen. I did watch *Alien* and its creature with the huge dinosaur-like teeth and dripping saliva. And more recently the film *Silence of the Lambs,* about a psychiatrist who devours former patients—a chilling metaphor at this point in history. When psychiatrists, mothers, and healers of any kind haven't healed the wounds of their own inner devouring hunger, they are liable unconsciously to devour the energies of their children and patients. More casually, it goes by the name a devouring mother. Or as the psychologist Melanie Klein would say, a "bad breast."

In books we have horror represented by Stephen King. In *The Shining,* the main character is a recovering alcoholic and writer, who becomes an off-season caretaker at a hotel called Overlook so he can finish his book. In living there alone, unfed by any human contact, he has to meet his own demons of starvation and abandonment, as all addicts must. After his wife and son finally arrive, he becomes a monster of a man, crazed from his own demons, having written a thousand pages of one line: "All work and no play makes Jack a dull boy."

Every night on the news we hear of murder and cannibalism in the form of Jeffrey Daumer, school bus crashes, U.S. government contractors charging nine hundred dollars per bolt on construction contracts, and Bosnia gobbling up human lives in a blood bath of carnage. Blood is often an essential aspect to images of horror. It is the life energy, the life "water" that flows through us. When it is contained within our bodies, we hardly see it, except in the innocuous pink blush of the cheeks and the blue tint to the veins in our hands. When it is let out to spill all over, it becomes a bright, shocking red reminder of the bloodletting and death that is possible at any moment of our lives. Some people faint at the sight of uncontained blood.

During the time I was writing this chapter, a story came on during an evening television tabloid program about a man who drinks blood. I wanted to turn it off immediately, but I made myself watch the first minute. He said that as a young kid in the schoolyard, he had gotten into a fight with a boy who landed on top of him. The boy was bleeding and some blood dropped into his mouth. He said it was the first time he had tasted human blood and it was "exhilarating." From then on he had a hunger, or thirst, for it. The program was about to break for a commercial but said they would be back to tell us how he acquired his blood. I didn't want to know. I changed the channel.

These examples are horrible. They terrify and disgust most of us. They make us think of evil and the devil. Everything ugly, bleeding, and dying must be from an evil source. This perspective on the body, the earth, and the feminine came into being with Christianity's efforts to separate itself as far as possible from paganism. Western culture has since tried to sanitize the dirt and blood out of religion, society, and consciousness to the point that it can only be relegated to horror films, books, cellophane-wrapped meat and the evening news. But in separating the light and the dark, the bloodless and the bloody, the pure and the dirty, we have also separated our psyches from the deep, inner hunger for love and sweet milk that form the very basis of our bodies and souls. It is in this separation from our true hunger that it gets pushed underground and becomes devouring. In bringing our hunger up into the light of consciousness, we claim our humanity, our dependency, and our need for both spirit and matter, God and mother, love and food. We claim the need to merge with our Creator.

In India during the festival of Kali, the Hindu and Tibetan goddess of death and destruction who clears the way for rebirth, a bowl is filled with blood and milk to represent the two life liquids of which we are formed and for which we hunger, which Kali drinks to represent hunger, life, death, and rebirth. In Christianity, we take communion, which represents the blood of Christ in the form of wine, plant blood (grapes), and the body in the form of bread or wafers. Before his crucifixion, Jesus sat with his twelve disciples at his last Passover meal, called the Last Supper in Christianity. In breaking bread he gave it to the disciples and said, "Take it and eat. This is my body." He then took a cup, which the later Arthurian legend would call the Grail, filled it with wine, and handed it to them saying, "Drink from this, all of you, for this is my blood, the blood of the new covenant poured out for many for the forgiveness of sins." The disciples consumed the wine and bread as his blood and body, his life force, so that when he died, he would still live within them. In the reenactment of the Last Supper, called the Eucharist, Christians eat of the body and blood of the one who combines spirit and matter, father and mother, purity and dirt, milk and blood. We consume the savior into ourselves to experience God living in every cell of our bodies. And in experiencing God living in every cell, we become one with our Creator.

✳ ✳ ✳

I kicked the refrigerator—hard. I had on very sturdy clogs, so I didn't hurt my foot. It felt good. I could hear another shelf fall inside, and I kicked it again. A rage of hunger denied and suppressed and turned into sleeping and eating and constant tiredness and overwork.

I had gone downstairs to fix dinner and opened the refrigerator. The shelf inside the door broke and spilled its contents out onto my kitchen floor. It was the last straw in a day in which nothing had gone right. I found myself growling and bellowing. And kicking the refrigerator. I couldn't remember when something had felt so good. I felt the full force of my foot slamming into the door. I was surprised I wasn't injuring myself. I felt flames of energy course through my body. I felt like the Egyptian goddess Hathor or the Tibetan Kali on a rampage. My cat came to watch. She crouched on the floor and looked up at me with her green eyes meeting my green eyes. For a moment I felt as though we locked energy and she recognized my fierceness in her own collective psyche, a species known for its hunger and its hunt.

I found myself feeling fully alive for the first time in weeks. I found myself growling out loud: "I want energy. I want food. I want love. I want strength. I want joy. I want health. I want healing. I want beauty. I want friends. I want safety. I want it *all*. Now. Here. In this moment. All of Life. Fully awake. I want it all." I heard thunder. For a split second in eternity I could not distinguish whether it was coming from inside of me or outside of me. It was all the same. I stood in the middle of the kitchen floor with all my eyes open and saw and felt circles and pyramids, suns and moons, stars and planets, animals and plants, blood and milk, light and dark, love and rage all pouring out of me at once. In my total hunger, I was completely full with Life.

✳

9
Wild Angels

A menagerie, I believe it's called—three cats and a dog. Within three months, I went from living alone for six years in my small early 1800s saltbox to living with three cats and a dog.

I began by adopting one homeless cat. A former student told me that she had a handsome white and gray cat with green eyes parked on the doorstep of her apartment building in Queens, New York. He sat looking longingly in the window at her other two cats. She could not take in a third because she had just acquired the second, and the two were having difficulty getting along. She called him Elijah and gave him food and water every day, but it had been two weeks, and she could not find anyone to take him. She thought she would have to remove him to a shelter, as he looked desperate and frightened, and several little boys were chasing him.

As she was relating this tale of woe, I heard a voice in my head tell me, "Take the cat." No! my rational mind replied. I could not take any animal. Too much responsibility. Too much mess. I traveled a lot and how would I cope? I had lived with dogs, Weimaraners, as a child, even helping a litter of six to be born to my female dog, Heidi. I loved them. We had kept the largest male puppy after the others were sold, and I had lived with two dogs for a long time. Then, I had a cat in college. The cat that went to college for a year, until the school decided they had made a dreadful mistake telling students they could bring their animals with them to college dormitories. A little mess, a little chaos. As though college wasn't chaotic enough. The college sent the animals packing, and my cat went home to live with my mother, where she seemed happy and stayed until she died almost twenty years later.

The voice was insistent: "Take the cat. It's yours." No, no. I couldn't. My student kept going on and on about the cat. I finally said: "Stop! I'll take the cat." She looked stunned. "You will?" She couldn't believe her ears. Yes, I will. I told her that she would have to take the cat to the vet first, have him checked for fleas, ticks, and feline leukemia and given shots. I was standing in the shower several days later and all of a sudden I thought: What's the worst case scenario? That this cat is female and pregnant. Half an hour later the phone range. It was my student: "I think we're going to have to rename the cat. Elijah is a female. A pregnant female." I knew it. I took a deep breath. How could I turn a pregnant female cat back on the street or send it to a shelter? Okay. I'll take her.

I got off the phone and thought of the dog I had when I was married, a beautiful golden retriever named Ezekiel's Golden Chariot, or Zeke for short. My husband had given him to me for a birthday present. When we separated several years later, I decided to leave him at the house with my husband. I didn't want to rip him from his home, and I didn't know where I would be living at first. He was also very attached to my husband, and I wanted him to have a yard and large house to play in. I also didn't think I could cope with him alone, traveling so much. It never occurred to me to hire someone to take care of him while I was traveling. I don't even remember whether there were those kinds of pet services at that time, and I didn't know who my neighbors would be.

Years later I would feel that I had abandoned him. My husband had tried to take care of him alone, as well, taking him in the car to his place of work. But it had become too much for him, and without telling me, he gave him to his daughter, who loved him and had recently been married. Zeke was abandoned twice, and my husband's daughter said he wouldn't eat for three weeks. They wondered whether he would live. Luckily, he did. When I heard about Zeke, I was devastated. It put me in touch with the reality of my abandonment of him, and then in touch with all the issues of abandonment in my own life.

I immediately thought of my father and how his alcoholism had led to his emotional abandonment of me. How one moment I had been the small baby he soothed in the rocking chair by singing lullabies, and the next I was the small child who was pushed off his lap because I was "too big," and then completely replaced by his own bottle. When I questioned my mother many years later about his alcoholism and emotional dissolution, she told me that my father had been abandoned by his own mother in childhood. She had apparently left her abusive husband, taken her newborn to live with her parents, and then went off with a man on a yacht. My father was left alone on a farm as a toddler with harsh grandparents, who probably did the best they could to take care of him between his mother's intermittent visits. Like me, he was an only child. I saw a photo of him at the age of four or five. He was the saddest-looking child I had ever seen.

He later married and had a daughter, my half-sister. Again the history of abandonment continued. I got the story that his wife took their daughter and went home to live with her parents. My sister was told that our father abandoned them. To this day, no one knows the real truth, and I'm too close to the issue to see clearly what actually happened.

My mother's history of abandonment is also deep. My grandmother, her mother, was left an orphan in childhood because both her parents died. The woman who took her in died when my grandmother was sixteen years old, and she was left completely alone in the world. She married my grandfather, who came from Sweden. He died young and left her with four children: my mother, her two sisters, and a brother. My mother adored her fa-

✳

ther and was devastated by his death. Many years later, her mother and all her sisters and brothers died, and my mother was alone in the world except for me.

When my mother was a young child, she was continually ill. She had been brought home in an open-sided horse and buggy soon after she was born in the middle of winter, contracted pneumonia, and almost died. What a welcome into the world. To a newborn baby, it must have felt as if she were being murdered. She was told later that her father commented on what a sickly child she was and that she couldn't belong to their hearty Swedish family. Rejection. She had barely left the womb and already she was barely alive and being rejected. In addition, she was the third girl. Her parents wanted a boy.

My mother was sick most of her childhood with upper respiratory illnesses and allergies. She was sent off to a farm every summer "for her health," where she was given lots of milk, butter, and cheese to eat, and exposed to lots of pollens, hay, and flowers. No one knew she was lactose intolerant and had environmental allergies. Her parents thought they were doing the best thing for her, but she felt abandoned, rejected, and sick. The truth is that she was being force-fed poison. Almost murdered, once again. The Buddhists are right when they say the source of all suffering is ignorance. Ignorance does not mean stupidity. It means not knowing. It is what we do not know, or choose not to know, that can destroy us and those we love.

I remember a woman who stood up in one of my workshops and told her story of having been born with a congenital defect that required several surgeries and hospital stays in her early childhood. She said she felt as though everyone was torturing her, and she had been left with repressed rage from being abused. It was only now, thirty years later, that she could understand and forgive the people who had been trying to help her. And appreciate the care they must have put into her recovery.

Feelings are not rational. The awareness of being born into this physical, material world of suffering is one of experience. When we are newborn babies, we do not have a conceptual process and cannot make rational leaps. We cannot talk ourselves out of feeling murdered, abandoned, rejected, and abused by telling ourselves that people are trying to do the best they can to take care of us. First we have the experience, at a body level, then we have the emotions, and only later when we are several years old, do we start to think about things and ask questions. But even then, the questions are more like: Why are there clouds in the sky? Where do babies come from? It is the rare child that expresses deep inner emotional distress. As we now know from all the thousands of children who are abused each year, most young children hide their real pain and despair, being afraid to lose whatever attention and love they have. Their ego structure is not strong enough to support confrontation if it means loss of love and abandonment. Most children would rather idealize their parents than risk losing them, which in a child's experience equals death. So the fear and rage get repressed, usually until we are adults, when we find that people other than our parents start triggering them with their behavior toward us.

My mother thought she was marrying a kind and loving man when she married my father. She did not realize that the abandonment he had experienced in his childhood would come back to haunt him and turn into alcoholism. She probably thought she could give him a stable, loving marriage and home, and he would give her the same. At a conscious level, people usually start out with the best of intentions. It is the unconscious poverty of soul and heart that gets triggered, however, at the first sign of abandonment. First my father's mother died, then my mother's, with whom he had become close. Abandonment through death. Then he had to fire someone at work, a woman who had worked for the company for twenty-five years. He didn't want to do it, but he was ordered to do so. She had a family. He felt terrible. Abandonment through rejection.

Over and over again, life kicks up abandonment issues. At some point the ego structure breaks down and is forced back down into the original wound that usually takes place at the preverbal level and in connection with the mother. A newborn baby is entitled to unconditional love. A newborn life is the most precious thing we have on this earth. It is totally innocent, dependent, fragile. The people who brought it into the world are responsible for making sure it is fed, protected, nurtured, and loved unconditionally. A newborn life, whether it is a human baby or an animal, is helpless and unable to make decisions for itself, or tell right from wrong. You cannot reason with a newborn and tell it not to be hungry, not to urinate or to make a bowel movement, not to bite or annoy you when you want to sleep. A newborn is acting from instinct and its need to stay alive.

Puppies are some of the most annoying creatures on earth. Unless you have several, who can take out their aggressive play on one another, they turn their attention to you. You become part of their pack. Dogs, like wolves, are pack animals and in the wild are never alone. They pounce, nip, bite your heels, put their teeth through your pants leg, and shit all over the floor. They don't do it to make us angry. They do it because they are happy to be alive, happy to play, happy to see you, and they use their mouths to express that. They want to taste life and bite into it, just the way newborns nurse as one of their first experiences of life, using the mouth to take in their mother's bodies as the first food of a new life. My bookkeeper told me that her baby used to suck on her jawbone. Babies put everything in their mouths. Taste, ingest, digest, excrete. A cycle that continues our entire lives.

So I decided to give a home to an abandoned pregnant cat. One cat. I could take care of one cat. I would give the kittens away. I started asking friends and family even before the cat arrived. I had tentative homes for four of them, and the vet said cats usually have about four to six kittens. I wanted to name the mother cat Psyche, which means "soul" in Greek. A pregnant soul, to me a beautiful image. I was feeling pregnant with my own soul's healing process, and I felt that Psyche had come to me as a reflection of my own inner pregnancy. I was finally learning how to create a safe home, a nourishing womb, for my soul to grow. The growth of the soul includes new birth, new life, which usually means the inner development of a whole, healthy child at a deep intrapsychic level that

*

shows up in dreams. Instead of starving the hungry child within, or finding gratification through material things and people, I was focusing attention and self-love at a soul level. I was finally giving more attention to my inner life than to the external world and all its demands.

Animals often show up in dreams when the person needs to pay attention to his or her inner instinctive life force. Acquiring an animal, or pet, to care for also can bring us into an awareness of these instincts. Over the years many people have contacted me regarding animal healing. Pets become part of the family. They usually provide unconditional love, something not always available from human beings. Nursing homes have found that dogs and cats can be healing for older people who are ill. The very act of having a living, loving, soft, and furry being to caress is a wonderful balm for the soul and the body.

I once received a letter from a woman whose small dog's hind legs had become paralyzed. She wanted to know whether there was anything she could do, or whether I could heal the animal. Since she lived quite far from me, I told her that I would do a distant healing, but that she could also participate. I explained how she could do a laying-on-of-hands. Several weeks later I received a lovely letter from her telling me that her dog was now fully recovered and jumping around like a little puppy. I decided to create a "Laying-on-of-Hands" meditation that could be used for animals, children, or even adults (*see* "Healing Meditations").

A week before Psyche came to live with me, I went to Saratoga for the horse races. One of my faculty members, Nini Gridley, was living closeby at the time, and her father had box seats at the finish line. I had a vague memory of visiting Saratoga when I was a child with my parents. They both loved horses, my father having trained and bred Arabian stallions in the army during World War II at a base in Pomona, California. I remember my father telling me that he could run his hand down a horse's flank and tell exactly which muscle was strained or torn. A functioning intuitive in uniform. I know I received some of my deep intuition and the sensitivity in my hands from him. My parents spent their honeymoon in

*

Kentucky bluegrass country and met Man O' War, the horse that won the Kentucky Derby in the 1940s. When my father died my mother gave their large beautiful painting of the horse to my half-sister, who was living in Pennsylvania trying to raise horses.

My father had bought a horse, Baby, before they were married and kept it boarded at a stable in Manhattan, and sometimes at a ranch in upstate New York. I remember going to the ranch as a child and horseback riding. They told me that sometimes the ranch was used as a backdrop in movies. I can still remember being on the back of a sweet old mare and enjoying my ride until we had to squeeze between two trees on the trail. My knee got caught behind one of the trees but the horse kept moving forward. What my knees were doing sticking out so far I don't know, but I can still remember the pain. It imprinted the ride in my mind forever, as pain often does.

Nini and I were in the car on the way to lunch and the first race of the day, when we encountered terrible traffic. I assumed the traffic was all heading for the races, but Nini said it was never this bad. Very slowly we inched our way up to a traffic light, where we were able to see the results of a terrible accident. A bus had hit a horse van. I didn't want to look. The driver's cab of the van seemed to be completely crushed, and the police and ambulances were all around trying to extricate the man. All I could think of was the poor innocent horse. "Look! Over there!" Nini cried out. I opened my eyes and looked to my right, where off to the side of the road was a beautiful chestnut stallion. His rear right leg and hip seemed to be injured, and he couldn't put any weight on them. There was some blood down by his hoof. A man was holding the reins as they waited for help. I felt sick to my stomach. I have spent twenty years dealing with ill and injured human beings, but a suffering animal is almost more than I can bear. I wanted to jump out of the car and rush over to the horse but I didn't dare. I didn't want to frighten him, and with so many lines of traffic and so much commotion, it seemed dangerous. I suggested we send the horse healing. As we inched our way past this horrendous scene, I closed my eyes, opened my heart, and prayed for the horse's healing and anyone else injured in the accident. I imagined the horse surrounded by healing white light, and gently visualized pale blue light, used for pain relief and healing, flowing through his hip and leg. I called on the angels of animal healing, on St. Francis and Mary, on Jesus and Buddha and everyone I could think of, especially God. It took us about twenty minutes to get past the scene, and during this time Nini and I sent the horse healing. My eyes were filled with tears of compassion, and I didn't think I would be able to get through the rest of the day's festivities.

We got to the restaurant and greeted Nini's father and guests. The table was already full, so Nini and I took a small table to the side. We stared at each another knowing exactly what the other one was thinking. Nini voiced it first. She felt a strong connection with the horse during the healing. So did I. We would have to wait for the television news later that night to see the results. We had done all we could do. One of the most important rules of healing is that you do everything you know how to do, and detach from the results. It is in God's hands. We had lunch and went to the races. Mr. Gridley showed us to a wonderful box seat right by the finish line, and Nini and I settled in. I felt elegant in my long ivory dress, platform sandals, and a wide-brimmed hat loaned to me by Nini. I had never worn one before. I decided to test my intuitive abilities and make small two dollar bets on the horses I thought would win. This was a completely new experience for me, and I decided to have fun. There were nine races. I opened to the list of horses for the first race and my eyes immediately lighted on Toomuchpleasure. I squealed with delight. This had to be the winner! My rational mind looked over all the other horses for that race, but I knew which one I was betting on. I placed my two dollars. As I was waiting I read through the picks by two experts. My choice was not among any supposed to win. I had bet a long shot. That was fine with me. According to conventional thinking, my whole career as a spiritual healer was a long shot.

In the meantime I looked around. Thousands of people seated in dark green bleachers. Most woman had hats. Thank goodness no one wore white gloves anymore. Mr. Gridley introduced us to

✳

friends of his and we chatted. The air was electric with expectation. The gong sounded and we knew it was time for the first race.
We took our seats. We couldn't see the starting line from where we
sat, but we could watch it on television. The gun went off! As the
horses rounded the first bend and the names were called out, my
horse was not among them. But around the second bend! Here he
(she?) came! It was a short race and Toomuchpleasure won! First
place! Being as conservative as I am, I realized to my dismay that
I had not bet the horse to "win," but only to "show." My take was
only eight dollars. But that was all right. I was happy. When Mr.
Gridley heard I had bet on the correct horse and no one else, including himself, had done so, he was so impressed he made up the
difference between win and show. Later that day he would bet on
a long shot in another race, get us each a ticket for it, and we
would win almost two hundred dollars each! I bet on all nine races
that day, and I had a horse win, place, or show in each race.

I thought of my father that day. Not at the races, so much, but
later when a friend of Mr. Gridley's took us into the owner's circle
to see the horses before the race. His friend owned a filly, a beautiful horse who was not expected to win, but who would show that
day. It was a thrilling experience to see the beauty and power of
such sleek and elegant animals. I would have preferred to see them
out in the wild, running free. But I knew they were well cared for
and appreciated, and at least they would not be eaten by cougars.
I thought of the horse Nini and I had sent healing to, and wondered
what the result would be. Photos were taken and proud owners
looked over the competition.

At the end of the day we retired to the restaurant for drinks, hors
d'oeuvres and an assessment of the day's fun. And though tired
from a long, hot afternoon that reached into the nineties, we decided to go to the polo match, where a table was reserved for us. I
watched as the horses and riders seemed to float past with ele-
gance and precision, working together as one body. Primal animal
aggression, contained and focused on a goal—winning, of course.
The thundering hoofs, the smack of the wooden ball and mallets.

Nini and I went back to the house, satiated with an almost perfect day. We turned on the television and waited with trepidation as the eleven o'clock news began. Almost immediately they announced that they would be coming back with news of a "bizarre" accident involving a horse. We waited. Minutes went by and we could hardly stand the anxiety, trying to make small talk about the day. Finally, the newscaster told of a horse van and bus accident that had taken place that day. He said the driver of the van was in the hospital in guarded condition. The horse, which had been thrown eight feet into the air and landed on top of the bus, then fallen off, was fine. That was what was bizarre. The horse was fine. Nini let out a shout of "Yes!" My eyes filled with tears and I took a deep breath, thanking God and everyone who had participated in the healing. The horse was fine. My day was complete. No amount of money won at the track could have given me the feeling I went to bed with that night.

A week later Psyche arrived. I was a few minutes late getting to the office and my assistant had let them in. I walked into the kitchen to find a beautiful white and dark gray cat with green eyes crouched in the corner of the kitchen. Green eyes. I have green eyes. I knew we would get along. A short-haired, sleek, Egyptian looking cat. She reminded me of the cat with the gold earring in the Metropolitan Museum of Art in New York City, where I had worked for a few years after I graduated from college and traveled in Europe and the Mediterranean. Psyche had the same regal bearing.

I talked with her softly, telling her I would give her a good home. I had private sessions with patients that afternoon, so I kept her in the kitchen, where she had bowls of food and water and a litter box. At the end of the day I let her out to wander around and explore the office. She seemed quite curious and bold. I then took her home, where she seemed to adjust almost immediately, eating well and drinking lots of water, something many cats avoid. The next morning I found her curled up at my feet on top of the down comforter. I met her green eyes with mine, and I knew we would be happy together.

I took her to a female vet that had been recommended to me.

She seemed to be healthy and about one month along in her pregnancy, which meant she had about a month to go. I had planned to spend ten days in Maine on vacation, a rest I desperately needed. I checked the calendar as to when I would be returning and when she was due to deliver. My inner intuitive voice said that both vets were wrong and she would probably deliver the week I was in Maine. I did not want her to be alone in a strange house delivering kittens. Even though everyone told me that cats are great mothers and usually have easy deliveries, I felt uncomfortable about abandoning her so soon after she had arrived. I canceled my trip to Maine.

Week by week she became rounder in the abdomen. She was underfed when I got her, and because most of what she ate probably went to the kittens' growth, she remained quite slim. She seemed content to be near me, and often curled up on top of my shoes in the bottom of the closet in my study. She wandered around the house, discovering new spots that seemed to promise safety and comfort for birthing. I found a cardboard box, just as the vet had suggested, and placed newspaper in it. She liked my shoes better, and I had a feeling she had already chosen her birthing location.

Sure enough, Psyche delivered a week early, at 1 A.M. on Sunday of Labor Day weekend. At about 10 P.M. she started getting very restless, roaming about the house, making a funny chirping sound in her throat. Even though it was a week early, I could sense that she would go into labor. I tried to sleep, but I lay there wide awake. She jumped on my bed and started circling and scratching. She never liked the birthing box I had made her. I turned on the light and saw her stomach contracting. I gently picked her up and put her on the floor, so she would not give birth on the bed. She went right for the bottom of my shoe closet. I had removed all the shoes, and now I put down several old towels, which she lay on. I sat by her side, softly talking with her. The contractions stopped for a while, and she seemed to settle down. I pulled the comforter off my bed and lay down next to her, knowing I was probably in for an all night delivery. I called the vet, and her service said she

*

was away. I felt as though I was trying to get a hold of a plumber in the middle of the night on a weekend. I contacted the emergency animal hospital just in case I needed help, and they gave me some advice about what to look for in case Psyche didn't take care of everything.

About 11:30 P.M. her contractions began again in earnest. I kept eye contact with her the entire time, and she did with me. It was a full hour and a half before the first kitten was born. The first breach seemed very painful and Psyche let out a cry. Newborn kittens are not the most attractive creatures in the world, looking a little like drowned mice. A friend of mine had scared me when she said that sometimes cats eat their young, and when Psyche started gnawing on something immediately after the kitten slipped out, I felt terror go through my body. "Don't eat her!" I cried out. She was, of course, chewing free the umbilical cord, but never having watched kittens being born, my anxiety got the better of me. I soon realized what was happening and calmed down as I watched the process of instinctual mothering take over. I watched in awe as Psyche licked her completely clean and the kitten took her first squeaky breath. Part of the vigorous licking is to stimulate the lungs and intestines, as well as to clean them off. Psyche licked her for a full hour and a half, until the most perfectly pale dove gray kitten emerged from beneath the slimy membrane. I watched for the placenta to emerge, which it did, and made the mistake of not turning my head away fast enough as Psyche ate it. I had watched the entire birth, but at this point had to get up, go into the bathroom and regurgitate whatever was still left in my stomach at 1:30 A.M. As Carl Jung wrote, there is no birth of consciousness without pain. He should have added that sometimes it is also a messy and nauseating process.

When I came back, the newborn kitten was starting to wiggle around, blind for the moment but instinctively searching out a nipple for milk. I was amazed as this tiny creature smaller than my hand sprang to life in front of my eyes. Psyche lay on her side, opening her belly for the kitten to feed. It took almost half an hour for her to find a nipple, but when she did, she eagerly started sucking for milk. Psyche seemed to relax. It is almost impossible to tell what sex newborn kittens are, but my intuition told me that the first one was a female. I hesitated to touch her, having read that many people handle newborn kittens much too soon and too often. They are so fragile that they need time to develop strength and to bond with their mother, just as human babies do. Neonatal intensive care units around the world are now monitoring closely how much handling newborns receive so as not to over stimulate their delicate nervous systems.

The first veterinarian in Queens had said he thought he felt three kittens in her belly, so I was expecting the birth of two more. I saw no more contractions, and my vet in Connecticut had warned me that, unlike many other animals, the mother cat can control her contractions and sometimes choose to do so. I lay awake almost all night waiting for the second kitten, stretched out on the comforter by Psyche's side. Finally, at 4 A.M. I got up and went to sleep in my own bed. At 7 A.M. I awakened to look in on the new mother and her first kitten. Mother and daughter were doing fine and I saw no further contractions in Psyche's belly. I sat and talked with her for a few minutes and then went to make my own breakfast.

All morning I kept checking on them in the closet, looking out for more contractions. There were none. By 10 A.M. I began to worry that something was wrong and called the emergency veterinary clinic—Sunday of Labor Day weekend. They told me that if she didn't give birth to another kitten by noon I would have to bring her to the clinic, an hour's drive from my house. I put down the phone and went upstairs. I knew moving her from the bottom of the closet would traumatize her. She looked so comfortable and content with the first kitten. I could definitely see that there were more kittens in her belly, however. I lay down by her side and talked with her. I told her how worried I was about the other kittens and that I wished she would give me a sign of kitten number two, so we wouldn't have to go to the clinic. She stared me straight in the eyes, and I was hit with the fact that I was a healer, and I wasn't using my healing abilities to help her. To this day I believe she relayed the message to me telepathically. I took a deep breath, closed my eyes, and dropped down into my heart. I let my heart open with love and concern for her well-being and prayed that God's will be done. I could feel my hands begin to get warm as my heart opened. I placed my right hand on her belly and lay there by her side. I could feel the deep warmth of healing energy transfer from my hand into her belly, and she seemed content to lie there soaking it up. I closed my eyes, as she did, we lay there together for several minutes. At a certain point I could feel that the healing was enough, and I slowly pulled my hand away, got up, and washed my hands. I sat and rested for a few minutes. When I got back to the closet I could see that her belly was beginning to contract. About half an hour later the second kitten was born, more quickly and easily than the first.

As with the first, she licked it off for over an hour. Instead of turning pale gray when it was dry, the second kitten stayed dark, a deep gray black with white underbelly, paws, and nose. It was a strange shade of gray black, and I admit I did not find the second kitten particularly attractive. It looked as though it had been rolling around in the cinders and ashes of the fireplace. It seemed smaller than the first. My intuition told me that it was a male, although it was too tiny to see anything, and I did not want to pick it up so soon after its birth. Psyche's belly looked fairly flat after the second kitten emerged, and when I used my intuition to tune in, I felt that there were no other kittens waiting to be born. After she had nursed both of them for several hours, she got up to drink some water and eat. I gently picked up the kittens and placed them on a clean towel at the bottom of the closet. Psyche sniffed the new towels with great suspicion when she came back, but she could see that her babies were safe and lay down by their side. I was amazed at how adroit she was in wrapping her body carefully around them so her nipples would be ready and waiting for their eager mouths. I watched with trepidation, wondering whether she would accidentally lie on them and suffocate them. I sat by ready to pull one out if necessary. Once or twice she did manage to lie on one while trying to avoid the other, but the kitten underneath would just wiggle its way out again and get right back in line for its feeding. The less interference from me the better. I was an observer, a student of Mother Nature at work bringing new life into the world.

I was also amazed at what a natural instinct Psyche had for motherhood. She was a good mother, carefully sniffing each new towel I put in the closet. When I realized that she wanted control over everything that went into that closet, I would let her sniff each towel first before I put it down. It had to pass her inspection. I was the only one she let handle the kittens. When my housekeeper and friends came to the house and tried to sneak a peak, she kept them at bay on the other side of the room by placing herself between the kittens and them. She sat in the middle of the floor and gave them a warning sound. She would only leave the closet to eat, drink, and relieve herself. All her time was spent taking care of her young.

I kept expecting more of a mess to clean up, as with puppies, but a few days after the birthing, I realized that Psyche was cleaning up after the kittens herself. There was nothing for me to do but provide fresh towels every other day and to make sure that Psyche always had fresh food, water, and a safe, quiet home. I was mesmerized by the process of such perfect mothering. I had spent twenty years as a healer, as many years doing my own psychotherapy and analysis, and was being given a living example of the best mothering I had ever seen right in front of my eyes. Psyche surrendered her body to the process. She knew exactly what the kittens needed and when. She didn't have any other job but this one. Not all animal mothers are so good. Some abandon their young, and it is true, some eat them if there are more than they can care for. Animals who are kept in zoos and have no former role models sometimes don't know what to do with their young when they are born. Most animals, like humans, are observational learners. But we all have encoded in our DNA the basic instinct to take care of, to mother, to protect, and to heal.

Of all the instinctive behavior I had witnessed with Psyche and her kittens, the most frightening happened once they were out of the closet. Several weeks later they crawled over the side of the towels and onto the floor for the first time. Psyche began to attack them, grabbing them by the throat, turning them on their side, and biting down until they squealed with fear or pain. At first I wanted to stop it. It was hard to listen to such plaintive cries. But I knew that she was teaching them submission to her as well as modeling attack and self-defense methods and that I should leave them alone. Over and over again, everyone would be playing, and then the attack would happen. Sometimes I had to walk out of the room. Sometimes the cry was so loud that it sounded as though the kitten was being murdered and I had to yell "Stop it!" because I couldn't tolerate any more. But I would observe the kittens either sit up or just lie there waiting. Instead of running away from their mother, they were ready for more.

This teaching of self-defense to the kittens made me realize just how poverty stricken my own childhood was when it came to learning any kind of aggression or self-protection. When I was two and my mother was still working, she had a friend of the family come to take care of me. Her name was Mardee. While she sat for me, I played with a little red-haired boy my age named Johnny. Years later Mardee would tell them that he would hit me, take my toys, and generally bully me. I would come to her in tears and her advice would be to go hit him back. This was a new concept to me, and apparently her good advice didn't get very far. My mother would come home and undo it by telling me never to hit another child, even in self-defense. I then became totally dependent on whatever adult was around to protect me, rather than learning to do it for myself. Such a simple thing as this imprinted my entire life.

I never learned to protect myself from negative energy and hostility until I became a healer and realized how much pain and suffering I was absorbing from others. As discussed in previous chapters, I developed "Psychic Self-Defense." But the blessing of the kittens and their training ground in my home placed the concept of aggression and self-defense in a new context. I realized how utterly dependent we are on the parents and adults around us to teach us how to cope with life. We are not born prepared. If the people around us have not developed adequate coping skills, they teach us inadequate ones. We then experience failure in our ability to feed, nurture, and protect ourselves. Basic instincts for survival. Basic mothering instincts if we are taking care of someone else; self-mothering instincts if we are trying to mother ourselves.

One of my training students presented a case study of her client to her classmates. She told of a woman in her thirties who had been having constant uterine bleeding for the past two years. She had been to doctors and had tried medication, but to no avail. The woman had been in psychoanalysis for ten years and was a massage client of my student for over four years. The bleeding had started when she entered into a relationship with a man for the first time. There were very few details of her childhood, since my student knew she was in therapy, and the woman was reticent to discuss it with her. Several times she had broached the subject and had been rebuffed. What we did learn, however, was that the patient had decided to try to lose weight when she entered into the relationship with her boyfriend. She went about this by eating three frozen Weight Watcher's meals a day and, thinking that would be enough to lose weight, stopped all exercise. My student had suggested to her that she wasn't getting adequate nutrition and needed some exercise, but she had refused to consider that possibility. She was openly hostile to considering any kind of relationship between her body and her emotions, and when my student questioned how angry she seemed, she denied it. She sucked on ice chips all day long, despite the fact that she was always cold and covered herself in blankets even while sitting around the house. When my student took her though a "Communicating with Your Body" meditation, having her get in touch with her uterus, the woman felt "empowered." It was the first time she had ever related to her uterus.

My immediate internal response to this case presentation was What kind of mothering did this woman have? She didn't know how to feed herself. Instead of preparing healthy fresh food for herself, she relied on preprepared, processed food, or "instant breast," as I call it. She had no aggressive energy, which is what one needs to exercise. And in analytic work, ice is the "negative mother," Demeter's grieving at Persephone's being stolen away by Hades, after which she left the world with no warmth, fertility, or abundance. This woman was in deep cold and keeping herself there with more icy food and ice chips. What was she trying to stay in touch with by keeping herself frozen? What was she trying to stay *out of touch with?* Both issues are always involved. The ego is trying to suppress something that is about to overwhelm it, yet the soul chooses just the right symptoms to make sure that the real key to healing is not lost forever.

She had never been with a man until her thirties. Very unusual in this day and age. Not married, no children. I wondered silently whether she had been sexually abused by a man in her childhood. Or was she a lesbian? In the tradition of acupuncture and Chinese medicine, all the ice and icy food had led to her losing all her heat, her blood, her female energy. But blood is also sexuality, passion; and chewing hard ice is an aggressive act. It seemed that an old emotional wound had gotten triggered in this woman as soon as she entered into this relationship and the bleeding was a result of this trauma. Most likely the bleeding was also the way that this woman was protecting herself against being "violated" sexually by the boyfriend. As one of my faculty pointed out, it is very difficult to have sex if you are constantly bleeding. What did the bleeding symbolize? If she had been violated in childhood and had no means of protecting herself, the relationship could have triggered her body's memory of this trauma. Her body and soul were bleeding as a result of this trauma, as well as a protection against its perceived recurrence.

My student had recently begun to use laying-on-of-hands along with the massage and had focused on moving energy with her hands through the woman's spleen and liver meridians. In Chinese medicine these energy lines participate in blood formation. She was improving and had her first normal menstrual cycle in two years. In addition, she and her boyfriend had broken up. I imagined that the healing, combined with the dissolution of the relationship, had taken the stress off the old psychological wound,

*

allowing her body to heal and balance again. My student was providing good mothering for her in the form of feeding her healthy, whole energy, and being compassionate. Her body was soaking it in, responding to it as nourishment, and using it to create hormonal balance and healing. Unfortunately, unless the childhood wound that had gotten retriggered by the relationship was being addressed in analysis, it might get repressed again until someone or something else came along, and then reemerge. I wondered what was happening in this woman's analysis that, after ten years, she was still incapable of feeding herself more than instant breast and that she was so out of touch with the relationship between her body and her emotions. But it was not our position to challenge her therapy, and we probably would have put her into a conflict of loyalties between the therapist and the healer.

If my intuitive diagnosis was correct, this woman represents what so many women and men suffer as a result of not learning good self-mothering. Unlike Psyche and the kittens, this woman was not taught to feed herself, nurture herself, and protect herself. She had repressed her aggressive instincts and was trying to starve herself into a shape she thought a man would find pleasing. Underneath, especially if she was abused as a child, she was repressing tremendous fear and anger. She was out of touch with her past, her anger, her connection between her body and her soul, her psychology. Psychology comes from the Greek *psyche,* soul and *-ology,* knowing. A knowing of soul, she didn't have.

Animals learn healthy mothering in two ways: instinct and observational learning. What they observe their mothers doing, as well as what they experience their mothers doing to them, gets imprinted in their brain and memory. As far as we know, they don't think through their lives from a conceptual position, as human beings do. They don't talk themselves into and out of instinctual feelings and behavior because they have been told by an adult that these are "good" or "bad," and they will be good or bad children if they feel or do such things. Domestic animals can be trained somewhat to be aware of trying to please their owners. All animals are different, however. Cats are only slightly trainable, tending to remain more wild than domestic dogs. This means that they don't sublimate or suppress their needs and instincts for the wishes of others. If you try to pick up a cat that doesn't want to be picked up, it will struggle out of your arms unless overpowered. Pull on a cat's ears, it will pull away from you, or you will get bitten. If a toddler is pulling on a dog's ears, many dogs will allow the discomfort, knowing that the child is harmless, and wanting to please the owner.

As children we are taught to please our parents. We are taught to be submissive to our parents, just like dogs and wolves in a pack. But, unlike those animals, we are taught to ignore our basic wild instinctual nature. Screaming, crying, running, destroying things, eating, laughing, loving, being happy, exploring. As children we react instantly to things and people unless taught to ignore those reactions and to please our parents or another dominant adult. If we are being physically, sexually, or emotionally abused, the dominant adult teaches us to ignore our feelings of pain and to submit to what the adult wants. In school we are taught to be submissive to the teacher and to the school system; in a job we are taught to be submissive to our boss and to the organization; in a marriage we are taught to repress our personal needs and desires for the good of the marriage.

A certain amount of containment is necessary to produce a healthy adult. If we all did exactly what we felt at any one moment, there would be a lot more murder, uninhibited sex, unwanted children, and suffering in the world. But containment does not mean repression of awareness or action. If a child grows up with an alcoholic mother and is taught to ignore her own needs in order to care for her mother, the child may grow up to be an adult who looks to be a caring, giving individual. She may get along well in society, be a skilled organizer, and make someone a terrific marriage partner. At some point, however, this woman will wake up to the fact that she is suffering internally, deep down where her wild, instinctual, creative nature exists. She will realize that she doesn't live for herself and has no life of her own. She is what is popularly called "co-dependent," living out her needs by projecting them onto other people and taking care of them. She may be so busy feeding others that she doesn't even eat in a healthful way. Her rage will come bubbling to the surface, and she may want to destroy everything she has created: her marriage, her job, her old self. To go about destroying these areas of her life through having an affair, quitting her job, or trying to slash her wrists, is acting out the homicidal and suicidal rage. Containment means that this woman will allow herself to feel her rage, her desire to destroy everything and everyone, rather than to repress it as she has done in the past. She will ask for help and support from someone qualified so she can be fed, given to, mothered. She will contain her feelings by building herself a strong ego, a strong self-mothering nature, a true sense of self-worth. She will express her feelings to people who need to know and will allow these honest feelings to give her the fuel to build a new life, eat properly, and live for herself. One of my students has done these things, having come from just such a background.

One of the greatest barriers to creating a new life is the desire to make all the instinctual, wild needs within us go away. Another female student of mine, who also grew up with an alcoholic mother, is still struggling with those needs. She told me that she had a frightening nightmare. She woke up in the middle of the night hitting her bed with a pillow. She had dreamed that there were two or three "fuzzy, round yellow things with feet" jumping in bed with her. They felt "evil" and "out to get her." She just wanted them "to get away from me and leave me alone." I asked her what had happened that day. She told me that it had been a very difficult day at work for her. She works in a hospital taking care of ill and frightened people. That day she had worked thirteen hours. Many patients had been jumping at her with their needs, trying to devour her, just like the yellow fuzzies in her dream. She had spent the entire day trying to fill other people's needs, trying to feed their hunger and ease their suffering. I asked how she had attempted to protect herself from being overwhelmed. She hadn't. She said she usually takes a shower when she gets home from work, but she hadn't even done that. She was too tired. I reminded her of the

"Psychic Self-Defense" techniques I had taught her: shower when you get home from work to get everyone's energy off your body; place your clothes in a place where they can air out, not in your bedroom where you sleep; eat something nutritious; and meditate before sleep, allowing the energy of each person you have encountered during the day to be released from your body. The next morning, surround yourself with a golden ball of light in your meditation session, so that you will be energetically protected when you go into work. Eat well during the day, and take several rest breaks, going outside for fresh air.

I asked what she had eaten that day: a grilled cheese sandwich for lunch and a bowl of pudding for dinner. Both bought from the cafeteria at the hospital. She is allergic to milk products and reacts badly to sugar. I asked why she had eaten so poorly. She said she didn't have time to eat better, and all the other food in the cafeteria is inedible. I told her it would have taken less time away from her job if she had taken some nuts, whole grain crackers, fruit, and instant soup with her and kept them in her desk or purse. She agreed grudgingly. So time was not really the factor. People use time as an excuse for bad self-mothering. It probably took more time for her to get up from her desk, go to the cafeteria, purchase comfort foods that mimic mother's milk like pudding and grilled cheese and get back to her desk, than it would have to bring food with her from home. It is part of her not wanting to pay attention to her own needs. I pointed out to her that she spends her day taking care of other people's needs and ignores her own. The "yellow fuzzy things with feet" are very uncontrolled, primitive, childlike images. They are her needs. Yellow is the color of the third chakra, the stomach and digestive system, and the will, motivation and vitality energies. The feet are grounding, first chakra survival and security. I suggested to her that they *were* out to get her: out to get her to pay attention to her stomach, her security, and her will to take care of the starving child within her. She said she wished those needs and that child "would just go away." I asked her if her mother ever felt that way about her. "All the time," she replied. That's why her mother abandoned her and her brother and sister, three children, to their grandmother and left, to die later of alcoholism.

I suggested to her that she needs to stay in touch with the fact that she is carrying around inside her a two-year-old child who needs her, is very hungry physically and emotionally, and will not disappear. By feeling that she wants this child and her needs to "just go away," she is acting toward herself the way her mother acted toward her. She was stunned at the analogy. I suggested that she needs to stop abandoning herself and her needs and learn to be a good mother to that small child within her. She said she would try.

I drove home that afternoon and thought about my two women friends in real estate. One day we had gone to look at houses late in the afternoon. Neither of them had eaten lunch, and one had not eaten breakfast. I suggested we stop so they could eat, but they refused. The latter was sitting in the back-seat popping glucose tablets as a way of leveling her blood sugar. I tasted one. It made me dizzy—pure fructose. When I asked why neither had eaten, they both replied that they were too busy with work. They are both mothers with children; or, should I say, both starving children with children. No mother to be found. A motherless culture. I went home and ate dinner.

✳

10
Home

He was howling and barking and whimpering. A small white wolf of fur sitting in a wooden playpen, alone. I felt an immediate connection. I walked over to the box and knelt down at the other end. In a low sweet voice I began to tell him "It's okay. You're all right. You're safe." He stopped and looked over at me. For a moment we just sat there staring, our eyes locked in some kind of recognition. He walked over and sat next to me. I reached my left hand into the box and gently stroked his neck as he looked up into my eyes with his head back. I fell in love.

A half-dozen children crashed into the pet store and over to our box. They started oohing and aahing and reaching out to pet him. I got up and went over to the cat litter. He looked back at me for a second before being overwhelmed by the children. I was in the store twenty minutes and the entire time he remained quiet, even after the children left. I took my cat litter and food out to the car after giving him a few strokes. I sat in the car ready to leave and I couldn't. I walked back into the store and asked the girl at the desk what kind of dog he was. A white German shepherd. I had never seen one before. Male, ten weeks old. I asked where he was from, who the breeder was. Amish. He was from an Amish breeder in

Pennsylvania. My father grew up in Amish country, Lancaster County, Pennsylvania. One of those moments when you're struck by the coincidence, or synchronicity as Carl Jung would say.

When I wanted my first dog as a child, at the age of ten, my father said there were two kinds I could not have: a German shepherd and a Doberman pinscher. My father had trained and bred horses in the army during World War II in Pomona, California, and had worked with both breeds. A Doberman had turned on him once, almost taking off his arm. He was afraid that both breeds were too vicious, too unpredictable, too dangerous. We settled on a Weimaraner, a German hunting dog, similar in looks to a Lab.

I left the store and went home. I couldn't believe I was thinking of buying a dog. I could barely cope with three cats. How could I take care of him? Who would tend to his needs when I was traveling? Would the cats and the dog get along? I must be crazy. I called the pet store and spoke to the owner. I asked about puppy mills. He assured me they only used a broker who went around to individual breeders and picked out the best dogs. Six times a year he went and looked at the breeders himself. I told him I needed the weekend to think about it. I would put down a deposit for the dog and be willing to lose it if I didn't take him. He agreed and we decided I would call by noon on Monday.

I couldn't get this dog out of my mind. All day, all night I thought about this dog. I didn't know what to do. I did not want to buy him on impulse. I wanted to give this animal the best possible home or let someone else take him. He deserved that. I did not want to buy him and then abandon him. When my rational mind gave out, which is always a blessing, I meditated. I closed my eyes and went into my breathing, and then into my heart. I burst into tears. All the losses of my other dogs came back. Especially Zeke. Poor Zeke. Abandoned twice. I hadn't been able to take care of myself adequately, much less an animal. Such desperation, such suffering at the end of a marriage. All I could do was run for cover and nurse my wounds. Like a wolf in a den, in the dark, waiting to heal. Ah yes. A wolf. The classic archetype of wild hunger and gold eyes. Several years before I had had a dream of a wolf asleep in a suitcase. I kept looking for signs of life on its body, even a tiny parasite. I could find none. Finally my inner wild wolf was waking up and feeling hungry. Primal animal strength, beauty, hunger, instinctive life force. Life with a bite.

I let myself feel my loss, grief, and suffering. I mourned not only for Zeke but also for myself, for my own inner animal, for my own inner unmet dependency needs of hunger, attention, care, trust, intimacy, and love; for the loss of innocence, freedom, and home. All the things that I thought I was finished mourning for, this dog aroused in me. I realized that life is nonlinear that it keeps spiraling back on itself, touching deeper and deeper levels of insight and meaning, experience, and love. I had thought I might save this dog from his abandonment, howling in that lonely wooden box. I didn't expect him to save me from mine. What a surprise.

The next day I went back to look at him again. The young woman in the store put him in the playpen with a rottweiler and the two of them tumbled around, growling and playing like dogs in the wild. They reminded me of my two kittens and how they appear to be killing each other while playing. At one point she removed the rottweiler from the pen so the shepard could focus his attention on me. Like the day before, he stared up at me and we began to bond. I talked to him gently, stroking his neck and back. I asked him if he wanted to come home with me. As psychic as I am, I couldn't tell his answer. I was too anxious. I left the store. After I returned home I called them and asked for his papers to be faxed to me. His father is Frosty Hansen; his mother, Sheba's Winter White. I called information for the number of the breeder—unpublished. I called the store and got the broker's number. He said the Amish didn't have phones and he always had to write. The shepard had been examined by two veterinarians, had his shots, and had been dewormed. He was all set to go.

Sunday night I went back a third time to look at him and brought him home. I couldn't wait until Monday at noon. The kittens had never seen a dog before, but I was sure Psyche had. She pretended to be friendly and curious, walking right up to his nose.

In a flash she hissed and swiped at his face with her claws. She just caught the side of his face, but drew no blood. He yelped in fear and pain and began to tremble all over. I carried him upstairs to my study, where he could be near me all night, and shut out the cats. Not a good welcome to his new home.

I left him on his bed for a few minutes to get newspapers and his food and water, and by the time I came back he had all already messed the floor in my study. I told him it was all right and petted him gently. I spent some time talking with him and gently stroking him. When puppies are excited they nip, bite, and chew. I had forgotten how much. He started nipping my hands, my pants leg, my shirt. Anything he could reach. He wanted to play. He was wagging his tail and seemed happy to have someone all to himself. I tried to get him to play with his toys, but my body seemed more appealing to him. Maybe he wanted to taste his adoptive mother. Like all babies, everything goes in the mouth. I played with him a little, hoping to tire him out. He tired me out. When I left the room again, he started to whine pathetically, desperately trying to get into the bedroom up and over the top of the treadmill. The possibility of abandonment was too much for him. I decided the only way to get him to calm down was to go in and lie down on his bed with him, which I did. I curled up around him and placed my arm and hand over him for weight, knowing that body warmth and heartbeat were what he was used to when he was with his other eight brothers and sisters all lying on top of one another. He closed his eyes and went to sleep immediately. I lay there cradling my new baby in my arms and filling him with healing and love. I was exhausted. About half an hour later I began to drift into sleep and decided to see if I could get up without waking him. I grabbed a large heavy beach towel and placed it over his small body so he would still feel weight on him and think I was there. I got up and went to sleep for two hours.

Every two hours I awoke. Was he all right? He was asleep. I was awake. What had I done? What would happen in the morning with the cats? I would have to carry him downstairs and out the front door for him to go outside, which is exactly what I did when he awoke at 4 A.M. I carried him up and downstairs every few hours for the next twenty-four hours until I could barely do it again. I called the vet and got her advice, which was to place him in the kitchen, put up child gates across the doorway, and relegate the cats to the living room. I moved all the cat paraphernalia out of the kitchen, and all of his possessions into it. This way I could take him out the kitchen door to the outside. I would only have to carry him down four front steps until he could manage for himself. Psyche took a few more swipes at him when he put his nose close to the gate to smell her. Cinder, the male kitten, seemed quite curious right from the start and sat on the other side of the gate and stared. Pearl wanted nothing to do with him.

The veterinarian also told me that in the wild, dogs and wolves have an order of dominance and submission. There is one male and one female who are dominant, while the others and the younger ones are submissive. Among them, there is also a pecking order, and they fight among themselves to take their position. One training theory is to make sure the new puppy never gets into a dominant position in the household, controlling everyone and everything that happens. The pamphlet the vet gave me stated that the owner should always be louder and more assertive than the dog when dealing with unacceptable behavior. I began to understand male testosterone poisoning, as some women call male dominance. The louder and more aggressive a show you put on, the more dominance you exhibit.

Thinking that the more time and attention I gave the new puppy, the happier he would be, I let him out of the kitchen and into the rest of the downstairs living room with me in the evening. He lay on the floor next to the couch while I enjoyed a fire roaring. I loved this aspect, nice and quiet, gentle and affectionate. But after a couple of hours, he would, of course, rouse himself and want to play. He would run around looking for something, anything, that he had not yet destroyed and try to chew it up. Something new was the most fascinating, forsaking his already familiar toys for anything else he could sink his teeth into. My hands. My clothes. Magazines, mail, my coffee table. Not wanting to be as punishing and angry as I remember my father being at times with me and the dogs I had as a child, I tried to be patient and understanding, gentle and firm with him. Over and over again, I would take things out of his mouth, tell him no, and replace it with a hard chew bone.

He took over. Given a taste of freedom from the kitchen, he ran rampant. In addition to chewing everything in sight, he followed whenever I left the room. If I went upstairs to get something, he would sit at the bottom of the stairs, too steep and slippery to climb, and bark and whimper until I reappeared. His abandonment fear was intense. I couldn't get anything done. The vet told me to crate him or keep him in the kitchen, no matter how much noise he made. I put him in his crate and stayed in the room with him, cleaning up the kitchen where he could see me. As I knelt to turn the spring locks on the gate, he came right up to my left ear and barked loudly. It almost knocked me over. My ear rang and then went numb. Pain. That was it. I shouted back at him "Quiet!" Stunned by the loudness of my voice and the anger in it, he stopped barking and sat down. He looked at me with his big brown-black eyes as if to say, "Wow! I didn't know you could be so dominant!" I was amazed as well, and realized that I had been too lenient with him, too understanding of his abandonment fears, maybe even identifying with them. I had thought he was afraid, needy, just like a child. But I had forgotten that, just like a child, he needed to trust that I could create safety for both of us. And if I was so worn out that I couldn't get anything else done but pay attention to him, I was not creating a safe, contained environment for either of us.

I also realized that I had placed my own need for company, for a companion, before his need for training. He was not yet good companion material. He was only twelve weeks old. I had let my own dependency needs interfere with his. Not a perfect mother. I would have to start over again. Safety and love always come first. If I had let his dominance control my life, it eventually would have led to such resentment and hostility in me, triggering my inner "bad mother" complex, that I would not have been able to treat him with love, care, and patience. I might even have wanted to get rid of him, abandon him, give him away, like the poor twelve-week-old black Lab I saw the notice for in the vet's office. The family had decided they couldn't cope with him and wanted to get rid of him. Only 35 percent of all dogs end their lives with their original owners. The rest are abandoned, sold, given away, or destroyed. It is a crime against life and love. It is the crime of the bad mother. I knew for the healing of my own inner mother complex and for the integrity of my heart and soul that I had made a lifelong commitment of love to Star. I had chosen him. I would have to choose him in all my actions. I would have to create a life of love, healing, and safety for him. I could not save all the dogs in the world, but I could save him—and myself.

For weeks I went through evenings of Star's trying to chew and shred everything in sight. It was a battle trying to get him to behave. One evening I finally gave up. I let him run around the living room and play with everything he could sink his teeth into: Kleenex boxes, boots, newspapers. Two hours later he calmed down. After going outside for a few minutes, he came back in and climbed up on the couch next to me. He had never done this before. He nudged his way between the couch back and my right side and lay down with his head on my shoulder, looking up into my eyes. I told him he was a good boy and stroked his head and neck. I closed my eyes and drifted into a light sleep. Heaven. When I awoke it was after midnight and he was lying on top of my feet at the bottom of the couch. I smiled. Bonding. This puppy had driven me out of my mind for a full month, when all I wanted was gentle affection and companionship. After two hours of expressing his wild aggression, he was ready to cuddle. I cringed to think of how I had been trying to suppress his activity, thinking it was too wild, too destructive. This dog didn't have a behavior problem. I did. My behavior hadn't been meeting his needs. I realized that he was a high-energy, assertive dog who needed more exercise and opportunity to play, more appropriately, outside. He needed more chance to bite into every new thing to come his way and taste it. More opportunity to be wild with life.

The next morning I awoke at 6 A.M. and took him out of his

crate, where he slept. He immediately went outside. It had gotten warmer during the night. When we came back in the kitchen I fixed myself some breakfast with no disturbance from him. He lay quietly looking at me. No jumping. No nipping. No barking. I took him out to play. I threw his ball over and over again, and he raced to get it and bring it back to me. After close to an hour of hard play, for the first time he came back in the house, lay down, and was completely calm and quiet for three hours while I was upstairs writing. I went into the kitchen several times to get some coffee and a second breakfast, and he just lay there dozing, looking up at me and then falling asleep again. Quiet. Time. Peace. This was a miracle.

When my morning writing was finished, I came down to the kitchen to find him chewing on one of my boots. In a soft gentle voice I looked him straight in the eyes and said: "Be gentle with that boot. I like it." He looked at me as though he understood and dropped the boot from his mouth. He left it on the floor and didn't pick it up again. I couldn't believe my eyes. This was a new dog. He walked over to the door and, for the first time, motioned to me that he wanted to go out. I opened the door and he walked out by himself. This was a first. For four weeks I had had to put on my coat, gloves, and boots and stand outside with him. He had never gone outside on his own before. All day he did this, exploring all around the perimeter of the yard. I watched him from my second-story window. It was as though he had grown leaps and bounds in his development from one evening of wild freedom. It made me wonder about human children: how we try to get them to fit into what is comfortable for us, so they will grow up to be "well adjusted." What is well adjusted for one child may be dysfunctional for another. What appears to be wildly destructive behavior for a puppy, may just be his wolf nature testing his strength.

Chaos is the elephant in the room. The one thing that we spend our lives defending against. We want to build a safe protected predictable life that never catches us unprepared. We want a full breast all the time, at our beck and call, the way it should be when we are newborn and needy and dependent. We want to test our strength and find it up to the task of life. Unlike the mountain climber who hangs without his safety rope off the edge of the sharpest rock thousands of feet above the ground and knows that he could die at any moment. We want to know we won't. We want to be in control of our lives and know that even our biggest risks are safe. That we have mastered this game of life and won. Everything around us is a construct of just this wish. And when this wish is threatened, all hell breaks loose. When the perfect marriage and family fall apart, people reach for guns and knives and words that are as lethal to the heart. When the stock market crashes and we lose the game of money, people jump out of buildings or run for other countries. When the pain of life is perceived as becoming too much to bear, people try to control the one thing they can—death: when, how, and where.

We will do anything to place our universe in an order we can understand. We blame others for our emotional pain, our bodies for betraying us, our government for letting us down. We perceive other people's religions as wrong, ours as righteous. We call other countries Satan, and creatures from other planets alien. We construct belief systems and ways of perceiving our world that keep us separate from anyone or anything that threatens to throw our personal world into chaos. All the time shifting the blame onto others, we want them to be the ones to fix what is wrong with our world.

If, as the field of psychology tells us, one of the measurements of mental health is the ability to tolerate anxiety, and if anxiety develops from confronting chaos over and over again, then the basis of spiritual health must be the ability to face the dark void of chaos, breathe in patience, sit with love in our hearts, and wait for Creation to form a seed of light to show us the way. We need to realize that we are in a perpetual state of being and becoming, constancy and flux, as is every other living creature and every other galaxy. Within the dark chaos, there are many lights in the process of formation, shooting colors into thin air, whether our eyes perceive them or not. We are in a pregnant womb, dark and rich with fertility. Just because we cannot perceive where the next cell is going to form does not mean life is without meaning or creative plan. The most horrendous calamities may be the most saving of graces bringing untold treasure into heart and soul. I will always remember one of my patients telling me that her illness saved her life. New life out of perceived chaos, feared death. It is only suffering. Just suffering. A gift in wolf's clothing. A treasure with teeth. And if, in the end, it is only chaos and all the love and care we have given over to our lives has no plan or meaning, then how rich a tapestry we have woven in the midst of dark nothingness. How deep a peace we have been willing to create from chaos.

* * *

Journal Entry, mid-November

The first heavy snow of the season. Six inches of deep brightness. Star is confused at first step into this cold white fluff. He puts his nose down, sniffs its chill up into his nostrils, and snorts. I walk down the steps in front of him so he can see he is safe, and tentatively, step by careful step, he sinks his paws down into the snow. Once down safely on the ground he surprises me by tunneling through the snow with his nose. Once he realizes that the snow is compliant to his play, he runs around and around in circles of flying sparkles, joyfully enticing me to follow. I run down the back field with him at my heels.

I shift realities for a moment and I am back in my childhood with my dog Heidi, playing in the snow. We run and run and don't get tired, glad to be alive and young. Play. I am playing. Star and I run around the perimeter of my half acre. The snow is up higher than his belly and he looks to me to tell him this engulfing white ocean is safe. Every time I tell him "good boy" he runs farther ahead, wagging his tail and dancing in circles. I feel fully alive. All my senses, all my muscles, nerves and organs. I breathe in cold crisp air into my lungs. I feel the wet chill of snow getting down my boot. There is nothing else in my life right now except this moment of joy. I race Star up the front of the property and down again. I am flying on two legs. I am a child. I hear myself

*

giggling and squealing with delight, like a toddler who has dis-covered living out loud. I am all the children who have ever played in the snow with their puppies. I lie down in the snow and make an angel.

We run four times around the property and back to the front door. I kick the snow off my boots and open the door. Star's small body is covered with snow and I dry him off with a towel and give him his favorite treat, a pig's ear. It is a smelly, hard piece of dark brown fat. When the pet store gave him one I asked what it was made of. The girl at the counter looked at me askance to check my reaction, and then admitted that it is actually a pig's ear. I guess it is better than him catching a live pig and eating it. Better for me.

I walk upstairs to my study and look out the window with my favorite view. It stretches out across the back of my property, which slopes gently downhill to a back field and forest line of maples and pines. They are blanketed in pure white, the dark brown and green etching a beautiful contrast to the snow. The shrubs and tall grasses in the field poke themselves up through the blanket. The one pine tree, a one foot baby when I first moved into the house, is now ten feet high and its arms cradling heavy white powder, just waiting for Christmas lights. I had thought of moving that tree, since it will eventually block some of my view of the back meadow, but now I see it as a perfect Tree of Life, waiting to remind me of how precious each and every tree is to our planet.

I wonder if the people of Bosnia have snow today. I wonder if they see it in the same way as I am doing right now. I wonder if the children play and feel joy. I wonder how many children are left. What is it, I think, that makes men run red blood through the joy of white snow and try to grasp another piece of dirt to call their own, when God exists within their soul. If only they would direct their quest within and eat of the fruits of their own inner Tree of Life, no one's soul would starve. The promised land is not a neigh-bor's piece of property. It is not something to capture with bullets and rage. It is something to find with peace and patience. Such courage it would take for freedom fighters to wait for a tree to grow inside their hearts.

Across the long view to my left I can see for several miles. The animal farm where elephants greeted me with their sounds when I first moved in. The rolling hills in the distance, with a small red farmhouse on top and a pure white field to their left. At times I have thought my house too small, too old, too run down, too much work. I have imagined someday being able to afford something grander. A black raven cuts the gray sky with its flight. To my right is the back of my neighbor's field, which she has mown for hay every summer, and where foxes play. I let my eyes scan across this expanse of pristine peace. I take it in with my soul and breathe it in with my heart. At this moment there is no more perfect view in the world. There is no place on earth I would rather be. I am home.

✳

11
Revolution

A revolution within the stone that Peter laid. Marble Collegiate Church in New York City invited me to speak on healing during Lent, and the following year to lead the first laying-on-of-hands healing service given in the church. Healing seems to be in the tradition of this church, founded in 1628 and known throughout the world as the church of Norman Vincent Peale, who was its minister from 1932 to 1984. Emotional, mental, and soul healing had always been given attention. Now they had invited a hands-on healer into their midst, and a lay person at that. Quite a risk.

I had always prayed that laying-on-of-hands would come back into the Christian churches. In the Four Gospels of the New Testament, there are over seventy instances of Jesus' doing healing through his touch or word. When I did my master's thesis in Pastoral Counseling, I described the interconnections between pastoral counseling and the healing work I had already been doing for ten years. I talked about the relationship of the soul and the body and how the churches had decided to focus only on the soul, losing touch with the command to "Go forth and heal." If Jesus had done laying-on-of-hands, I could not understand why the Church had lost the tradition.

I remember having dinner with a friend of mine and her boyfriend, a former priest. My friend had wanted him to meet me, thinking he would be interested in what I did. He was polite, but incredulous. I'll never forget his asking, after an interminable pause in the conversation at his turn to speak, "Do you really believe that God comes into physical form to heal?" I was stunned. Of course I did. Didn't he? Wasn't that the message of the New Testament? Jesus as God in physical form come to heal us. He never answered definitively in the negative, but I could see from the pain on his face and the tone in his voice that he did not. He then asked whether I really believed that I could heal. Yes, of course. Everyone can heal if they open themselves to God's presence. His head hung, he stared at the dining table for a long time. It was obvious to me that he did not believe he had the power to heal. In that moment I knew why he had left the priesthood. He had not seen any evidence of God's healing presence in the world, and he had obviously not experienced it in his own body and life. I felt sorry for him. A person without a living God inside is dead to Life.

It stunned me that someone steeped in the message of the New Testament would believe that God no longer exists as a living presence, a healing presence. I wondered how many more priests, ministers, and clergy of all denominations had entered the Church trying to find a living God for themselves, not because they had already discovered God and wanted to share the discovery. I wondered how many had failed.

When my mother was in the hospital with a life-threatening infection, taking antibiotics and hooked up to intravenous fluids, the hospital chaplain came in to comfort her. I was there at the time, fortunately. He had a cold and was obviously not feeling well. This was someone my mother knew from years of working at this hospital, so I tried to be friendly. But the protective mother instinct in me wanted to usher him out as soon as he came in the door. I was incensed that he would bring new germs into the room of someone trying to recover from a serious illness. He sat at the foot of the bed and they talked of her condition for a few minutes. He then asked her if she went to church. She had, for a long time, but told him that she had a rich spiritual life, which she practiced on her own. He proceeded to give her the party line about coming to church. I began to get angry. He kept coughing and blowing his nose. I couldn't stand it any more. I confronted him about his cold and suggested that he should be home in bed taking care of himself. He said that yes, he should, but he had many patients to see and to comfort. The steam started coming out of my ears. I told him that he was exposing my mother to his cold and endangering her well-being. I told him that the best way to be a healer was to take care of himself first. He looked at me with a stunned expression. This thought had obviously never occurred to him. My mother explained to him that I practiced spiritual healing. I told him that we would send him healing for his cold. He responded that he didn't believe in healing. I looked straight into this man's eyes and knew what I had to do: "A hospital chaplain who doesn't believe in healing? Why are you in the ministry?" His jaw fell open. He tried to weasel his way out of it. But he had said it. He didn't believe. He left. The following week, fully recovered from his cold, he came into my mother's room and apologized to her for his behavior. He said he had done a lot of soul searching after he left us. I had done my job. Protected my mother and helped him wake up. Maybe even helped awaken the healer within him.

I believe that the real value of religion, and any religious tradition, is to help its followers wake up to the living presence of God within. The goal of a healer is the same: awaken the healer within the other person. What is so extraordinary about the job, is that to be a healer means to become healed. The healing is never one way. We experience being healed in the process of healing others. Buddha experienced his own enlightenment while sitting under the Bodhi tree, the Tree of Life, and helping others. Jesus lived out his own journey of exploration, death, and resurrection, while calling to him followers who heard a message of love as the only law and experienced it through his touch and teachings. Mother

Teresa has evolved her soul in the process of giving service to the dying. Thich Nhat Hanh has found inner peace from years of torture in Vietnam while teaching a message of peace to others.

True service is a deep religious experience. And experience is sacred. It is a transformative process that is new at every moment. Everyone who is learning the practice of self-love and self-healing, while giving service to ease the suffering of others, is a spiritual healer. It does not matter whether we practice on our own or within a church or temple. It does matter, however, that we follow our inner guidance, our direct connection with God, rather than rules and laws laid down by other people. Mystics from all religious traditions, Eastern and Western, tell us that the healing of one's soul is like taking God as a lover. Allowing the inner experience of union with God to provide the healing. Any actions that come out of this union will be true, loving, and healing. If one has lost or never had this connection, religious rules can be helpful in building a life that simulates a spiritual life. But we still need to find heart, to find the soul of love.

I was thrilled and more than a little nervous to be invited to speak in a church. I had always wondered what my connection to conventional religion might be. I felt like an outsider practicing the laying-on-of-hands on my own. When people asked me what church I was affiliated with, I tried to be as tactful as possible in telling them that I had a private practice and was open to working with people of all religious backgrounds. Several years before, I had met the Episcopal priest and author Morton Kelsey at a retreat. I had read a number of his books such as *Healing and Christianity; God, Dreams, and Revelation; Companions on the Inner Way; Dreams: A Way to Listen to God;* and *Afterlife,* and used some of his material for my master's thesis. I was fortunate enough to be placed in his small discussion group during the retreat. When he heard that I did spiritual healing, he invited me to do laying-on-of-hands with him at the closing service on the final evening. It was a very moving experience, standing next to a man I respected so much and placing my hands on each person who came up for healing. He said something to me I shall always remember. He told me that if he had his own church, he would invite me to do healing there. No one had ever told me anything like that before. I felt honored and deeply moved.

Now Arthur Caliandro, the minister of Marble, and Florence Pert, the associate minister, had the courage to invite me, a lay healer, to speak about laying-on-of-hands. I remember the first time I saw the inside of Marble's sanctuary. It is a large high-ceilinged church with carved wooden beams and deep maroon cushions with gilded fleur-de-lis forming an all-over pattern. There are pews on the main floor facing the Chancel, with balconies around the second floor. The Chancel is framed in a gilded wooden arch, and the gilded lectern has a large gold angel as its base. Completely full, Marble can hold twelve hundred people. I could feel the presence of the Holy Spirit as I entered this sacred space. One hundred years of love filled this sanctuary. Living love. True healing.

My first talk at Marble was on a Saturday during Lent. A half-day workshop in which I talked about awakening the healer within each of us by opening ourselves to God's presence in our bodies as well as our souls. About two hundred and fifty people came. I reminded them that Jesus as a healer reached out and touched people with his hands as well as with his words. I talked of the Holy Spirit working through us when we open our hearts and minds to Christ and ask for healing. I discussed the value of prayer, guided imagery, and forgiveness. Since most people had not experienced laying-on-of-hands as a form of healing, I described my experience as a healer and the way I believed that it worked. Because the audience sat in pews, it was too difficult to send my training students out to do laying-on-of-hands, so I took people through several guided meditations and had them place their hands over their own hearts during the final self-healing meditation. Many people came up to me and told me they felt tingling and heat in their hands. Others felt relief of their symptoms. Some experienced an opening of their hearts. The response was wonderful, and some of my oldest students and faculty members, like the healer Gene Jennings, heard me first at Marble Collegiate Church that Saturday.

The following year I was invited back to lead a healing service during Lent. I spoke from the pulpit in robes. I had done something that I did not usually do: prepare. I had written a sermon and brought my notes with me. While in the waiting room off to the side of the sanctuary, one of the assistant ministers asked whether he could put anything on the pulpit for me. I handed him the pages of my sermon. When I went up to the pulpit to speak, I got through the first page, turned it over, and there was nothing else there. Nothing. The rest of my sermon had disappeared. I looked down at the lectern in shock. I looked out at the six hundred people in the congregation and took a deep breath. What was I going to do? I couldn't tell whether they knew that something strange was going on, so I made a joke that the rest of my sermon had disappeared and I would proceed as best I could. The congregation chuckled, the ministers looked nervous. Later Gene Jennings told me that no one would have known if I hadn't said anything, and that I scarcely missed a beat. If they only knew that my heart missed several beats. So I did what I seem to do best: improvise and talk from inspiration. It taught me a lesson, which I had to learn twice more. I am not someone who should prepare or write down her talks. God seems to have given me the gift of filling with Spirit when I stand in front of an audience. What I am supposed to say just flows through me like a river. If I let my ego prepare what to say, I negate that process and lose my connection with Spirit and the audience.

The church had set six chairs at the front for the laying-on-of-hands. At the end of the sermon, Arthur Caliandro, Florence Pert, myself, and three other assistant ministers took our positions behind these chairs. The congregation stood in line and one by one took whichever chair opened next. I lost track of time, but almost everyone in the congregation came forward. There were only a few seconds for each person to state his or her need for healing, and then a few words of prayer as the healer laid on hands. One man caught me in his desperate story. He went on and on, sucking me into his vortex, and I couldn't stop him. I could feel my psychic protection disappear and my throat close off as I tried to resist him and tell him there was no time for talking and only a minute for healing. When I finally got him out of the chair, I had to walk out the back of the sanctuary to the nearest ladies' room. I was coughing so hard I could scarcely breathe. One of the church's assistants came back to see whether I was all right and to tell me there were many more people to heal, something of which I was only too aware. But I had gotten sucked in by the man's demon of starvation and suffering, and it took me a couple minutes to release it. Healing can be dangerous work. Without meaning to, some people let desperation act as a psychic vampire, draining as much life force as it can from the healer or whoever is around to supply them with energy. These are the demons that Jesus threw out. I wasn't quite as facile with demons yet.

The healing service was a moving experience for all of us who participated, and Marble decided thereafter to continue these healing services during Lent every year. They also invited me to speak at their Ten O'clock Hour on Sunday mornings before the service. Each month a different speaker presents a topic on all the Sunday mornings of that month in a large room off to the side of the sanctuary. The first year I spoke on "Awakening the Healer Within" during March. Between eighty and one hundred people attended each Sunday morning. I had invited my training students to come and do laying-on-of-hands. Ten students arrived and Gene Jennings, by then the head usher, assigned each one to certain rows. In one hour I was able to talk about healing and lead the audience through a brief healing meditation, during which everyone received laying-on-of-hands. People commented on how much heat they felt, or tingling, or energy. I watched as people opened their hearts and got in touch with the healing energy and power with which God has imbued each of us. I tried to explain that Jesus Christ the healer lives within each of us today, and that awakening the healer within means awakening to His presence and allowing the healing to take place in physical, emotional, mental, and spiritual ways. People came up to me with tears in their eyes after the meditation. I was grateful to be doing healing within a church, where it should be done.

The following year Florence Pert invited me back for another round of Sundays, also during March, this time on "Forgiveness and Letting Go of Judgment." After I spoke, I would sneak a peak at the program for the service that day, and invariably Arthur Caliandro would be talking about the same topic. One Sunday we both talked about dealing with anger. I decided we had some special telepathic bond. It was similar to the way my assistants usually dressed in the same colors I did, even though we had not coordinated beforehand. One Sunday everyone would come in red, the next in blue. We enjoyed such simple examples of telepathy. Most people would say it was just coincidence, but we knew better. It happened all the time.

March and I seemed to agree, so Florence asked me whether I would like to come back to Marble Church every March for the Ten O'clock Hour. I happily agreed to do so. The third year I wanted to speak on "Resurrection and Healing," because it was Easter, but Florence thought that might be "too heavy." Crucifixion might be heavy, but resurrection seemed a lot lighter to me. I found in the schedule that my topic had been changed to "Creating a New Life." I dutifully proceeded to talk about this topic, but kept slipping the idea of resurrection into my talks. I had a developing awareness that healing and resurrection were really the same: that in healing our body, heart, mind and soul, we are in a process of resurrection. Moment by moment, here and now.

Years before I had announced a special Easter healing circle entitled "Resurrection and Healing." Forty people responded and I had to split the group into two circles on different nights. The topic of resurrection fascinates and inspires everyone. Christians and non-Christians. As Gerald Epstein states in his book *Healing into Immortality,* every Jew speaks of resurrection in his or her morning prayers. In the East, Hindus and Buddhists speak of resurrection as both reincarnation and enlightenment. They believe that lifetime after lifetime they are reincarnated in a new body so that the soul can evolve and heal the suffering it carries with it. Once this suffering is released completely, one experiences a state of enlightenment, or complete resurrection. Further lifetimes are not needed. New bodies are not required, unless one decides to come back as a Bodhisattva, someone who chooses to be reborn to help relieve the suffering of others.

I began seeing and talking about the parallels between healing, reincarnation, enlightenment, and resurrection. The Book of Revelation talks of resurrection at the end of time in which everyone who has ever lived will come back in physical form. In the East, there are endless cycles of death and rebirth, with no end of time foreseen. Depending on one's karma, or accumulation of actions and consciousness, a soul can evolve toward enlightenment in human form or be reborn as an animal, bird, or insect. Bodhisattvas take a vow that they will not attain enlightenment until all sentient beings, including animals, attain enlightenment, which is fairly well understood to be something that will not happen for a long time, if ever.

What about now? If, as scientists are now beginning to tell us, time is really just a construct of the mind and everything in the universe evolves in cycles of death and rebirth, then human beings are also evolving in cycles of death and rebirth. Our bodies, our minds, our souls. For a Christian, if every moment is an opportunity to experience the living Christ alive in our lives, then aren't we talking about the resurrected Christ? Carl Jung felt that Jesus symbolized the living embodiment of the Self, the whole consciousness aligned with and expressing God. Body and spirit together, in one being. So each of us is a living embodiment of healing in evolution. An evolution through birth, persecution, death, and rebirth. We evolve in God's presence, and God evolves within us. We are meeting, touching, moment by moment, until there is no more separation. Until we rise again and there is union and healing, resurrection.

It is this union with God that I experience when I do laying-on-of-hands. In reaching within to heal myself and reaching out to heal another, I experience God's presence awakening in my heart and body, my mind and hands. I fill with an awareness of Divine presence and light. When I stretch my hands out to hold them over someone's body, I am searching for that place within the person where I can touch the Spirit of God. The meeting ground. Holy ground. In touching this place within the person, I can often help awaken God's presence deep within his or her soul. I bring to the meeting ground an energy of consciousness, an embodied life and light that can spark the same within the other. In physical touch, the Divine gets taken out of the realm of disembodied Spirit, and becomes manifest. Spirit touches us, we touch Spirit. Touching Spirit.

Searching for the living God, the real Healer, within a person, is like trying to find the new molecule of carbon that scientists call C60. When they first began the search, all their instruments and theories told them that this molecule must exist. But no one could find it. No one could put their hands on the evidence for what they believed would be one of the strongest molecules. They thought it might be in soot, but could not titrate out the molecule. They theorized that C60 existed in stardust. They kept trying to postulate what atomic form it would take. In playing with the atoms of carbon and hydrogen, one scientist came up with a round molecule of hexagrams interlaced with pentagrams. It formed a perfect ball. A Bucky Fuller ball, the geodesic dome he constructed for the World's Fair in 1967. A soccer ball. Dozens of scientists spent years trying *to touch* C60, but it was so elusive that it remained a theory for a long time. Finally a scientist in Arizona heated graphite, placed it in solution, and came up with a red liquid that contained C60 crystals. Other scientists were stunned that it was so simple.

The laying-on-of-hands is a simple way to touch the living presence of God within each person. It does not depend on complicated theology, doctrine, canon, or ecumenical agreement. It is the organic reality of love in action. It is the feminine component of religion. The mother holding her child with her hands and feeding its hunger with her breast. This act of love is instinctual, organic, dependent on the body. I believe that laying-on-of-hands was lost from the Christian churches because Christianity became trapped in the mind, in rules and canons, doctrine, and power struggles. The patriarchal disconnection with the organic feminine body of healing love disappeared. The feminine became relegated to an idealized Virgin Mary, and the churches forgot that Jesus himself invited the dark, organic feminine, in the form of Mary Magdalene, to be part of his journey and message of love in physical form.

The organic feminine is threatening to a world that prides itself on control and domination. This is as true at a personal level within each of us as it is in the greater whole. In many ways we are afraid of physical touch. It makes us aware of the child within and that child's organic need for love, warmth, gentleness, sweet tastes and smells. We never lose those needs, no matter how old we become. The mother is the first experience we have as a newborn after we leave the realm of disembodied spirit. Our soul moves through a feminine body of warmth and blood into a physical world, and we begin to forget our previous lives and experiences. Our mother temporarily takes over God's role of creator, birther, nourisher, and lover. If our mother does not touch us with love and create safety and comfort in the physical and emotional world of childhood, we learn to fear the feminine organic world as chaotic and threatening, punishing and painful, or remote and rejecting. The physical body becomes a resented residence rather than a safe home. Living in a body means learning to live with limitations and separation from complete union with God and mother.

I was listening to Connecticut Public Radio one afternoon when a priest came on to tell a story about a little girl with a newborn brother. She kept insisting that she wanted to be alone with him. Her parents were nervous about his safety, but the little girl was loving and gentle with him, so they finally agreed. The little girl walked into the bedroom and closed the door. But she did not push it shut completely and it stayed opened a crack—enough for the parents to hear her speak to the newborn brother: "Tell me what God feels like. I'm beginning to forget." She didn't ask to be told about God or have God described. She wanted to remember what God feels like. The organic, feeling realm of reality. To be at one with the energy of the Beloved is what the child within us wants. As Jesus said, unless we become like little children, we shall not enter the Kingdom. The Kingdom is within us, and within us is the organic feeling level of our Divine being.

I was invited by the Catholic Health Association to speak at its annual convention. They asked whether I could lead a half-day workshop on laying-on-of-hands. They called it "Reach Out and Touch." I hated the title at first, thinking it sounded like an ad for AT&T. They expected several hundred people to take my workshop, since the total registration for the convention was twelve hundred. A few weeks before the event they called to say that I had received more than 80 percent of the initial registrations for the whole convention, and my workshop was full at four hundred people. Could I open up the registration? I agreed, and called on more student assistants to go with me to St. Louis. By the time I arrived, there were 650 people in my workshop, and it had to be held in the main ballroom of the hotel. I was stunned. I had never before spoken to so many people at once, and I had certainly never taught this many people to do laying-on-of-hands in four hours.

That morning I walked into the ballroom and up to the front, where I stood on stage. I looked out across this vast sea of faces and bodies. I had been told that there would be clergy from all denominations, Catholic and Protestant, maybe some Fundamentalists. There were as many men as women. As I started looking around more carefully, I noticed many priests in collar and sisters in habit. I couldn't believe my eyes. Some were in their sixties and seventies. Why were they here? Why did they want to hear a much younger lay woman, a spiritual healer, talk about laying-on-of-hands? I had prayed. I had meditated. I had asked for God's guidance and the right things to say. I decided I would probably be burned at the stake right there on stage.

I waited for the attack. It never came. I talked about my background as a healer, initially being careful not to use the word *psychic* in any way. I explained what I did and how I believed that we are all healers, in and outside of the churches. I took them through a meditation and played beautiful healing music in the background. Halfway through the morning I asked for questions. There was a microphone in the middle of the center aisle. Now was the time. I was sure someone would come up with a scathing attack. No one did. Everyone seemed genuinely hungry for information about healing. Many people described moving and powerful experiences during the meditation. Relief.

The second half of the morning I asked all 650 people to pair up. My assistants and I had carefully planned how the healing would work, and much to my amazement, it did, easily and quickly. The couples decided who would be the healer and patient, and they took their places. The patients sat in chairs, with the healers standing behind them. I guided them through a laying-on-of-hands process. There was music playing softly in the background, and everyone closed their eyes. I looked out across these servants of God, opening their hearts with love, praying for their egos to get out of the way. The room softened, my heart opened. I saw faces filled with light and smiles, shoulders relax. For more than twenty minutes, people remained deeply still, resting in the healing heart of God's presence. I watched as 325 pairs of hands reached out with love to touch the Spirit of God within their partner. I felt the power of this love in the room. I looked at my assistants. They were awestruck and humbled, and looked to me with tears in their eyes. I looked out at this miracle with tears in mine.

When the healings were finished, people sat with one another and shared. Instinct took me down to the floor to speak with an older couple, a priest in his seventies and a woman of about the same age with a back problem. They were both glowing and smiling. She was telling him how she had felt heat from his hands and white light flowing through her body. Her back felt better almost immediately. I looked at his face. Even his wrinkles were beaming. I smiled back at them and asked whether he had ever before done a laying-on-of-hands. He said no. How did it feel? Wonderful. As I looked into this man's shining face, I imagined that God had come alive for him in an organic way that he had never participated in before. He felt God alive in a stranger's body with his hands. He experienced his hands filled with God's love.

After the sharing, we reversed the pair-ups so that everyone could experience giving and receiving the laying-on-of-hands.

People were amazed at what they felt. Skeptics were smiling. The man in the front row who had sat through the first meditation with his arms and legs tightly crossed and his eyes open was chatting excitedly with his partner about the heat he felt in his hands. People asked good questions. They wanted to know how they could take this healing technique back to their congregations and hospital patients. I described the healing services at Marble Collegiate Church in New York City and also suggested they use healing in their private pastoral counseling sessions. All they had to do was reach out and touch the person who was suffering. Hold their hands, touch their heart or head in prayer. They probably already did this without intentionally focusing healing energy. The intention was important. Opening the heart first was essential. I was overwhelmed with the appreciation I received from this group of 650 people who had devoted their lives to God. I was touched deep in the heart.

I left St. Louis that afternoon aware that something momentous had happened. I never really thought I would see the day that I would be standing in front of priests and sisters talking about laying-on-of-hands, much less teaching them how to do it. There really was a grass roots revolution in the churches. And I was part of it. What a magnificent blessing. I sat on the plane that day, filled with tears of gratitude, feeling as though my heart would burst. Thank you God, I kept saying. Thank you.

I flew from St. Louis to Louisville, Kentucky, to talk with a group of hospital administrators from the Sisters of Nazareth Hospital System, made up of seven hospitals over several states. I had been invited by a kind and visionary man, Mark Dundon, the president. I explained to them what I did and how I saw spiritual healing integrating into the medical model and hospitals. I presented "The Healing Journey" model that I had created several years before and used in my TOUCHING SPIRIT® Training Program.

I also took the group through a guided healing meditation that combined insights from "Communicating with the Body" with the healing power of the "Self-Healing Meditation." The individuals in the room that had seemed most skeptical before the meditation

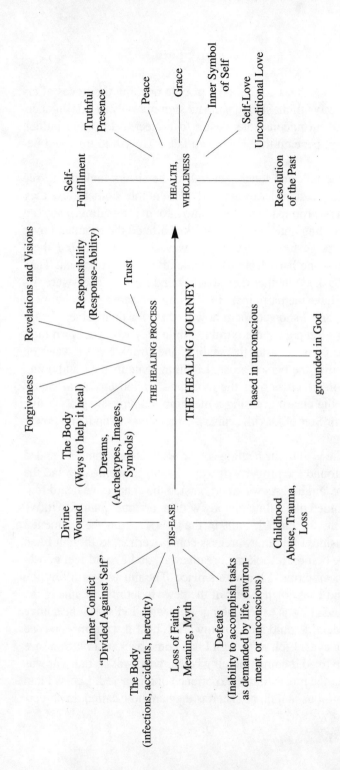

The Healing Journey
TOUCHING SPIRIT® Training Program

were the ones that had the most trouble opening their eyes afterward. I always think skepticism is a sign not only of intelligence, but also of an unconscious desire to protect a deep and hidden wound. But beneath the skepticism is a real wish to trust and believe.

After the talk and lunch, several of the sisters took me to see their healing center. I was amazed. Here at the Motherhouse they had taken one room and turned it into a room for healing. They did both counseling and massage. I walked around the room and over to the massage table. The energy was not good. I asked them whether anyone had cleared the table after the last patient. They said no. I asked whether they would mind if I did. They were delighted to have me participate in blessing and setting the energy in the room, and I showed them how to do it for themselves. I suggested they keep a candle burning while they worked, wash their hands in cold water after the healing, and sprinkle some water on the table after the person arose. Lighting some incense and doing the sign of the cross over the table and around the room would complete the clearing. Using a meaningful spiritual symbol, like the cross or Star of David, brings a dimension of depth and power to the ritual.

After the visit to the healing center, Ruth Dundon and I decided to walk around the property. It was a beautiful spring day and the birds were singing. As we stood outside the chapel, we heard music. It sounded like a flute melody with an oriental quality to it. We walked into the chapel, built in the 1800s. From the moment I walked inside, I felt an awareness come over me, as though I had been there before. It took my breath away, and I could feel goosebumps on my arms. I knew this place. The music was filling the chapel, and I sat down in one of the pews to let myself take in the power of what I was experiencing. Here was God's presence, alive and abundant. I could feel it in my body, hear it with my ears, see it with my eyes. I felt as though I had come back to a place where I had once lived. I could not tell whether what was so familiar was the chapel, the music, or the experience of the sacred. I knew I had been a religious, a nun, or sister as they are now called, in at least

one other lifetime. Maybe one of those was right here in
Louisville, Kentucky. It didn't matter. In this moment in eternity I
was home within myself. I sat in deep bliss for a long time, until
the music ended. I told Ruth that I wanted to find the person playing the music. We went looking and soon discovered an older sister in a room behind the altar. She smiled at our pleasure and
showed us an old cassette tape of James Galway playing Japanese
seashore music. We went over to the bookstore on the other side of
the property and each bought a copy.

This organic experience of the sacred, the awareness of God's
presence in life, is the very foundation of healing. We are spirit
embodied in matter. In Judaism the word for soul, *nephesh,* includes the physical body. There are many ways to look at the
physical universe and the body. Ultimately, we all have to admit
that this feminine, Mother Nature realm is messy and seemingly
chaotic. It can take us off guard with illness, pain, lightening,
wind, snow, tornadoes, and plague. Most people would prefer to
think that God's bequest in Genesis of having dominion over Nature is permission to attempt to control everything that seems out
of our control. What seems to be out of our rational control is often seen as bad, evil, and something to be ignored or punished.
Until a few hundred years ago in the West, all illness was believed
to be the work of evil spirits, and the body not something to be
catered to or treated kindly. Wisdom resided in the mind, evil in
the body.

Nikos Kazantzakis, author of *Zorba the Greek* and many other
books, struggled his entire life with this dichotomy between the
body and the spirit. I discovered Kazantzakis in college while
completing my Comparative Religion major at Hobart and
William Smith Colleges. His life fascinated me. My senior year I
decided to do my honors thesis about him, with the help of my religion professor and advisor Ronald Gestwicki, who was completing his Ph. D. on Wallace Stevens's poetry. Like my life until then,
Kazantzakis's was filled with illness and poor health until his
death in 1957. His love for God and all things spiritual drew him
into examining the question of suffering in the world and the di-

chotomy between light and dark, spirit and matter. He wanted to understand Jesus and his mission as savior, a topic he explored in all his writings, especially the novels *The Greek Passion, The Fratricides,* and *The Last Temptation of Christ,* which Martin Scorcese turned into a film. Kazantzakis agonized about how a good and just God could allow suffering in the world. He wanted to live the best life he could live as a way of transforming suffering. In some novels his heroes affirm life, the feminine, the body, and its pleasures; in others, Kazantzakis takes pleasure in an almost ascetic, sacrificial stance. Spirit seemed pure and light to him; the body and the feminine appeared dark and chaotic. Yet he kept coming back to the body and an affirmation of life.

I identified with Kazanzakis's struggle between the body and spirit, life and death. For me, being embodied, even being alive, was a painful challenge. At that age I had no idea of just how deeply these issues would touch my future. Twenty years later, I have become a healer whose intention is to bring new life, resurrected life, into consciousness in a physical way—exactly what I believe Kazantzakis had in mind when he wrote in *The Fratricides:* "Christ had, in reality, come down to earth and lay dead within us, and we all wept and waited for Him to be resurrected." In *The Rock Garden* he writes:

> We must understand well that we do not proceed from a unity of God to the same unity of God again. We do not proceed from one chaos to another chaos, neither from one light to another light, nor from one darkness to another darkness. What would be the value of our life then? What would be the value of all life?
>
> But set out from an almighty chaos, from a thick abyss of light and darkness tangled. And we struggle—plant, animals, men, ideas—in this momentary passage of individual life, to put in order the Chaos within us, to cleanse the abyss, to work upon as much darkness as we can within our bodies and to transmute it into light.

Years later, after receiving my master's, I would often think of going back to graduate school to get my Ph.D. in pastoral counseling, especially to further explore issues of spirituality and religion. I wondered what it would be like to engage in deep discussions of healing and spirituality with people whose life paths were journeying with God. So when Harvey Cox, Thomas Professor of Divinity at Harvard Divinity School and author of *Fire from Heaven,* called to ask me to speak there on healing, I was delighted. It was especially moving to hear from him because he and I had not seen each other for many years. In the early seventies, after graduating from college, I had been traveling through Europe. David Miller, then Professor of Religion at Syracuse University and author of *Gods and Games,* had been the outside examiner on my honors thesis on Nikos Kazanzakis, and when he heard I was going to be in Switzerland, he invited me to stop by a residential conference he was presenting. It was held on a beautiful old estate on the lake in Vezia, Switzerland. Jean Houston was there leading a workshop about getting in touch with deeper potentialities. This workshop was the first one I had ever taken that had to do with the New Age or anything alternative. At one point in the workshop she asked us to find a partner. Harvey Cox and I, total strangers at the time, paired up. We had to look into each other's eyes, letting go into an altered state in which we could see other realities. I remember seeing his face change from his age at that time, to that of a small child, and then to that of an old man. It was as though I could see all the masks of time on top of his soul, while his soul remained constant.

As with speaking at Marble Collegiate Church for the first time, I made the mistake of preparing what I was going to say. I suppose I was anxious that the audience of graduate students would want something more than just my life and work as a healer, so I went back to my master's thesis and pulled out several pages that felt essential to my perspective on healing. Professor Cox had taken me on a tour of the campus and into the chapel in which I would speak. There was no cross, no star of David, nothing in the way of

symbols or ornamentation. He told me that it had all been removed because of controversy. That should have been my warning.

That night I walked into the chapel to speak. My student assistants who lived in Boston had arrived early and set out candles and
my tape recorder. About seventy people showed up and filled the
pews. I began talking about spiritual healing. I acknowledged that
all religions and shamanic tribal societies have traditions of healing that use touch in some way. I wanted to make sure to let audience members know that I was aware there were people from
various religious backgrounds listening to me. I have spent my entire career being especially careful not to step on anyone's religious toes, having had several past lives in which I was persecuted
for my religious beliefs. I have always tried to use nondenomina-
tional and nonsexist language when speaking about healing, and
my training students, many of them not Christian, have always
told me how welcomed and included they felt in my program.

I continued to speak about how we are all healers and can
awaken the healer within us. I spoke about the body and the spirit
working together, and the need to communicate with the body. I
talked about the white light and healing energy, about how we can
heal ourselves and, if we wish, participate in healing others. I described several patients I had worked with over the years and the
results of my healing work with them. I brought up the laying-on-
of-hands, and then I made a terrible mistake. I read from my master's thesis. I spoke of a statue of Jesus that had been damaged in
Europe during World War II. A bomb had blown off the hands of
the statue, and instead of replacing them, the community decided
to leave the statue without hands. I believed it was a lovely symbol of how we can all reclaim being the hands of the Divine at
work in the physical world. We can become those healing hands,
reaching out to heal each other.

Slam. Someone walked out. Slam. Another person walked out.
I could feel waves of anger hit me from the back of the chapel.
Four or five people walked out. In twenty years this had never hap-

pened to me. I imagined, rightly or wrongly, that the people walking out thought I was shoving Christianity down their throats. This was far from the truth, but they didn't wait around to ask me about it. I was shaken, but I went on with my talk. I took the rest of the group through a healing meditation, bringing white light into their bodies and feeling God alive in every cell. My students did laying-on-of-hands as best they could, considering people were sitting in pews. One man toward the back refused the laying-on-of-hands, and sat with his eyes open part of the time. Still, the meditation was beautiful and I could see from the expressions on people's faces that most of them were experiencing a deep state of connection with God. At the end, a number of people sat in silence without opening their eyes. At least I had gotten through to them.

Then the questions began. A few people commented on how peaceful they felt. A woman at the back said she couldn't do the meditation because I used white light, and since I had spoken of Jesus earlier, she thought maybe the light was Jesus. She was Jewish, and she didn't want Jesus in her body. I told her that white light is Divine Light, the basic energy of Creation, the energy of which we are all composed. Even African tribal societies speak of white light in their spiritual traditions. The man who had refused laying-on-of-hands turned out to be a Fundamentalist minister. He stood up and preached at me for five minutes. He told me that I had failed to convert and heal the patient I had been speaking about because I hadn't described heaven and the saving power of Jesus Christ. I told him that my patient was completely without any religious upbringing. Her lineage was Jewish, but she had never been introduced in any way to her spiritual heritage. In the five years that I had been working with her, she found a deep inner connection with God and prayed and meditated daily. Despite the fact that she did not heal physically, she explored her spiritual life in a way that she never would have if it hadn't been for her illness.

When my talk was over, many people came forward to tell me how much they had enjoyed it. But I knew that I had just experienced one of the most difficult audiences I had ever encountered.

I tried to remember what it was like to be a graduate student. I recalled how argumentative everyone was, how important opinions seemed to be, and how intent students were on proving their own perspective. I became aware of how different it is to *feel* the presence of God in one's life and body rather than to discuss and read about it. I wondered how many of the students at Harvard Divinity School were struggling, like that priest, with their own religious backgrounds and the loss of faith and meaning in their lives. I wondered how many of them were caught in their heads, their minds. I remembered that as an undergraduate Religion student, I refused to use the word *God.* I felt it was so overused that it had no meaning for me. It was not until I became a healer that God really had meaning for me—word or no word. I wished I could have reached those students who walked out in anger thinking I was just another proselytizing Christian. On that evening I did not. I was not revolutionary enough for them, and too revolutionary for the Fundamentalist preacher. Professor Cox told me later that most of Generation X, the one following the baby boomers, is "suspicious of religion and longing for spirituality." He said I had incited two weeks of heated discussion in the classroom. Heated means impassioned. Where there is passion, there is feeling. The heart gets touched and the healer within can come alive. Maybe I had done my job after all.

I have never understood what is behind the motivation to convert other people to one's religious viewpoint, unless it is the need for power or validation. I believe, as do most Buddhists, that there are many spokes in the wheel, many paths to God. Every religion has its beauty, its stories and parables, its ways to put love into action in the world. I have often thought I would stand up some day, the next time I am attacked, and ask my attacker, "Do you love God?" I imagine the answer will be "Yes." My response will be "So do I. What's the problem?"

I cannot imagine God turning anyone away from heaven who has lived a life of love in action. If Jesus and Buddha are right, that the kingdom of heaven is within us, then opening the heart and living one's life from this openness is to be in heaven here and now.

There may still be suffering in the world, but heaven can exist within our own hearts. To meet the suffering of the world with love is truly to manifest healing. To touch the suffering of the world with hands of love is to bring revolution back into the churches. The kind of revolution that created them a long time ago.

12
Seed Pearls

I unlock the door to my home and walk upstairs to my study. I have just returned from speaking about resurrection and healing at Marble Collegiate Church. The view from my back window meets me with its line of trees and open meadow of grasses. Without taking off my coat, I sit at my computer. I open a new document and begin

> *bare and full*
> *I walk the grass*
> *to the edge*
> *of straw*
> *lines of trees*
> *plant life*
> *in my path*
> *offering chances*
> *to hold*
> *a solid*
> *miracle*

The words flow from some new river in my soul. I do not think about them, plan them, or edit them. They just flow through me the way healing energy flowed through my hands twenty years ago. It is 2 P.M. and for six hours these waters of soul flow from my fingers and into the computer screen. My coat is still on. I stop and make dinner, sit again, and continue writing poetry until I go to bed at 11 P.M. The next morning I get out of bed and sit outside with my morning coffee. The sun is shining, the birds chirping, a true spring day of rebirth. I go upstairs and bring my notebook computer outside and sit on the deck in the morning sun. The poems burst into creation like Zen koans or haiku with each new spark of consciousness like a bird's flight across my vision.

swooping birds
bobbling
in the breath
of God

By 2 P.M. that afternoon, twenty-four hours after I began, I have written almost one hundred pages of poetry. Healing, spiritual poetry flowing open its energy from new life in my soul. As I reread what has come forth, I feel my heart open and tears flow. This is my healing happening before my eyes and moving through the cells of my body. In my dreams good men begin to appear, positive male figures, positive animi are being born. I dream of Michael Crichton, the writer, handing me a book. The cover is blank. I know it is mine.

I remember that my father loved poetry and used to read it to my mother when they were engaged. He kept small leather books of poems on his bed table. As a child I loved to look through them and always remembered Rudyard Kipling: "If I built a wall I'd want to know who I was walling in and who I was walling out, and to whom I was like to give offense." And "If you can keep your head about you when all are losing theirs and blaming it on you." Early "Psychic Self-Defense" training. That's as far as the lesson progressed. My former husband had written poetry, a few treasured ones to me. He was good, very good. The soul of a poet in the guise of a warrior. I remember his poems fondly.

But me. I would never in a million years have imagined that I would write poetry. A book maybe, but never poetry. "Useless but essential," as I think I once heard it described. I was brought up to be useful. On the other hand, Winston Churchill, when confronted during World War II with members of his Cabinet who wanted to cut the budget for the arts, replied that he would not. If we are not fighting for freedom of expression, he replied, what are we fighting for?

I was giving birth. To poems. Finally, the lifelong pregnancy was coming to fruition. Within a week I had written another fifty. Every day I sat and allowed them to flow through. For one of the only times in my life I was able to get my judgmental, rational, male animus mind out of the way and let the birth process happen unimpeded. I would usually hear the first line of a new poem and know I had to sit down immediately to catch it or risk losing it. Like Annie Dillard's comment about writing: "One line falls from the ceiling." Within six months I had almost six hundred pages of poetry. I had no idea whether they were any good, but I didn't care. They were healing for me, and for the first time in my life I would keep these children and not offer them up too quickly to be devoured as food for other people. I would let the full impact of their birth be felt down in the healing ground of my soul before I shared them with anyone:

> *long years*
> *carrying*
> *a pregnant womb*
> *as soul solutions*
> *struggle in mud*
> *to raise a whole*
> *spirit*

It was months before I allowed anyone to see them. Finally, I shared some with my dear friend Camille Hykes, the editor of magnificent and award-winning books like *Shelter* by Jayne Anne

Phillips and *Platte River* by Rick Bass. She loved them. I had the courage to share a few more with intimate friends. They loved them as well. I found on the rare occasion that a poem would come through for a patient or student, and I knew I was meant to share it with them as part of their healing process; like the dark one I wrote after hearing that one of my young and vulnerable patients was almost raped in her own apartment by her landlord:

> *see straight*
> *accept your dark eye*
> *not everyone is so nice*
> *there are hungry ghosts*
> *living in bodies*
> *who would swallow your sweetness*
> *and digest your juices*
> *there are raging rapists*
> *who would overpower*
> *your politeness and*
> *steal your pearls of beauty*
> *there are murdering monkeys*
> *who distract your soul from love*
> *and eat your heart with words*
> *so wake up, young Persephone*
> *to danger's presence*
> *choose the night witch*
> *Hecate as your guide*
> *before Hades steals*
> *your virginity and separates*
> *mother and child*
> *from the illusion*
> *of lifelong play*
> *and men on white horses*

I found myself writing poems about my former husband, my father, former lovers, and friends. Each poem was its own healing,

offering insight into the past and forgiveness in the present. I had
the courage to send my former husband one poem written for him
before his trip to the World Triathlon competition in New Zealand.
He liked it. Months later I called and asked him if he would read
some more of my poetry. He agreed. We met on a bench in the late
summer sun and had a picnic lunch. When we were finished eating,
I handed him a selection of poems, including several for him. He
laughed at some. I was insulted. He reassured me he was laughing
because the imagery was so stark, so impactful that he couldn't
quite believe it. He kept reading, for a long time. At one point he
looked into my eyes and said "You're a poet." My heart smiled.

I began to take some of my poetry to my workshops with me. I
was terrified. This was unknown territory. I could fail. I could get
up in front of a hundred people and they could hate it. Think I was
silly. Worse, I had never read poetry out loud before. What if I was
awful. Just for this reason, I knew I had to do it. I knew I had to
face my fear, stand my ground, and place it all on the line. I had to
grow along with my soul.

In Boston, at Interface Center at the conclusion of my Friday
night talk on "Awakening the Healer Within," I pulled out a few
sheets. I read one. No one walked out. I had warned them, so if
they wanted to leave before it started, they could. No one did. I
kept reading. People smiled. I could feel a deep stillness permeate
the room, and the words seemed to be absorbed as I sent them out
into space. I got to the final poem and I choked. Part way through
the reading my eyes filled with tears and my voice cracked and I
couldn't go on. I commented that reading this poem was harder
than I expected. I took a few deep breaths and looked up. People
were still there with me. A man to my right, who looked as though
he had been bored to death through my talk, was all of a sudden
leaning forward in his seat with his eyes wide open. I started
again:

> *I have spent my hands*
> *laying down love*
> *in the hearts*

of those who come
for tender care
and words that melt
hope into the bones.
I have filled holes
of broken loss
and moved settled expectation
out of its orbit
until it turns on
face light.
I have stared down
demons of starvation
and kept the ground
under my feet like
a sacrificial altar
welcoming the child
to eat self-love.
I have spent my heart
laying down love light
to repair the path
of broken dreams
and restore the mirror
to its rightful place
in the eyes of Divinity.

When it was all over, I thanked everyone for listening and bid them Namaste ("I bow to the Divinity within you"). Several people came up to thank me. One had tears in her eyes. Another wanted to know when they would be published. As I went back to my room that night I knew something extraordinary had happened. A marriage of light and dark, feminine and masculine, ground and spirit. My healing work would never be the same. I had found my true soul voice, and it was touching Spirit in the souls of those who listened, and growing roots.

* * *

Journal Entry, late October

I awake at 5:30 A.M. with seed pearls germinating in my mind. Poems with the soft round shine of pearls that glow in the stillness of laid out strings, but can only be tested by biting down with teeth.

I am staying in a brownstone apartment on the Upper West Side in New York City. Strangers to me, friends to my friend. A large, spacious expanse of oak and glass and fireplaces without burn. On the mantel in the living room is a large framed photograph of a round mirror reflecting back a dark cross perfectly centered top to bottom and side to side. The bedroom in which I am staying faces the back courtyard. After writing down the seed pearls on a piece of scrap paper, I have coffee and a small fruit muffin. It is warm in the apartment and I go to the door that leads out onto the balcony to open it for air. I place my hand on the knob and look through the glass. There, diagonally stretched out before me, is a long black cable from the left corner of my building to the brick one across on the other side of the courtyard. In a row, like pearls of cooing grace, are several dozen pigeons all facing in the same direction towards me. I stand motionless, like someone in Mesmer's gaze, not daring to move or even to breathe, knowing that I have happened upon a sight that holds its magic in only this moment upon the earth. As though all of Creation has met for breakfast and agreed to hold still for the eyes of a poet awakening at dawn. For timeless moments the pigeons all balance on this tightrope. I let my eyes stretch across the cable, counting twenty, across to the other building, where I count twenty more. Exactly forty.

My eyes scan down the line. Some are dark gray all over. Others have variances of dark and light. A few have one round white patch in the middle of their backs, while two have wing tips of pure white light that flash on air's edge as they take a training run across the airspace between the cable and the balcony's black ornate railing. One is almost pure white, with only a little gray on its wings and back feathers. This one reminds me of a pure white pigeon that I saw many years before on Broadway. It stood there in the middle of the sidewalk with one or two other nondescript gray friends. I couldn't believe my eyes as I noticed its presence upon the pavement. Neither could anyone else. Dozens of people slowed their gait. Some, like me, stopped completely to look down upon this pure white bird treading lightly upon the hot cement. I felt as though I were looking upon the Holy Spirit, who had deigned to take the embodiment of a pigeon to remind us that Divinity lives at our feet even on a New York City street.

While writing this book I saw another pure white pigeon on Columbus Avenue. Once again, I stopped and gazed in wonder. Twice in a lifetime. I could scarcely believe my eyes. I, who am so used to miracles that they are daily occurrences, was awestruck. I remembered reading an article in some New York City publication by a writer who found a hatchling in a nest on the ledge outside his kitchen window. A single, fluffy little thing breaking its way into this world. It survived several days and then disappeared. He was saddened and fascinated. He read everything he could and asked experts about pigeons. He was told that another more aggressive bird had probably eaten it, or that it had fallen from its nest to its death. He was told that very few pigeon hatchlings actually survive in the harsh environment of New York City, which is why no one ever seems to see them or their nests.

I gazed down at this splendid white angel walking in the middle of the sidewalk at the corner of Eighty-third Street and Columbus. I looked up to see how many people had noticed and stopped to admire it, as many had done years before. No one. Not a single person gave it any recognition, or even a glance, from what I could see. I wondered what had changed in these years, two avenues over, that the deep beauty of grace should be lost in this place. In a flash of light I wondered if this pigeon was a child of the former. Somehow it did not feel like the same bird, although I suppose it could have been. I do not know how long pigeons live. But a child. A new carrier of Holy Spirit come to visit Columbus Avenue. I could scarcely leave that corner and go on about my business.

Now I watch as these forty pigeons sit gracefully, preening their feathers now and again; and then, two or three at a time to lead the line, swooping down through the air to test their landing gear on the edge of balconies and back up to the cable and the building's roof. At one point all of them take to flight and the entire airspace between the buildings is filled with the gentle sound and sight of flapping wings and cooing. I wonder if they do this every morning; if they have nested back in this oasis of space and trees and windows that appreciates the awakening of Creation. They seem to feel safe here, as though they have found a home in which to play and nest and start their day. It occurs to me that each pigeon is like a human being, with shades of gray, handed down through generations of shadow. The darker the gray, the more they blend in with their surroundings. The white wing tips and flutters of light catch the eye. They are dangerous. And yet I imagine, that like people, these pigeons are somehow evolving out of the dirt and dross, the earth and shadow of Creation, into a state where maybe it is safe to show one's light and catch the bright shine of Spirit's play.

And then they come. The black crows. Three of them. Big, sharp beaked, menacing. Thirty-nine pigeons fly away. There is one brave gray one who is willing to stay on the opposite edge of the building top. They just stand there, like statues or scarecrows, etched against the sky, lest I forget that the sharp beak of shadow exists in the world. When they have accomplished their mission of claiming territory, one by one they fly off. The courtyard stands empty for a few minutes. I wonder if they are relatives of the seven who had eaten all the pears off my pear trees at the end of summer when there was no rain and they were probably thirsty. Hunger. That's what they represent. The ravenous hunger of the black beak. Come to take what it seeks. I should remember.

I look up again and the pigeons begin to come back. A few brave ones, including the white one, swoop in and stand on the building where the crows have been. Twelve disciples. Then some tiny brown wrens. Two seagulls soar at the tops of high rise buildings. A silver metal bird, belly full with human flesh, cuts its mark going southwest. A lone bluejay sits on the railing to my right next to my writing window. The day has started with seed pearls of awakening round shine on which to bite my teeth. On which to re-

*

member that we are all members of some great cooing Creation dancing its grace in front of our faces and healing our souls into whole embodiments of Spirit.

I get up from my writing and stand at the door once more. Across the courtyard there is one pigeon standing on the chimney stack. It is the white one. I look at it more closely. It has some light gray on its wings, and a beautiful black stripe through the gray. It stands tall in the light. From the left, floating across my field of vision, is one plant seed shining its filaments in the air. I wonder where it will come to rest and take root.

*

Healing
Meditations

✳

Opening the Chakras with Color
Communicating with Your Body
Pain Relief
Self-Healing
Laying-on-of-Hands
Strengthening Your Aura
Self-Forgiveness

Introduction

These meditations may be used while you are alone, or you may wish to slowly read them to a friend, family member, or patient who needs healing.

If you are using a meditation alone, you may wish to read completely through the meditation before beginning so that you have an idea of how your experience will progress. You may then attempt to guide yourself from memory or, occasionally, open your eyes and refer to the text of the meditation.

If you are reading a meditation to another person, remember to pause at the end of each sentence (5 seconds) and paragraph (20 seconds) to allow the person time to process your direction. These times are approximate and open to adjustment, depending on the feel of the meditation and the person's needs.

Healing meditations are valuable adjuncts to medical treatment. Please do *not* use them in place of medical treatment.

Opening the Chakras with Color

The chakras are the wheels of energy in our subtle body that contain and distribute life force. In opening these centers, we mobilize healing throughout our physical body as well as balance our emotional, mental, and spiritual levels of consciousness. Sometimes the chakras move clockwise, sometimes counterclockwise. Allow each chakra to find its natural flow.

Find a comfortable position, either sitting or lying down. Uncross your arms and legs and close your eyes. Take a long, deep breath and let it out slowly. Allow your breathing to become full, deep, and relaxed.

As you count from ten to zero, allow your rational mind to rest, and you will become more receptive to the wisdom of your unconscious and its healing power.

10, 9, 8, 7, 6, 5, 4, 3, 2, 1, 0. You are now very deeply relaxed.

Focus your attention way above the top of your head, out into the heavens, and get in touch with a brilliant, powerful, white light and energy flowing down toward you.

Allow yourself to experience this light energy flowing all around you and through you, filling your body with its radiance. With each breath you inhale this light. As it fills and surrounds you, it gently permeates your entire being and joins the river of life energy already flowing through your body.

Focus your attention at the base of your spine, where your coccyx bone is located. This is your root chakra, your center of security, safety, and grounding in the physical world. Get in touch with the white light in your first chakra as it gently moves in a circular motion.

As the light energy slowly opens your root chakra, it becomes a bright red. Feel the energy and vibration of this red light as it gently moves in a circular motion.

Feel this red light energy flowing down through your legs and feet and into the ground, connecting you with Mother Earth.

Notice any sensations and emotions that arise as you connect with the physical nature of your body and Mother Earth.

Now gradually allow the energy in your first chakra to continue flowing upward in a spiral motion into your second chakra in the center of your pelvis.

This is your center of sexuality and creative life force. As the light energy opens your second chakra it becomes a bright orange and moves gently in a circular motion.

Notice any sensations and emotions that arise as you connect with your sexuality and creative life force.

Now gradually allow the energy in your second chakra to continue flowing upward in a spiral motion into your third chakra at your solar plexus between your rib cage.

This is your center of physical will power, motivation, and vitality. As the light energy opens your third chakra it becomes a bright sun yellow and moves gently in a circular motion.

Notice any sensations and emotions that arise as you connect with your physical will power, motivation, and vitality.

Now gradually allow the energy in your third chakra to continue flowing upward in a spiral motion into your fourth chakra, your heart center in the middle of your chest.

This is your center of love and compassion. As the light energy opens your fourth chakra, it becomes a bright green and moves gently in a circular motion.

Notice any sensations and emotions that arise as you connect with your heart.

Now gradually allow the energy in your heart chakra to continue flowing upward in a spiral motion into your fifth chakra in the center of your throat.

This is your center of self-expression. As the light energy opens your fifth chakra, it becomes a bright sky blue and moves gently in a circular motion.

Notice any sensations and emotions that arise as you connect with your self-expression.

Now gradually allow the energy in your fifth chakra to continue flowing upward in a spiral motion into your sixth chakra between your eyebrows.

This is your center of psychic sight and true vision. As the light energy opens your third eye, it becomes a bright indigo (blue-purple) and moves gently in a circular motion.

Notice any sensations and emotions that arise as you connect with your ability to see clearly.

*

Now gradually allow the energy in your third eye to continue flowing upward in a spiral motion into your seventh chakra at the crown of your head.

This is your center of spiritual consciousness and direct knowing. As the light energy opens your seventh chakra, it becomes a bright violet and moves gently in a circular motion.

Notice any sensations and emotions that arise as you connect with your spiritual consciousness.

Now allow your awareness to slowly scan down through all of your chakras. As you see each color, allow yourself to feel the energy slowly moving in a circular motion in each center.

When you reach your first chakra at the base of your spine, reconnect with the red light energy moving down through your legs and feet as it gives you a feeling of grounding.

On the count of ten, you may open your eyes. 1, 2, 3, 4, 5, 6, 7, 8, 9, 10. Give yourself a minute or two to become accustomed to being back in the room with your eyes open.

✳

Communicating with Your Body

This meditation will assist you in using the wisdom of your unconscious to gain new insights into the nature of a physical symptom or illness, and to understand some of what is needed for healing to take place. Before beginning this meditation, choose the physical symptom, illness, or location in your body that you would like to focus on.

Find a comfortable position, either sitting or lying. Uncross your arms and legs, and close your eyes. Take a long, deep breath and let it out slowly. Allow your breathing to become full, deep, and relaxed.

As you count from ten to zero, allow your rational mind to rest, and you will become more receptive to the wisdom of your unconscious and its healing power.

10, 9, 8, 7, 6, 5, 4, 3, 2, 1, 0. You are now very deeply relaxed.

Focus your attention on a symptom or illness that you would like to understand, communicate with, and heal. Get in touch with all the sensations in this area of your body.

Allow yourself to remember any sensations you have experienced previously.

Now temporarily increase the intensity of these sensations.

Notice how you are doing this. Is there anything you are thinking or feeling that is increasing these sensations?

Now take a deep breath and release it. As you do, allow yourself to decrease the sensations.

Notice how you are doing this. Is there anything you are doing that is allowing you to decrease the sensations?

Now use your imagination and become the symptom or illness. Imagine being a child who is pretending to identify with the symptom or illness. What are you like? What personality do you have?

What is your life like?

What do you do to this person whose body you are in?

What are you trying to tell this person? What message are you trying to convey?

As this symptom or illness, how have you changed this person's life?

How have you changed this person's relationships?

What emotions have you provoked?

Do you express something that this person cannot?

Is there something you help this person avoid?

Is there something you do for them? Are you useful in some way?

Are you protecting this person from anything or anyone?

What can this person do to heal you?

Now become yourself again. Tell the symptom or illness how you feel about what it has told you.

What feelings are you in touch with that you were not aware of before you developed this condition?

What needs and desires are you now in touch with?

Is there anything in your life you want to change as a result of this condition?

Now picture your life beginning to change in the ways you desire. Visualize yourself incorporating whatever you need for healing to take place.

See yourself as whole, healed, and filled with self-love.

On the count of ten you may open your eyes. 1, 2, 3, 4, 5, 6, 7, 8, 9, 10.

✳

Pain Relief

This meditation will assist you in releasing physical pain and place you in a deeply relaxed condition. The most effective position is to lie down so that you can allow yourself to fall asleep at the end of the meditation.

Find a comfortable position, either sitting or lying down. Uncross your arms and legs, and close your eyes. Take a long, deep breath and let it out slowly. Allow your breathing to become full, deep, and relaxed.

As you count from ten to zero, allow your rational mind to rest, and you will become more receptive to the wisdom of your unconscious and its healing power.

10, 9, 8, 7, 6, 5, 4, 3, 2, 1, 0. You are now very deeply relaxed.

Focus your attention on the location in your body where you experience pain. Allow yourself to become aware of all the characteristics of this pain.

Is it sharp or dull? Hot or cold? Do you feel throbbing or pressure?

Are there any other characteristics?

How large or small is the pain? Over what area does it extend? What shape is it? Allow yourself to feel it as three dimensional with depth and height, width and volume.

What color is the pain?

Now allow yourself to temporarily increase the characteristics of the pain.

Notice how you are doing this. Is there anything you are thinking or feeling that is increasing the pain?

Now take a long, deep breath and release it. As you do, allow the pain to decrease.

Notice how you are doing this.

Now use your imagination and place yourself inside the center of the pain. As the pain, what are you like?

What is your life like?

What are you trying to say? What message are you trying to convey?

Now begin to change your size, shape, and color in any way you wish.

What are you like now? What color? Shape? Size?

Now become yourself again. Visualize the pain projected onto a movie screen.

What do you see? What color is it? Shape? Size? What is it doing?

Visualize it as changing color, shape, and size again. Watch it like a movie.

Visualize the screen as moving farther and farther away from you.

As you are watching the screen disappear, feel a cool blue light surrounding your body and head.

With each breath you are taking in more of this cool blue light. Your entire body fills with its gentle presence and produces a deep state of relaxation.

Every cell in your body is filling with this gentle, cool blue light. Cooling, comforting, healing.

With each breath you are taking in more of this cool blue light. Your entire body fills with its gentle presence and produces a deep state of relaxation.

Every cell in your body is filling with this gentle, cool blue light. Cooling, comforting, healing.

Flowing throughout your entire body, you rest in a deep peace. Deeper and deeper.

You may wish to remain in this deeply peaceful and healing place. You may even wish to drift into sleep.

Completely comfortable, relaxed, healed, . . .

✳

Self-Healing

This meditation will assist you in focusing healing intention on a symptom, illness, or area of your body. By connecting your awareness, brain, and physical body through visualization, you are creating an opportunity for messages of healing to be sent where they are needed most. The immune system has been known to respond to healing imagery.

Find a comfortable position, either sitting or lying. Uncross your arms and legs, and close your eyes. Take a long, deep breath and let it out slowly. Allow your breathing to become full, deep and relaxed.

As you count from ten to zero, allow your rational mind to rest, and you will become more receptive to the wisdom of your unconscious and its healing power.

10, 9, 8, 7, 6, 5, 4, 3, 2, 1, 0. You are now very deeply relaxed.

Focus your attention way above the top of your head, out into the heavens, and get in touch with a brilliant, powerful white light and energy flowing down toward you.

Allow yourself to experience this light energy flowing all around you and through you, filling your body with its radiance. With each breath you inhale this light. As it fills and surrounds you, it gently permeates your entire being and joins the river of life energy already flowing through your body.

Focus your attention on the area of your body that needs healing. Breathe deeply and let go.

Allow yourself to feel and image the white light energy gently circulating through this area of your body. Light energy is the energy of Creation, reminding your body of its power to create healing and new life.

Watch your blood circulation cleansing your tissues as it removes toxins and unwanted cells.

See and feel your bright red blood bringing new oxygen and nourishment to your tissues and bones.

Feel and visualize your nerves beginning to balance, relax, and send messages of healing throughout your body. Breathe.

Allow your body to harmonize all its healing energies while strengthening your immune system, muscles, nerves, organs, and bones.

See and feel this area of your body healing.

On the count of three, see your body as being totally and completely healed, and hold this image. 1, 2, 3.

Imagine your body functioning exactly as you wish, and while holding this image of healing, repeat the following affirmation three times:

I accept my healing and acknowledge the light within me. Breathe. I accept my healing and acknowledge the light within me. I accept my healing and acknowledge the light within me.

Feel and see yourself in a complete state of healing.

See your body and your whole being as healed, joyous, and radiant with light.

See yourself doing all the things you love to do and have always wanted to do.

Feel yourself radiant with healing energy and light, love and joy.

Experience your true nature as healthy and whole.

On the count of three, you will receive a symbol of healing. 1, 2, 3. This is your symbol of healing. Visualize this symbol in the area of your body that is now healing and trust that it will continue to generate healing energy and new life.

Allow the meaning of this symbol to be a mystery, knowing that at some point you will understand its importance. Feel its presence within you and experience it radiating light and healing.

You may open your eyes on the count of ten. 1, 2, 3, 4, 5, 6, 7, 8, 9, 10.

✳

Laying-on-of-Hands

This meditation will guide you through a basic form of the laying-on-of-hands. It can be used with adults, children, and animals. To begin, place the person or animal in a comfortable position either sitting or lying down. They can even be asleep. Position yourself so that you will be able to rest your hands either above or lightly on the afflicted area. Make sure you are in a position that will be comfortable for you to hold for fifteen to twenty minutes. If you become uncomfortable at any time, raise your hands, change your position, and replace your hands. Remember to breathe!

Begin with your hands at your sides or on your legs, uncrossed, take a deep breath, and close your eyes. Allow your breathing to become full, deep, and relaxed.

Begin with a prayer that is simple and appropriate for your spiritual beliefs, such as: I ask that my ego be put aside and that this healing be for the highest good of the person (or animal) receiving it. I ask for God's healing love and power to be present.

As you count from ten to zero, allow your rational mind to rest and become even more deeply relaxed. 10, 9, 8, 7, 6, 5, 4, 3, 2, 1, 0. Breathe. You are now very deeply relaxed.

Focus your attention way above the top of your head, out into the heavens, and get in touch with a brilliant, powerful, white light and energy flowing down toward you.

Allow yourself to experience this light energy flowing all around you and through you, filling your body with its radiance. With each breath you inhale this light. As it fills and surrounds you, it gently permeates your entire being and joins the river of life energy already flowing through your body.

Focus your attention on your heart chakra in the middle of your chest, your center of love and compassion. Visualize the white light concentrating its energy here, and begin to feel it moving in a gentle, slow, and circular motion.

As it flows, it begins to open your heart center. Breathe deeply and allow your chest to open fully, making room for this light energy.

As you do, you can feel the love and compassion in your heart for the being in front of you. This love and light energy combine into a powerful healing energy.

As this healing energy becomes stronger and fuller, it moves up into your shoulders, down your arms, and into your hands. You may begin to feel a tingling, pulsation, or even warmth in your hands and fingers.

Now lift your arms and place both of your hands palm to palm in front of you, about six inches apart. Keep your hands and fingers relaxed, move them slightly toward and away from each other. You will begin to feel the sense of energy between them. Almost like a gentle magnetic pull.

Now lift your arms and place both of your hands, palms down, about two feet above the body of the being in front of you. If

✳

they are sitting in a chair, you can place one hand in front and the other in back of the body.

Close your eyes again and allow yourself to begin to feel the energy from your hands meeting the energy emanating from their body.

If this being is in pain or discomfort or has some kind of infection or inflammation, you may feel this in your hands. If your hands become uncomfortable or painful at any time, remove them and shake them gently away from you. Replace them slightly higher or farther away than they were previously placed.

Healing is usually pleasant and comforting, but if the person, child, or animal experiences any kind of agitation or discomfort as you place your hands over the body, remove them and replace them several inches farther away.

To clear the energy field, gently move your hands in a sweeping or brushing motion above the body.

When the area feels smoother and clearer, replace your hands above the location that needs healing, and visualize the white light and love flowing out of your hands and into the body. Breathe.

Wait patiently as the healing energy begins to flow. You may notice that your hands begin to lower or move closer on their own, as the animal or person allows the healing to be received. You may even find that you can lightly rest your hands on the person or animal receiving the healing.

Drop all thinking and breathe easily and gently.

Focus all your attention on your hands, allowing the healing energy to flow through you.

See the receiver as whole and healthy.

Feel the love and energy flowing from your heart through your arms and hands and into the receiver. Trust the process of healing.

Remember to breathe and allow your heart to remain open, always aware of the love and compassion that is essential to the healing.

Allow yourself to merge so deeply with the healing energy flowing through you that you lose track of time and surrender to the process. (Long, silent pause, five to ten minutes.)

Visualize the receiver as completely healed, whole, and radiant with joy. Visualize the receiver doing all the things he or she loves to do.

You may continue the laying-on-of-hands as long as you wish and it feels comfortable for you and the receiver. You will know instinctively when to complete the healing and lift your hands away.

Before ending the healing, say a short prayer of gratitude, such as: I am grateful for the healing taking place now. I trust that it will continue in both visible and invisible ways, and that the will of God will be done in this situation.

Lift your hands slowly, shake them away from you, and then, wash them in cold water.

Get both yourself and the receiver some cool or room temperature water to drink. Allow the person, child, or animal to rest as long as they wish before getting up. Sometimes the receiver will have fallen asleep or drifted into such a deep state of healing that you may wish to let the receiver rest alone in peace. Make sure that the receiver is safely positioned before leaving the room.

Once you have left the room, sit outside or in a place where you can rest.

When the adult or child arises, the individual may wish to share with you how he or she experienced the healing. Always allow the receiver to share first, then you may briefly share what you felt, as long as you keep it positive. After a healing, the receiver is still in a very open state and needs to hear only brief and positive feedback.

Strengthening Your Aura

This meditation will assist you in strengthening the energy field around your body as well as fortifying the life force within you. Gold has always been the substance of alchemical transformation. In the Middle Ages the alchemist's goal was to turn base metal into gold. It is a substance of beauty and strength. If you do this meditation on a regular, even daily, basis, you will find it easier to protect yourself from other people's negative emotions and thoughts, and to ward off the negative energy in your environment.

Find a comfortable position, either standing or sitting in a straight-backed chair. If you stand, separate your legs to shoulder width and slightly bend your knees. If you sit, uncross your arms and legs. Close your eyes, take a long, deep breath, and let it out slowly. Allow your breathing to become full, deep, and relaxed.

As you count from ten to zero, allow your rational mind to rest, and you will become more receptive to the wisdom of your unconscious and its healing power.

10, 9, 8, 7, 6, 5, 4, 3, 2, 1, 0. You are now very deeply relaxed.

Focus your attention way above the top of your head, out into the heavens, and get in touch with a brilliant, powerful, gold light and energy, like the sun, flowing down toward you.

Allow yourself to experience this gold light energy flowing all around you and through you, filling your body with its radiance.

With each breath you inhale this light. As it fills and surrounds you, it gently permeates your entire being and joins the river of life energy already flowing through your body.

Experience this gold light flowing all the way down through your legs and feet as it connects you with Mother Earth and a sense of secure grounding.

As you fill and strengthen with this gold light energy, you can feel yourself expanding. Your entire aura, your energy field, is becoming bright with gold light and energy, for three feet completely around you, like a golden egg of strength and protection.

With each breath, you inhale more power and protection. With each breath out, you release your fears and weakness.

Moment by moment you are feeling stronger, more secure, more protected.

All your muscles, nerves tissues, and organs are being filled and permeated with this gold light. All the cells in your body are beginning to gently vibrate. You can feel the transformation of energy all the way down through your feet and into the ground.

Both your physical body and your aura are becoming stronger as they form a whole system of protection and strength.

As you breathe deeply, you can feel your heart center becoming fortified with love and compassion.

You feel that you can confront any challenges to come your way and deal with any person you may have to face.

Breathe.

You are radiant with light, love, strength, and energy.

Feel your protection. Feel your internal strength merging with your external protection.

Allow yourself to visualize a situation in which you would like to feel strong and protected.

Feel your new strength and see yourself able to deal effectively with this situation.

Visualize yourself as able to remain centered and strong, safe and protected.

As you go out into the external world, you will feel protection from within and surrounding you. You will feel your radiant aura.

Whenever you feel the need for more energy and protection, you will only have to breathe deeply and focus on allowing the gold light to fill you.

Retaining all of this strength, energy and protection, you may open your eyes on the count of ten: 1, 2, 3, 4, 5, 6, 7, 8, 9, 10.

✳

Self-Forgiveness

This meditation will assist you in releasing the past, letting go of guilt and shame, and healing your heart. Self-forgiveness is an essential part of the healing process because it opens the heart with self-love and healing energy. During this meditation you will have the opportunity to experience this energy in your own hands and do a brief laying-on-of-hands on your heart.

Find a comfortable position, either sitting or lying. Uncross your arms and legs, and close your eyes. Take a long, deep breath and let it out slowly. Allow your breathing to become full, deep, and relaxed.

As you count down from ten to zero, allow your rational mind to rest, and you will become more receptive to the wisdom of your unconscious and its healing power.

10, 9, 8, 7, 6, 5, 4, 3, 2, 1, 0. You are now very deeply relaxed.

Focus you attention way above the top of your head, out into the heavens, and get in touch with a brilliant, powerful, white light and energy flowing down toward you.

Allow yourself to experience this light energy flowing all around you and through you, filling your body with its radiance. With each breath you inhale this light. As it fills and surrounds you, it gently permeates your entire being and joins the river of life energy already flowing through your body.

Allow your attention to focus this white light in the middle of your chest, in your center of love and compassion, your heart chakra. Feel it gently moving in a circular motion and opening your heart.

Breathe. Allow your heart to fill and open with love and compassion, light and radiance.

Now visualize an image of yourself seated in front of you. See yourself as clearly as possible, as though looking in a mirror or at a photograph.

Allow yourself to see and feel all your flaws, fears, anger, guilt, and shame: all the things that keep you from self-love.

See all the ways you try to protect and defend yourself.

See all the ways in which you fail to live up to your own expectations.

And send the white light of compassion and self-love out from your heart across to this image of yourself.

Feel and see this love light flowing through you and out to this other you, entering your heart and being received.

Allow yourself to forgive yourself. Allow this love light to wash away all the things you have held against yourself, past and present.

Allow this self-forgiveness to heal the wounds of your heart with new light and self-love.

Now switch roles and become the other you. Become the you who is being forgiven.

Feel the forgiveness and light entering your heart.

Feel the gentle power of this forgiveness and love.

Allow yourself to feel blessed.

And allow this white light and love to pour through you, pour through your whole body: all the way down into your torso, legs, and feet,

up into your throat and neck, face and head;

down through your shoulders, arms and hands.

Allow this love light to pour through you, cleansing you, healing you, releasing you.

And now, keeping your eyes closed, focus this light in your hands.

Very gently lift your hands a little and bring them together until they are about ten or twelve inches apart, palm to palm. Allow yourself to feel the energy between your two palms.

Move your hands slightly and feel the gentle pull of energy between them. This is the energy of healing, of love, of forgiveness.

This energy is tangible and real. It is your participation in Creation.

Keeping your eyes closed, bring your hands up to your head, so your palms are several inches from your face. Allow yourself to feel the energy between your hands and your face.

And then very slowly, bring them down over your throat.

And over your chest where your heart is. Feel the contact of energy between your hands and your heart.

As you now forgive yourself, you participate in the atonement and peace of your own heart.

And the atonement and peace of all Creation.

Allow yourself to stay in this deep state of healing as long as you wish, and only when you are ready, count from one to ten and open your eyes.

*

Acknowledgments

J ust as it takes a village to raise a child, it takes a community to write a book. My patients and students have provided me with the teaching ground on which I could learn the life lessons needed to be a healer: self-love, compassion, forgiveness, acceptance, strength, and courage. To all of them, I am deeply grateful.

If it were not for Michael Kaplan, the person who taught me how to use a computer, I would never have finished this book. His patience was endless. Gene Jennings provided me with constant spiritual support and encouragement when I needed it most, as well as Biblical sources for quotes and information. Nini Gridley read part of the manuscript and gave me valuable feedback and editorial suggestions.

Virginia Harris, friend and guide, helped me prioritize my work, reconfigure the TOUCHING SPIRIT® Training Program, and carve out the time and energy in my life to write the book. All the while giving birth to her own child.

My deepest gratitude goes to Camille Hykes, who was the first to see the book through my eyes and to believe in its potential. She shone a light and encouraged me to press on through dark moments of doubt. As if that were not gift enough, she introduced me to both my agent and my editor. Thank goodness Nicolas Dalton planted the suggestion to talk with her; and during the final crunch of finishing the manuscript, fed me wonderful French food and played with Star.

I express great thanks to my agent Lynn Nesbit for commanding me to find my voice, and to my editor Caroline Sutton for helping me to refine that voice. Despite being from another publishing house, Joann Davis deserves my thanks. It was she who originally approached me years ago about doing a book, and she who implored me to write my personal story rather than a scholarly book.

I am eternally grateful to my soul sister, Laurie Layton Schapira, whose love, truth, and dark eyes have provided a rock on which to build my soul.

My dear friends Elise and Bob Hall have given me constant encouragement during long years of struggling vision; as did my friend and colleague Roger Paine, who set aside his own dreams as a writer to direct and keep alive the vision of Interface Center in Boston as a place of healing.

And finally, as always, my most profound gratitude goes to loved ones: my mother, for a lifetime of love, support, encouragement, and faith; and to Psyche, Pearl, Cinder, and Star, for teaching me the meaning of family and providing me with rich compost for the soul of this book.